Battle for Moscow

Titles of Related Interest

Adragna	ON GUARD FOR VICTORY: MILITARY DOCTRINE AND BALLISTIC MISSILE DEFENSE IN THE USSR
Baxter	THE SOVIET WAY OF WARFARE
Bellamy	RED GOD OF WAR: SOVIET ARTILLERY & ROCKET FORCES
Gareev	M. V. FRUNZE, MILITARY THEORIST
Hemsley	SOVIET TROOP CONTROL
Laffin	BRASSEY'S BATTLES: 3500 YEARS OF CONFLICT, CAMPAIGNS AND WARS FROM A-Z
Messenger	HITLER'S GLADIATOR: THE LIFE AND TIMES OF SS-OBERSTGRUPPENFUEHRER AND GENERAL DER WAFFEN-SS SEP DIETRICH
Mikheyev	THE SOVIET PERSPECTIVE ON THE STRATEGIC DEFENSE INITIATIVE
Niepold	THE BATTLE FOR WHITE RUSSIA: THE DESTRUCTION OF ARMY GROUP CENTRE JUNE 1944
Simpkin	RED ARMOUR

Related Periodicals*

Armed Forces Journal International

Defense Analysis

Specimen copies available upon request

Battle for Moscow

THE 1942 SOVIET GENERAL STAFF STUDY

Edited by

MICHAEL PARRISH
Indiana University

PERGAMON-BRASSEY'S
International Defense Publishers, Inc.

Washington · New York · London · Oxford
Beijing · Frankfurt · São Paulo · Sydney · Tokyo · Toronto

U.S.A. (Editorial)	Pergamon-Brassey's International Defense Publishers, Inc., 8000 Westpark Drive, Fourth Floor, McLean, Virginia 22102, U.S.A.
(Orders)	Pergamon Press, Inc., Maxwell House, Fairview Park, Elmsford, New York 10523, U.S.A.
U.K. (Editorial)	Brassey's Defence Publishers Ltd., 24 Gray's Inn Road, London WC1X 8HR, England
(Orders)	Brassey's Defence Publishers Ltd., Headington Hill Hall, Oxford OX3 0BW, England
PEOPLE'S REPUBLIC OF CHINA	Pergamon Press, Room 4037, Qianmen Hotel, Beijing, People's Republic of China
FEDERAL REPUBLIC OF GERMANY	Pergamon Press GmbH, Hammerweg 6, D-6242 Kronberg, Federal Republic of Germany
BRAZIL	Pergamon Editora Ltda, Rua Eca de Queiros, 346, CEP 04011, Paraiso, São Paulo, Brazil
AUSTRALIA	Pergamon-Brassey's Defence Publishers Ltd., P.O. Box 544, Potts Point, N.S.W. 2011, Australia
JAPAN	Pergamon Press, 5th Floor, Matsuoka Central Building, 1-7-1 Nishishinjuku, Shinjuku-ku, Tokyo 160, Japan
CANADA	Pergamon Press Canada Ltd., Suite No. 271, 253 College Street, Toronto, Ontario, Canada M5T 1R5

Copyright © 1989 Pergamon-Brassey's International Defense Publishers, Inc.

All Rights Reserved. No part of this publication may be reproduced, stored in a retrieval system or transmitted in any form or by any means — electronic, electrostatic, magnetic tape, mechanical, photocopying, recording or otherwise — without permission in writing from the publishers.

First edition 1989

Library of Congress Cataloging-in-Publication Data
Battle for Moscow
Translation of unpublished manuscript: Sbornik
materialov po izucheniiu opyta voiny. No. 2.
Includes index.
1. Moscow, Battle of, 1941–42. I. Parrish,
Michael. II. Soviet Union. Raboche-Krest'ianskaia
Krasnaia Armiia. General'nyi shtab. III Title.
IV. Title: Sbornik materialov po izucheniiu opyta
voiny. No. 2.
D764.3.M6B33 1989 940.54'21 88–23881

British Library Cataloguing in Publication Data
Battle for Moscow: the 1942 Soviet General
Staff study.
1. World War 2. Battle of Moscow
I. Parrish, Michael
940.54'21

ISBN 0-08-035977-9

Printed in Great Britain by BPCC Wheatons Ltd, Exeter

Contents

EDITOR'S INTRODUCTION *vii*

1. *Operational Tactical Lessons of the Winter Campaign of 1941–42* 1

2. *Characteristics of Defensive Combat* 18

3. *Characteristics of Offensive Combat in Winter* 25

4. *Combat Employment of Ski Units* 36

5. *Combat Work of the Artillery in the Winter of 1942* 43

6. *Reconnaissance* 56

7. *Combat Employment of Large Cavalry Formations* 74

8. *Special Characteristics of Actions in the Karelo-Finnish Theater* 99

9. *The Struggle for Mastery of the Air on the Northwestern Front* 111

10. *The Defense of a Large, Populated Place* 118

11. *Antiaircraft Defense of a Major Center* 131

12. *Combat Employment by Ground Troops of Smoke for Cover and Camouflage* 155

13.	War Experience in the Topographic Support of Combat Troops	*172*
14.	Regulation Concerning the Organization and Work of the Army Rear	*185*

APPENDIXES

1.	Order of Battle of Soviet Forces during the Battles of Moscow	*199*
2.	Soviet Forces in the Battle of Moscow	*203*
	INDEX	*205*
	ABOUT THE EDITOR	*210*

Editor's Introduction

THE genesis of the Battle of Moscow was in the titanic struggle known in the USSR as the "Great Patriotic War," which quite possibly will remain the greatest land campaign of all time. Lasting 1,418 days, it caused total casualties of nearly 20 million dead on the Russian side alone. In the apt words of Gerald Reitlinger, "It changed the Russian State from a timid Asiatic country still licking the twenty-year old wounds of civil war, to the military power that dominated Europe from the Elbe to the Adriatic."[1]

The motives of Adolph Hitler to embark on this dangerous adventure are not the subject of the present discussion, which must remain confined to conditions that led to the Battle of Moscow. On June 21, 1941, a force of slightly over 3 million men attacked on the entire Russo–German frontier aided by Hungarian, Rumanian, and Finnish troops. Facing them on the Western military districts was a force of at least 170 divisions of nearly 2.9 million men, which was soon supported by an army that could mobilize nearly 6 million men in uniform. In terms of tanks and air units, the Soviet Union forces were comparable if not superior to the enemy, and yet the Soviets suffered massive defeats in the early fighting, particularly on the western front (formed on the basis of the Belorussian Military District) where the German blitzkrieg advanced faster than it had against the Poles in 1939. In the center part of the front, two pockets in Bialystok and Minsk destroyed the majority of Soviet forces that were deployed on the frontier, and by early July the Army Group Center had advanced nearly 300 miles into Soviet territory.

How could all this have happened? During the Stalin years the official Soviet line presented the early defeats as a part of a grand strategy worked out by the "greatest military leader of all time" to exhaust the enemy through a strategy of "active defense" and prepare the ground for a successful counteroffensive.[2] The fact that this thesis could be supported in 1986 by an American historian can only be attributed to the powerful temptations of revisionism.[3]

The most vigorous opponents of the Stalinist version are a number of Soviet dissident historians including Anton Antonov-Ovseenko, P.G. Grigorenko and A.M. Nekrich,[4] who document the state of unpreparedness in which the Soviet Union entered the war and the inability of the Soviet command to deal with the crisis. These historians place most of the blame squarely on the shoulders of Stalin and his close political and military associates who were guilty of serious mistakes in foreign and military policy including the decimation of the high command in the purges of the 1930s.

The books and memoirs published during the Khrushchev years take something of a middle stance between these two views. Although critical of the contemporary military and political leadership and of the weaknesses in arms and equipment, they also point out that the Soviets managed to survive the early setback and finally turn the tide. The Soviet histories written under Brezhnev delete such negative views and put the accent on the positive even to the point of including favorable albeit nonglorifying mentions of Stalin. With the ascendancy of Gorbachev we are seeing once again signs of a nascent "objectivity" and a more critical view of Stalin as *feldherr*.

The Battle of Moscow is usually considered to have begun on October 1, 1941, after the rout of Soviet forces in Kiev—quite possibly the greatest single defeat suffered by any of the combatants during the Second World War. It reached its climax on November 16, 1941, with the third and last German attempt to capture the city and the inconclusive completion of the Soviet counteroffensive in mid-January 1942.

Soviet histories like to claim that it was defensive battles in Belorussia in August and September 1941 that brought to a halt the Wehrmacht's first attempts to capture Moscow, when in reality it was Hitler's decision to concentrate on the Ukraine during this period that saved Moscow from being captured. By October 1941, Kiev had been captured and the Southwestern Front smashed, and once again Hitler's attention turned north toward Moscow. Within ten days the forces of the Germany Army Group Center had smashed through the west and Bryansk fronts, and six Soviet armies had been trapped in the Vyazma pocket where over half a million Russian soldiers were captured. The newly appointed Zhukov tried to stabilize the front with an improvised line near Mozhaysk with indifferent success. Despite the deteriorating weather, which hampered the German advance, Kalinin, the northern anchor of the Soviet defense, fell on October 14, and Stalin planned his own escape to Kuibyshev, but not before ordering the execution of a number of imprisoned officers. The German forces now intended to surround Moscow and force it to surrender with a line of advance from Yarsolavl' in the north and Orel-Mtsensk and Tula from the southwest.

By early November, deteriorating weather conditions, the long German supply lines, and some confusion on the part of the German high command in regard to its next move gave the Russians a breathing spell, and Stalin returned to Moscow to preside over the parade on the twenty-fourth anniversary of the Bolshevik Revolution and to appeal to, among other things, Russian patriotism. Stalin, finally believing Richard Sorge, his erstwhile spy in Tokyo, that Japan was not about to move west, began to transfer reserves from the Far East and to incorporate them mainly in defense of Moscow. Many of these units were decimated in senseless counterattacks ordered by Stalin during November, but the Germans were also bleeding.

By late November the Germans basically exhausted their manpower and tanks in their advance as the fresh but somewhat untrained Soviet reserves were arriving. The Soviet counterattack, largely the brainchild of G.K. Zhukov, was not so much designed to roll the Germans back as it was to upset their plans for a final offensive toward Moscow. On December 5, the Soviet counterattack against a tired and depleted Wehrmacht began and developed slowly and unevenly against an enemy who, although forced to leave much equipment behind, did not panic. This developing crisis in the center of the front, however, gave Hitler the opportunity to take over the leadership of the Wehrmacht and to get rid of a number of older generals who had led the blitzkrieg in the first two years of the war.

By mid-December the German spearheads toward Moscow had been pushed back, and the Soviets continued their offensive on a more ambitious scale. Fortunately for the Germans, Stalin decided to launch a counteroffensive on the entire eastern front, which divided the Red Army's strength. Added to this was Hitler's unorthodox but wise decision to secure the German positions behind the lines that further hindered the advance of the Red Army and bled its resources. Finally, by the beginning of 1942, the Soviet plan to encircle the Army Group Center had failed to materialize, and the Germans further managed to cut off and destroy large Soviet units such as the 33rd Army.

For the next two years the strong points of Rzhev and Vyazma proved to be thorns in the Russian side, providing potential starting points for a future attack toward Moscow. A new breed of German commander, such as Walter Model, managed to tie up in this sector substantial Russian forces, who continued to get bloodied in futile attacks while the main campaigns were being fought elsewhere. This history of "quiet" fighting during 1942–44 in the central part of the eastern front was not one of the proudest chapters in the history of the Red Army, and the Soviet commanders during this time showed an obvious lack of imagination. It was only in the summer of 1944 during the operation known as "Bargartion" that the Army Group Center was finally defeated by the Red Army.

The Battle of Moscow without a doubt was the first major German defeat of the war, but it was far from being a Russian victory. To learn the lessons of the Battle of Moscow, the Soviet General Headquarters and the General Staff appointed a section in the Operations Section of the General Staff headed by Major General P.P. Vechnyi. In May 1942, Vechnyi was sent to the Crimean Front as chief of staff where Soviet command, through sheer incompetence, managed to snatch defeat from the jaws of victory. After this fiasco an angry Stalin dismissed the entire command of this front including the chief culprit, the Grand Inquisitor L.Z. Mekhlis, chief of the political administration of the Red Army and Stalin's own watchdog in Crimea. In Mekhlis's case, this was a temporary setback, but Vechnyi, who could have been shot, was brought back to Moscow to labor in the back rooms of the General Staff and away from Stalin's immediate military entourage. A group headed by Vechnyi produced a number of studies during the war devoted to various campaigns: one of the first was called "Operational and Tactical Lessons of the Winter Campaign of 1941-2" (the subject of this book), which appeared late in 1942.

The *Battle for Moscow* understandably avoids any mention of strategy or how the Germans managed to end up at the gates of Moscow. It is primarily a study of Soviet tactics and the lessons learned from fighting in winter conditions. Later studies had more to say about Soviet strategy.

But this is a rare book, a Soviet scrutiny, warts and all, of a part of their own war effort and intended not for mass consumption—and thus not distorted by propaganda and imbalance—but as a guide to how battles were fought and why their results were not always satisfactory. This is a survey of the battleground as seen by the Red Army's frontline troops, junior commanders, and all the others who suffered the brunt of the fighting. Thus these pages are not about grandiose battles but about how to fight in the trenches, in the cold, in rough terrain, and about which weapons to use. The *Battle for Moscow* tells us of lessons learned in the bitter campaigns of 1941-42; the reader can decide whether these are applied to later battles.

The original Russian-language edition of this indispensable study of Soviet tactics is in the U.S. National Archives, and the English translation was prepared by the U.S. Army and is available through the U.S. Military History Institute. It is not known how the U.S. Army got hold of this report, but the editor assumess that it came from captured documents (although there is no definite proof). Neither the original nor the translation wins any literary prizes. The editor has tried to smooth out the roughest edges without affecting the flavor of the original, which, after all, was written by soldiers. As far as possible, attempts have been made to introduce consistency in grammar, translation, and transliteration.

For those who want to go beyond a study of tactics, there exists a large body of Soviet literature. Any study of the Battle of Moscow should include the appropriate volumes in the six-volume *Istoriia velikoi otechestvennoi voiny. Sovetskogo Soiuza* (History of the great patriotic war of the Soviet Union) (1962-65) and the 12-volume *Istoriia vtoroi mirovoi voiny* (History of the second world war), *1939-1945* (1973-82). General histories of the Battle of Moscow include *Bitva za Moskvu* (Battle of Moscow) (1966, 1968); *Ordena Lenina Moskovskii voennyi okrug* (Order of Lenin Moscow military district) (1972); *Proval Gitlerovskogo nastupleniia na Moskvu* (Defeat of Hitlerite attack on Moscow) (1966); A.M. Samsonov: *Velikaia bitva pod Moskvoi* (The great battle of Moscow) (1958); *Za Moskvu, za rodinu* (For Moscow, for motherland) (1964); *Besprimerynipodvig* (Unparalleled feat) (1968); A.M. Samsonov: *Porazhenie Vermakhta pod Moskovi* (1982) (Defeat of Wehrmacht before Moscow); and others.

Memoirs that shed light on this battle include those by G.K. Zhukov: *Vospominaniia i razmyshleniia* (Memoirs and reflections) (1974); S.M. Shtemenko: *General'nyi shtab v gody voiny* (General staff during the war years) (1968); A.M. Vasilevskii: *Delo vsei zhizni* (Affairs of life) (1973); K.K. Rokossovskii: *Soldatskii dolg* (Soldier's duty) (1968); L.M. Sandalov: *Na Moskovskom napravlenii* (In the Moscow direction) (1970); D.D. Leliushenko: *Zoria pobedy* (Dawn of Victory) (1966); F.I. Golikov: *V Moskovskoi bitva* (In the Battle of Moscow) (1967); K.F. Telegin: *Ne otdali Moskvy* (Moscow does not surrender) (1968); and others.

Two historical novels in the tradition of *War and Peace*—namely, A. Chakovskii: *Blokada* (Blockade) (1969), based on the unpublished memoirs of Marshal Timoshenko, and I. Stadniuk: *Voina* (War) (1972)—give the most vivid impression of the military crisis faced by the Soviet Union during the early months of the war. A detailed bibliographic coverage of the Battle of Moscow can be found in the editor's *The USSR in World War II* (1982).

I would like to thank the U.S. Military History Institute for use of the Soviet General Staff Study of the winter campaigns 1941-42 and Louis Rotundo, who discovered the original manuscript. Also, I wish to acknowledge the invaluable assistance of Wendy Cox, Nancy Cummings, Rhonda Hoopingarner, John Myszkowski, Kip Neal, and Terri Ogle in preparing this volume.

Michael Parrish

Indiana University
Bloomington, Indiana

Notes

1. John Erickson, *The Road to Stalingrad* (New York: Harper & Row, 1975), p. 48.
2. Matthew Gallagher, *The Soviet History of World War II* (Boulder, Co.: Praeger, 1963), p. 11.
3. Bryan Fugate, *Operation Barbarossa* (Novato, Ca.: Presidio Press, 1984).
4. Anton Antonov-Ovseenko, *The Time of Stalin, Portrait of Tyranny* (New York: Harper & Row, 1981); P.G. Grigorenko, *The Soviet Collapse* (Possev, 1969); and A.M. Nekrich, *June 22, 1941* (Columbia, S.C.: University of South Carolina Press, 1968).

In this chapter the study points out several factors that contributed to the partial failure of Soviet counteroffensive during the Battle of Moscow including insufficient cooperation among units ranging from fronts to divisions as well as between units and their support groups. There is also a critique of tactics deployed in fighting in winter conditions, night fighting, pursuit, and combat for populated areas—Ed.

1

Operational Tactical Lessons of the Winter Campaign of 1941-42

THE winter campaign of 1941-42 was characterized basically by wide offensive operations of the Red Army and by defensive operations by the enemy along the entire front. As a result of the campaign as a whole, the Red Army gained a number of victories, liberated a vast territory that had earlier been seized by the enemy, and caused him heavy losses.

However, the winter operations of 1941-42 did not lead to the immediate destruction of the main enemy forces on the field of battle, though the main enemy forces often found themselves in extremely grave difficulties and more than once were on the verge of total defeat. Toward the end of the campaign there was a degree of stabilization of the front line that was not greatly changed until the beginning of the spring and summer operations.

One of the basic reasons for these incomplete results of the winter campaign was in the major shortcomings in troop leadership during the course of operations. Among these shortcomings were

• insufficiently organized and thought-out cooperation among operational groups operating in various directions;

• insufficient cooperation among armies carrying out overall operational tasks and also within armies among divisions and formations of other arms (army support and special troops); and

• an inability to carry through major operations to conclusions resulting in the full defeat of the enemy on the field of battle.

Characteristics of the Operational Defense of the Germans in Winter 1942

At the beginning of the winter campaign the enemy had no established system of operational defense. The system was worked out and formulated during the course of the campaign itself. The basic characteristics of the defensive actions of the enemy in opposition to the offensives by our troops consisted of the following:

• stubborn holding of the most important areas from the operational point of view, consisting usually of a complex of sizable populated places and other terrain features suitable for defense involving road junctions or centers covering important directions (the region of Rzhev on the Kalinin Front, the region of Vyazma on the Western Front, and the regions of Balaklaya and Slavyansk on the Southwestern Front); and

• counterblows with operational reserves from the operational regions listed above or from near them against the rear or flanks of our most advanced groups, which presented the greatest threat to the enemy.

It is necessary to note that in holding the most important operational areas, the enemy showed the most extreme stubbornness. The German command, in requiring of its troops that they hold these points at any cost, did not attempt to maintain a continuous front line, since this would have been difficult to achieve in view of the considerable length of the front and the relatively limited number of available troops. A number of areas were in fact operationally and even tactically surrounded by our forces.

In the battles aimed at holding these places, the enemy expended his principal effort in the tactical defense zone and in delivering short counterattacks against our troops with his immediate operational reserves. Broad operational maneuver with substantial regrouping of forces as a rule was not undertaken by the enemy. The German High Command held the most important areas by moving individual divisions from one direction to another. Shock groups formed for counterblows were formed basically by gathering elements already on the front and reinforced with divisions brought from a neighboring sector of the front.

The Germans built the basis of their defense in the tactical zone through the holding of populated places and other important and suitable points, and they made wide use of mortar, artillery, and automatic infantry weapons fire in connection with counterattacks by tactical reserves.

Enemy tactical aviation was not used on a mass basis; separate groups went into action against our troops and immediate operational rear.

The tank formations of the enemy did not undertake independent operational tasks (with the exception of the offensive against Moscow); they were used in close cooperation with infantry.

The basis of the rear activities of the Germans in the defense was built on the employment of trucks and railroads, by which they accomplished the movement of supplies and evacuation. For the supply of their encircled elements, the Germans made wide use of transport aviation.

Characteristics of Winter Offensive Operations

Our offensive operations took place with the concentration of powerful groups at the main sector, along a broad front. Such operations led usually to the rapid penetration of the enemy tactical defense zone and the breaking through by our large groups into the operational depth of the enemy dispositions. The combat groups of the enemy were broken up into a number of separate and isolated small bodies, which made it easier to destroy them.

But sometimes an operation was able to bring about the total destruction of an operational grouping of enemy troops. Generally, our troops, having penetrated deeply into the enemy position, became spread out along a wide front, and even in the direction of the main effort, they became disorganized and lost cohesion, so that their offensive could be stopped by German reserves thrown in from other sectors or from the deeper rear. Half-encircled and fully encircled areas still held by the enemy were utilized as bases from which to launch counterattacks, in favorable circumstances, against the flanks' rear of our troops (as in the vicinity of Rzhev). Sometimes, with the aim of relieving their encircled garrisons, the Germans launched counterattacks with forces brought up from neighboring sectors.

When our offensives carried our forces into the depth of the enemy position, there was unsatisfactory coordination between our forces that had broken into the enemy position and those that still remained on the original front line. The initial tasks given armies by front commands and the initial missions given to divisions by army commands covered too long a phase of the operation, and flexibility was lacking in the change of correction of such initial missions in the light of the subsequent developments.

Within armies, coordination between individual divisions involved in the accomplishment of a common mission was weak. The commanders of armies generally showed weakness in organizing and conducting combat of all armies in the main direction of their attacks. The setting of the action for the artillery by army commanders more often than not was faulty in character. As a rule, without regard for the width of the army sector, the artillery was given missions covering the entire width of the army sector though it would have been possible to concentrate it.

Aviation was used in driblets for scattered missions when it was needed in decisive mass for systematic action against the enemy at the point of main effort. Mobile forces usually were given proper initial missions, but in the course of action they often got cut off, and cavalry corps ended up often operating in cooperation with the main forces. Ski units were poorly trained, both from the technical and the tactical point of view. There were examples of successful employment of separate ski battalions for carrying out limited tactical missions. Though there were several favorable opportunities for the employment of large ski forces to accomplish substantial missions on operational scales, advantage was hardly ever taken of such opportunities.

Our rear service organizations were not equal to the task of providing uninterrupted flows of supplies to the troops in winter conditions when the troops had made substantial gains from their initial positions. Troops periodically suffered shortages in materiel and in supplies as a result. A systematic casualty replacement system was not organized.

Conclusions Concerning the Conduct of Offensive and Defensive Operations

The experience of the winter campaign of 1941–42 gives a basis for the following operational conclusions.

Offensive Operations

1. Winter conditions do not make major offensive operations impossible (operations on the scale of an army group or several army groups operating together), but they do make it particularly essential to calculate forces and resources carefully in relationship to the missions to be accomplished by the operations.

Launching large-scale operations impulsively without regard to the available troops and resources leads to a scattering of forces and a failure to achieve substantial results.

2. The objective of actions in winter operations should be primarily the thorough defeat of a given enemy grouping.

The most appropriate operational form in offensives by army groups is the offensive carried out by several groups on several sectors, with subsequent encirclement and destruction of given operational enemy groupings.

3. In the course of operations, all arms (except ski troops) have less capability for maneuver than under summer conditions; in connection with this fact, planning of winter operations must be particularly thorough and well-integrated.

4. Simply continuing to advance is not always the best course to follow. The mere threat of encirclement does not cause the enemy to abandon important areas held by him. Encircled enemy groupings must be destroyed or captured; this, in the long run, facilitates the best rate of advance for our troops.

5. Winter operations basically should be planned on army group scale. Armies can carry out limited operational missions. As a rule, the army group

gives its armies daily immediate missions, with only general orientation concerning subsequent missions. The depth of the daily objective of an army in general should not exceed 15 to 20 kilometers.

6. For operations in winter conditions, the depth of echelonment of the troops is of great importance. On the army group scale of operations, in the offensive, there should be at the departure positions two or three operational echelons: the *first* for the initial blow and the smashing of the tactical defensive zone; the *second* for the development of the operation in depth; and the *third*—a reserve echelon—for the reinforcement of the armies as needed during the course of the operation for carrying out counterattacks and for destroying resistance in encirclements left behind by the advancing earlier echelons.

The deployment of echelons in winter conditions should be at reduced intervals, because of the imposed reduced mobility. Speed and flexibility of commitment of the second echelons depend largely on the conditions of the roads; they must be in good condition, and sometimes additional roads must be built.

7. The correct assignment of unit and formation boundaries through the depth of the projected operation is of great importance. The areas assigned to units and formations should include sufficient roads and populated places to facilitate the deployment and the combat actions of the attacking troops. The axis of advance and unit boundaries of armies, corps, and divisions should be so assigned as to ensure that the main direction of their attack will bring them to the objective of their assigned missions.

Higher headquarters, in accordance with changes in missions of troop formations, during an operation may order the necessary changes in formation boundaries. But a major change in the already assigned sectors of advance must be considered as exceptional during the course of an operation, and it should be undertaken only in cases where rapid and substantial changes in the situation make it essential.

8. The accomplishment of major operational tasks requires, as a rule, the joint efforts of several armies. Operational combinations employed in connection with the encirclement of operational enemy groupings must be worked out on army-group scale. The actions of armies on their assigned front sectors should be simpler; usually an army attacks in a single direction with one major grouping operating in the direction of the main effort.

9. The operational formation of an army attacking in winter conditions typically includes two echelons; in the second echelon there may be a rifle and/or mobile formations. The depth of the immediate missions of the divisions of the first echelon, depending on the situation, should not exceed 5 or 6 kilometers; the depth of a daily mission objective of the first echelon is 15 to 20 kilometers.

10. The organization of combined-arms combat in the main direction of an army-scale offensive is prescribed by the army command.

The army command, by organizing the reinforcement of divisions and the allotment of attack and supporting army troops, directly facilitates the accomplishment of the mission of the troops operating in the direction of the main effort. If there is a great number of formations in an army, the divisions operating in the sector of secondary effort may be formed into a provisional *operational grouping*.

11. Mobile formations in offensive operations under winter conditions are capable of carrying out independent operational missions. But the limitations imposed on their maneuver capabilities by winter conditions make it advisable for them to operate relatively near to the main body of the army and in close cooperation with it.

In armies carrying out the principal missions of an operation, it is desirable to have ski units of brigade size with heavy firepower, which can be effectively used to accomplish the envelopment and deep envelopment of opposing enemy groups.

Combat aviation is used under the centralized control of army group. In most cases, it is undesirable to place air units under army control.

12. The success of winter operations depends to a large extent on their careful planning and preparation and particularly on the organization and work of the rear.

The preparation of the rear before an operation is a most important task of the army-group command, and the preparation of the road network and the timely movement forward of supplies and materiel are particularly important elements of this task.

The rear and the road network are as a rule prepared before the concentration of the troops earmarked for the projected operation. Particular attention should be paid to reinforcing road-building and repair units, which should be given the necessary tools and equipment for their work. The leading troop elements, particularly mobile elements, should have transport with good traction and cross-country mobility. At division through army level, there should be adequate quantities of sleigh transport.

Defensive Operations

1. The operational defense takes its most definite form on army-group scale. The army group organizes the holding of a given operational defensive line, and it organizes the maneuver of the echelons into which its elements are divided.

2. The basis of the operational defense is the maintenance of an organized front and the securing of coordination among the various operational areas and sectors with the aim of accomplishing the overall defensive mission.

3. The depth of the defensive front is determined by the concrete circumstances and by the mission to be accomplished by the army group. Special attention should be paid in defensive actions to maintaining operational contact among the armies involved and to prevent the enemy from achieving penetrations to a depth that might enable them to threaten friendly operational flanks and rear areas.

4. The basis of defensive actions on army scale usually consists of holding the main defense area.

If the enemy succeeds in breaking through, the army continues to hold its defensive area while taking measures to keep control of major populated places, particularly those located at road junctions or center.

The army must organize a second echelon. If the enemy attacks with limited forces, the second echelon is used to smash enemy elements that may have broken into our defensive position. If the enemy has a substantial numerical superiority, the second echelon is used to reinforce the first echelon in its efforts to hold the main defensive area, to delay the enemy in order to give time for the maneuver of army-group reserves, and to maintain an organized defensive front along the whole army sector.

It is desirable to have ski units and formations as part of the second echelon.

5. Conduct of defensive operations under winter conditions depends to a large extent upon roads. The main sectors where it is expected that army second echelons and army-group reserves may be employed should be provided with adequate roads, prepared beforehand.

6. Mobile formations may be used—if satisfactory roads have been prepared beforehand—for independent maneuver against enemy elements that have broken through as well as for actions in close cooperation with combined-arms formations.

Tank units (brigades and lower) as a rule should be employed in close cooperation with combined-arms formations.

7. Tactical aviation is most effectively centralized at army-group level; its mass strikes should be directed against the most important targets in the formations and areas of the attacking enemy. If the enemy is having difficulties with his communications, tactical aviation can be effectively used against his roads and rear, in order to interrupt the regularity of the activities of his supply elements.

8. Operational counterblows on a large scale are organized and carried out by army group. In carrying out counterblows, it is especially important to deprive the enemy of communications with his rear quickly by seizing important populated places and road junctions in his rear areas.

9. The organization of the rear must be seen to as early as possible. Roads must be put in shape for night as well as day movement; heated shelters, baths, and laundries should be installed as near as possible to where the troops are deployed, and collection points for the evacuation of damaged equipment and salvage must be set up: these and other measures must be taken in good time by the appropriate command.

Characteristics of Offensive Combat in Winter

The combat actions of the troops of the Red Army on all fronts in the winter campaign of 1941–42 show again that successful offensive engagements are possible under conditions of the rugged Russian winter. In such combat our army has a substantial advantage over the invading enemy, for our army is operating under conditions with which it is familiar.

The characteristics of winter combat according to the experience gained in the offensive actions of the Red Army justify the following conclusions:

1. The enemy defense in winter is generally linked with populated places, particularly those that cover basic communications routes or are located along favorable tactical lines (high banks of rivers, lakes, road junctions, rail centers, or between large forest masses, or flanked by unfrozen marshes, etc).

The presence of intervals between individual strong points provides favorable opportunities for the infiltration between them of small mobile groups that can isolate centers of resistance; disrupt the fire system of the enemy; operate against his rear, his headquarters, and lines of communication; and disorganize control. Usually the offensive develops along roads; however, flanking movements and envelopments are of great importance and are often carried out through roadless terrain when this is possible.

2. Command reconnaissance by all arms determines the character of the enemy defense; the presence of obstacles, particularly of those characteristic of winter warfare—snow banks, frozen-over slopes, and ice holes; the accessibility of various secors for infantry, artillery, and tanks; and approaches and lanes for ski troops.

Terrain reconnaissance is of particular importance in winter. It should reveal the layout and nature of the road network, the depth of snow cover and the passability of the area in general for infantry and tanks. In the breakthrough of the enemy defense by the Fourth Army, a second attack was carried out by the 360th Division (reinforced) and by two brigades. Reconnaissance information indicated that in the area where the attack was to take place there were roads—though in poor shape—but in actual fact, there were no roads, and the snow was deeper than had been thought. As a result, in the course of the operation, it became necessary to shift the heavy artillery and tanks from this sector, where they had been intended, to other sectors.

3. Taking into consideration the characteristics of winter actions, including the rapidity with which men tire and the extra expenditure of fuel, the depth of immediate objectives as well as of subsequent objectives is reduced. In the breakthrough of the enemy defense by the troops of the Third and Fourth Armies in the winter of 1941–42, the depth of the daily objectives for divisions varied between 3 and 10 kilometers per day, depending on the terrain and the character of the enemy defense.

Combat is planned so that the blows of ski detachments, enveloping columns, and the troops attacking frontally are all coordinated simultaneously.

4. At the departure positions for the offensive snow trenches are prepared beforehand, together with shelters and heated lean-tos. If the snow cover is deep, the communications trenches leading up to the enemy positions are prepared.

The assault line is chosen so that it will be close to the initial objectives of the attacking troops. In the attack on Malaya Vishera on 11 November 1941, the 257th Rifle Division occupied a departure position some 800 meters from the forward edge of the enemy defensive position. And in moving forward to the assault, it took very heavy losses and failed to achieve significant results.

In order to avoid unnecessary losses from enemy fire, the troops should move up to the assault line under cover of darkness or smoke. The troops should delay at the assault line for the shortest possible time.

In most cases, infantry attacks without skis. Tanks attack along roads or at least along directions where the snow cover is most shallow; and they are accompanying guns that move on snow runners within the combat formations of the infantry. In order to make the approach of the infantry easier and hasten its passage over the areas most subject to enemy fire in front of the forward edge of the defense, it is useful to have the infantry towed on sleighs and similar transporters by tanks.

6. The forward attacking units and formations should not get involved in drawn-out actions for strong points and centers of resistance of the enemy; they should leave behind screening and blocking forces and then bypass them in order to penetrate into the depth of the enemy position. The liquidation of the bypassed centers of resistance is left to the reserve units and formations that are advancing directly behind the leading assault elements. If the initial units and formations are tied down in drawn-out actions, then the reserves, utilizing the intervals between enemy strong points, must penetrate behind them in order to take them under attack from the flanks and from the rear.

In combat in the depths of the enemy defense, ski elements operate in the enemy rear against his communication, with the object of disorganizing his rear areas and impeding the moving up of his reserves.

7. As soon as it is apparent that the enemy is withdrawing, pursuit detachments organized ahead of time are thrown into action; these consist of infantry on sleighs, ski detachments, and cavalry. These pursuit detachments advance as fast as possible along parallel routes to the enemy route of withdrawal, seizing important terrain and communications features in the enemy rear and forcing him from roads into trackless terrain and bringing confusion into his formation. Tanks carry out the pursuit along roads. Artillery and aviation, bringing their firepower to bear against the routes of withdrawal, seek to slow up enemy movement.

In breaking through the enemy defense, particular attention must be paid to bringing the supporting artillery and the rear area elements forward as rapidly as possible. When elements of the 360th and 249th divisions early in January 1942 broke through and reached Velizha, their artillery and rear elements fell a full day's or two marches behind, and consequently, the infantry was not able to accomplish any substantial results after six days of combat.

8. In encirclement battles in winter, the task of the attacking forces consists of preventing the enemy from organizing an all-round defense based on

populated places. It is essential to bend all efforts to keep the encircled enemy out in the frost and snow and to destroy him before he can dig in.

In winter encirclements, it is not necessary to establish a firm and airtight ring of encirclement. The main thing is to seize all the enemy's communications routes, all of the road centers in the area, the populated places, and the best positions in his flanks and in his rear. The main body of the troops should be employed to strike concentrated blows at the enemy in order to break up the encircled forces into smaller, isolated groupings, which can be hit with mortar and artillery cross fire, thus destroying these isolated groupings each separately.

On the Volkhov Front as a result of the winter offensive of our troops, a great part of the German garrisons found themselves encircled, but their destruction proceeded very slowly, even though most of the encircled garrisons were caught within firm and well-defined rings of encirclement. In the end, German relief forces were able to reach many of the encircled elements, and a number of our units actually found that they had fallen into encirclement.

9. The work of the rear is greatly complicated as a result of winter conditions. It is not possible to provide each individual formation with its own supply and evacuation routes. In such conditions, supplies are brought forward along main routes and then are distributed to separate formations along lateral routes. This was the case, for example, with the Fourth Army at the time of the Toropets operation. Movement of transport vehicles along roads takes place, as a rule, during the night. Army vehicles bring supplies up to divisional exchange points. Ski detachments and units, operating at a considerable distance from the main supply routes, forage locally for supplies and rations; their ammunition requirements are brought forward either by sleds or by air transport.

It is specially important to warn and train the troops against the danger of frostbite; rations must be brought to the troops under even the most difficult conditions, and above all, timely aid must be organized for the wounded. In the villages that have been seized from the enemy, it is necessary to organize warm shelters for the wounded and the frostbitten, and facilities must be provided for warming stations and places where soldiers can get hot meals.

Combat for Populated Places

In the winter campaign of 1941–42, the main battles and the most bloody ones took place for the defense and seizure of populated places. Such battles included the ones for Tula, Kalinin, Klin, Istra, Volokolamsk, Mozhaisk, Medyn, Maloyaroslavets, Yukhnov, Kaluga, Rostov, Tikhvin, Toropets, etc.

This is natural, for defense in winter, as has already been said, is organized on the basis of strong points and centers of resistance, most of which are built up on the basis of populated places. The latter can, with relatively little expenditure of effort and resources, be converted into defensive centers. Being located as they are on roads and at road junctions, populated places constitute serious obstacles for troops on the offensive. Bypassing them is difficult, for it forces the attacking troops off the roads; and they also require sizable blocking forces.

Nevertheless, despite the difficulties, the envelopment and encirclement of populated places occupied by the enemy is a matter of prime importance in winter offensive operations. Taking advantage of the less than continuous system of infantry fire, ski detachments and groups of submachine gunners infiltrate between strong points, isolate them, and clear the roads through the use of specially designated detachments earmarked for actions in the enemy rear and on enemy flanks, the whole of these actions being coordinated with those of the main body of troops that is attacking frontally.

In connection with combat for populated places, the following can be said:

1. Small and weakly fortified populated places—particularly if they are held by troops whose morale is not high—can best be attacked at once without preparation, in order to prevent the enemy from taking measures to organize their defense. In such a case, detachments of ski infantry with machine guns and light mortars move across country in order to cut off the enemy's withdrawal routes. Troops attacking frontally under cover of artillery fire seek to throw the enemy out of the shelter of the populated place with a rapid blow; and having forced him out into the winter weather, he is forced into combat in the open and destroyed.

The rapidity of maneuver and the energy with which actions are carried out play most important roles in such cases.

2. Night attacks, though they require precise organization and determination in the execution, are successful in most cases. In general they should be organized in such a way that the troops can use the cover of darkness to pass open areas subject to enemy fire and gain a solid foothold on the outskirts of the town by dawn. In January 1942, two brigades tried during two days without success to take Kresty in daytime attacks. Two regiments of the 358th Rifle Division that had come up seized a foothold in the town by a night attack; on the following day, they were able to take the entire town in a three-hour battle.

3. Action for a large or well-organized, defended populated place calls for a carefully planned and organized attack.

In organizing his attack, the commander must
- reconnoiter the enemy defense thoroughly, locating his strong points and the intervals between them and the character and system of obstacles;
- determine the depth and kind of snow cover and the most favorable approaches for tanks and for infantry;
- prepare and occupy departure positions for the attack, using for this purpose the nearest available populated places and woods or developing a system of snow trenches and shelters;
- prepare and occupy departure positions for the assault itself, making snow tenches when necessary; and
- provide hot meals and hot water for the troops.

4. The offensive takes place under the cover of fire from aviation, artillery, and mortars; in this connection, the use of incendiary rounds and bombs is of special importance. Part of the troops attack frontally without skis. The main forces carry out flanking maneuvers to attack from the flanks and from the rear against the most weakly defended sectors. Ski and submachine gun detachments cut the roads leading to the populated place under attack, cutting off communications and preventing the reserves from moving up or the garrison from withdrawing.

Reacting to the threat of encirclement, the enemy sometimes will abandon the populated place, if it is not of special significance to him in his overall defensive system; but as the experience of the winter of 1941–42 shows, the enemy will seek to hold the most important populated places at any price, notwithstanding the threat of encirclement.

5. The departure position for the assault is chosen with the depth of the snow cover in mind. The deeper the snow, the closer the departure position should be to the objective. Regimental artillery and antitank guns mounted on runners and operating directly with the infantry support the assault infantry with direct fire. Tanks begin the assault with the infantry, covering the infantry with their armor. Infantry helps the tanks to overcome barriers and obstacles. False attacks on secondary sectors, false lifts of artillery fire, and methodical artillery preparation involving the generous use of incendiary rounds and strafing and bombardment from the air—all these measures are used to wear down and weaken the enemy.

6. If an attack fails, the troops should not be made to hold their positions for a long period in the frosty cold; under cover of fire they should withdraw to cover, and after regrouping, they should attack again.

In the battles for Velish in January 1942, our attacks followed one after the other. The enemy, having figured out the plan and the order of battle of our forces, was able to repulse them easily with fire, and he inflicted heavy losses on our troops.

7. For the pursuit of enemy troops that have been driven out of a populated place, tank units may be used; operating along roads, they destroy—either with fire or with their treads—enemy personnel, transport, and guns that are dug in. In the action for Andreapol, a platoon of the 141st Tank Battalion, which was pursuing the retreating enemy, took advantage of the fact that there was heavy snow cover that made it impractical to leave the roads to catch and destroy up to two companies of enemy infantry, some ten guns, and seventy trucks.

Night Attack

The short winter daylight (six to eight hours) and the long winter night make it possible to make wide use of dark for active combat actions. The experience of the past winter [winter 1940–41—Ed.] shows that the Germans rarely held off night attacks. When the latter were resolutely carried out, they usually resulted in forcing the Germans to abandon their positions. It was in this manner near Rostov that we seized the villages of Gnilovskaya and Temernik, with a total loss of only eighteen men.

The basic factor in a night attack is surprise. Experience shows that if the enemy discovered the preparations for a night attack, then it was best to put it off till the following night, since otherwise it was almost certain to fail. In November 1941 a night attack by two regiments on Malaya Vishera ended in failure because the preparations for the action had been made almost immediately after a lengthy daytime attack, and they came to the attention of the enemy.

Night attack usually has as its objective the seizure of favorable departure positions or of strong points on the forward edge of the enemy's defense position, in order to make the development of the attack early the following day easier and in order to consolidate and develop successes already achieved in the depth of the enemy position.

The experience of the winter of 1941-42 showed that it is possible under cover of darkness for large detachments of ski troops to infiltrate deep into the enemy positions; these detachments then carry out disruptive actions in the enemy rear and disorganize his control and then, on the following morning, operate in coordination with the troops that are attacking frontally. In the attack by our troops on the town of Malaya Vishera in November 1941, two large ski detachments of some 500 men each infiltrated behind the enemy lines at night, and by a blow from the rear, they facilitated the seizure of the town on the following morning. Such night actions are possible in a situation where there is not a solid and continuous front, as was the case for example on the northern sectors of the German front.

The plan of a night attack, particularly in winter, should be simple, and the missions of all elements involved should be explicit and not overambitious. Night attacks in winter should be carried out within a brief period of time and should be quickly executed. As soon as possible after the mission has been accomplished, personnel should be put into shelters seized from the enemy or into some other similar cover from the elements.

Experience shows that usually in winter night attacks carried out frontally it was convenient often to designate objectives on open terrain, alongside villages or near the edges of woods; the Germans customarily withdrew part of their forces from such objectives in the open, sending them some distance to the rear in order that they could be in heated shelters.

A group that penetrated into the enemy position had to be prepared to conduct combat independently within the enemy position. The troops in the groups should be good skiers and as a rule armed with submachine guns. In addition, there were several company mortars and individual antitank guns and rifles. Communications with such a group was organized by means of radio.

A group that penetrates or infiltrates the enemy position does so in smaller subgroups that pass between enemy strong points; it assembles in a predetermined place behind the enemy line, assumes its combat formation, and proceeds to carry out its missions. The actions of such a group operating in the enemy rear must be sharply and energetically carried out. The group can accomplish the following missions:

• disruption of enemy control and command system, destruction of enemy artillery, rear installations, etc., as an independent mission, after which it can withdraw to its own lines; and

• infiltrate through to the enemy rear where it takes up favorable positions for a coordinated attack, in cooperation with troops attacking frontally; in this case, it passes by the flank of some enemy strong point or objective, takes up a position behind the objective, and prepares to attack it by morning in coordination with troops attacking frontally.

In the first case, the group should be sent out early in the night to have sufficient cover of darkness in which to accomplish its mission. In the second case, the detachment should be sent out rather later in the night so that it will have to spend as little time behind the enemy lines as possible before dawn and the attack. It can reasonably be sent out one or two hours before dawn, arrive at its immediate objective, and be prepared to attack very shortly after it has formed at its assembly area. In this case, the work of the artillery must be carefully organized so that artillery does not by error fire on friendly infiltrating detachments while they are bypassing enemy strong points.

If the snow is not deep, the attack takes place without skis and is the customary formation for night attack. If the snow cover is deeper than 30 centimeters, units are best advised to use skis, though ski actions at night, particularly in difficult terrain, are not easy. Therefore, if possible, it is best to approach the enemy position without skis, penetrate the position, and attack. In this case, the skis should be brought along behind, towed by a few soldiers detailed to this duty or towed on sleds; the skis of each small group should be towed close behind it so that at dawn and sometimes even at night the troops can take to skis on short notice.

Special attention must be paid to camouflage and to provide as much warmth as possible for the troops. Snow suits should be clean and free of mud; the troops should wear dry felt boots and be warmly dressed (better in jackets than in long greatcoats); they should have gloves and, if possible, heating devices such as hot water bottles.

In preparing for a night attack in winter, special attention should be given to staking out routes of advance over the snow cover. In winter, and especially in windy weather, all traces quickly disappear in the snow, and points on a given piece of terrain can change quite markedly. Each route must be clearly marked with stakes or other clear markers, and before the attack, the route should be checked. The guides must bring their groups without fail or error to the objectives.

The time of an attack depends on circumstances; sometimes it is best to launch it during the second half of the night. Experience shows that Germans at this time withdraw a part of their troops to heated shelters; the remaining troops, half-numb with cold, leave their weapons, try to get some warmth at improvised half-shelters, or sleep. Furthermore, the systematic illumination of the area that is carried out by the Germans during the first half of the night markedly diminishes during the second half.

In the course of a night attack—after the enemy has been alerted—routes can be indicated by light-markers, rockets, and searchlights. In this case, the troops should use light signals to hasten their advance and resolutely attack the enemy.

Having seized the firing points on the forward edge of the enemy defense, the infantry should hasten as quickly as possible to reach the enemy's shelters, isolated buildings, or small villages in his position in order to catch enemy troops there and destroy them. When necessary, these shelters may be utilized by the attacking troops as warming posts and as first-aid stations.

Pursuit

The basic mission in the pursuit is to deny the possibility of breaking contact with our troops and organizing a new defense. In winter, the enemy usually withdraws his units from combat along a wide front, then for a time the withdrawal takes place in the form of small columns retreating; finally these join together into march columns, and a normal march formation, with rear guards, is taken. In the withdrawal, the Germans gravitate toward roads, villages, and the edges of woods. The pursuit should prevent the enemy from achieving these ends in the retreat.

Immediately after a withdrawal is discovered, pressure on the enemy should be increased, and he should be denied the opportunity to break contact and organize into columns. In this case, mobile units should be thrown forward at full speed; tanks with submachine gunners, motorized infantry, and cavalry should advance rapidly along roads in order to deny them to the enemy and thereby to force him to move across country slowly and in small groups. At the same time, infantry units on skis and special ski battalions of submachine gunners should press forward frontally, enveloping the enemy rapidly, and taking the enemy under fire from the flanks and from the rear as he is struggling through the deep snow as he withdraws.

If the enemy succeeds, nevertheless, to form up into small columns, it is necessary to get on as quickly as possible with the job of destroying him. Ski troops envelop the columns even while they are forming up; they overtake the withdrawing formations and cut their route of withdrawal; their immediate mission is to halt the withdrawing enemy, and then in conjunction with troops pursuing frontally, they destroy the enemy.

In withdrawal during winter, the enemy seeks to organize and fortify populated places. Houses are quickly made ready for defense; tanks and armored vehicles are usually driven into enclosed cattle runs and barns from which they suddenly open fire on our troops as they appear. Elements that discover a populated place occupied and defended by the enemy should quickly encircle the place and attack it. In cases where the village is occupied only by enemy rear guard elements, the pursing troops should bypass the place and continue to pursue the retreating enemy main body. The destruction of the enemy troops in the village should be left to the reserves of the pursuing unit or to the second echelon of the army.

On the main withdrawal routes, the Germans leave groups (of five, ten, or more men) on motor vehicles or skis. These men with automatic weapons, and sometimes with machine guns, mortars, and antitank rifles, strive to hold up our advance elements, and then, taking advantage of their own mobility, they withdraw to the next convenient line. This type of action was used repeatedly by the Germans in the withdrawal from Moscow as well as on other occasions. Sometimes such groups of men with automatic weapons take up hidden positions along the routes of pursuit of our forces and open fire on our advancing columns.

In pursuing the enemy, it is essential to keep up continuous reconnaissance out ahead as well as on the flanks. Furthermore security for the flanks of columns must be provided on a broad front. Particularly in movements through forests, flank security elements should comb the terrain up to a distance of 1 or 2 kilometers on either side of the column.

In a withdrawal, the enemy makes a wide use of obstacles, especially of antitank and antipersonnel mines, which he carefully conceals in the snow. Obstacles and mines are placed along the roads, at bridges, on the shoulders of roads, in likely halting places, or favorable sites for artillery positions. Therefore, in pursuing the enemy, in the first place it is essential to speed up the tempo of pursuit, so that they enemy will not have time to set out mines or obstacles; and in the second place, it is necessary to carry out careful engineer reconnaissance, by assigning to forward elements enough sappers and enough equipment so that mines can be detected and disarmed.

In organizing the pursuit in the northern part of the theater, where for the most part the enemy does not have a continuous front, it is advantageous to send ski detachments deep into the enemy rear (10 to 15 kilometers), where by surprise blows they can disorganize enemy command control and cut main routes over which the bulk of supplies for the enemy front-line units moves. In December 1941, after our forces had taken the town of Bolshaya Vishera, a battalion of ski troops was dispatched in the direction of Gruzino where it cut the road, prevented the movement of ammunition and rations to the enemy at the front, and obliged two enemy regiments to withdraw.

The greatest success in the overthrow of the enemy forces can be achieved through parallel pursuit on one or both flanks.

In the pursuit, it is essential to thrust tanks, motorized infantry, and ski detachments along roads that enable them to deny the enemy important road centers, crossings, and defiles and thereby to force the enemy into terrain that is difficult to cross or even to force him into impassable terrain where he can be cornered and destroyed.

From the very beginning of the pursuit, it is necessary to organize the clearing of snow from roads and the repair of roads. Artillery taking part in the pursuit should have an attached sapper element that can facilitate its rapid displacement forward and deployment.

The troops should push forward, not delaying in villages that have been seized, the villages should be organized as warming points for later echelons of troops that are pushing forward and used for aid stations, rear installation, and so on.

The following is a critique of defensive tactics in winter conditions, including the difficulty of creating defensive lines because of frozen ground, the necessity of special camouflage, and the need for heat in shelters. The General Staff also covers the problems faced by tanks used as a mobile striking force to counter enemy penetrations. Emphasis is placed on coordinated countermeasures among air force, artillery, and armor to force the enemy to leave the roads and get bogged down in cross-country snow. The main objective of such winter defenses should be denial of roads to the advancing enemy. Also discussed are the characteristics of marches in winter conditions. The report admits that the German forces were well led during this phase of the war—Ed.

2
Characteristics of Defensive Combat

COLD, snow, short daylight hours, and bad weather do not interfere with the normal forms of defense, but they make necessary certain changes and additional measures. Winter defense, like any other, must be planned with a view to repulsing mass infantry attacks supported by tanks, artillery, and aviation.

In choosing the main defense area, it is necesary to determine whether the enemy has ski units or not. Troops not equipped with skis will attack along roads, and their deployment in deep snow will be slow. But if they have skis and sleds for transport, units can operate off roads, carrying out flanked movements and envelopments across country.

In winter the characteristics of terrain change. When they are frozen over, rivers, lakes, and swamps are no longer obstacles; but at the same time, readily passable hollows and ditches become impassable for tanks and difficult passages even for infantry. New roads can be made quite easily through the snow. Villages and other cover become particularly important for providing warming points and rest areas for the troops. Therefore it is desirable to

Characteristics of Defensive Combat 19

choose for a defensive area a place that has villages, woods, and other cover, which will make it possible to organize strong points and centers of resistance.

The forward edge of the main defense area is chosen in an area not easily accessible by the enemy. But in choosing it, one should avoid stereotyped layouts. It is best to site the forward edge of the main defense zone on the forward slope of a height, for this will make approach difficult and will facilitate friendly counterattacks. Cover in front of the forward edge that the enemy might be able to utilize should either be eliminated or made useless by means of engineer obstacles, and it should be taken under mortar and artillery fire.

In the security area in front of the forward edge of the defense, obstacles in the form of mines, booby traps, concealed obstacles, and blocks should be set up covering roads and approach routes available to the enemy. The security area must be defended by infantry equipped with skis by artillery on ski mounts, and by engineers.

The main characteristics of engineer preparation of the main defense area in winter include:
- the fact that the job of digging and moving earth in frozen weather is especially time-consuming;
- the making of trenches, shelters, antitank obstacles out of snow;
- the conversion of rivers and lakes into natural obstacles by breaking the ice cover and creating ice holes;
- the cutting through of ski trails for the movement of infantry columns and the preparation of routes for counterattack by second-echelon elements, by reserves, and by tank units;
- the clearing of fields of fire and the clearing of snow away from firing points, communications trenches, etc.;
- special camouflage measures, clearing away tracks in the snow, setting up cover, covering trenches with camouflage material and woven snow-covered branches, painting materiel and equipment white, and wearing white snow camouflage suits; and
- the setting up of warmed shelters including heated earthen shelters and covered dugouts for command posts and aid stations.

In the trenches there should always be observers and men to man machine guns, while the remaining troops are rotated by platoons to warming shelters.

Reserves should be deployed in covered places or in shelters, but weapons must be kept in position, manned, and ready to open fire.

Army second echelons and reserves should be highly mobile. They are likely to be called on for rapid and sudden actions. This is achieved by preparing routes for counterattacks and by mounting personnel on skis. Regimental and divisional commanders should have mobile reserves on skis available.

The system of infantry, mortar, artillery, and antitank fire in the defense must be organized in such a manner that

1. It can interfere with the enemy approach;

2. Artillery and mortars can deny the use of roads to the enemy;

3. By long-range fire on columns and on concentrations of troops, the artillery can support the actions of the front-line defensive elements;

4. It can disrupt and strike the enemy and his tanks while he is preparing for the attack and concentrating his forces;

5. It can repulse the enemy assault on the forward edge of the defense and separate his infantry from its tanks and destroy it;

6. It can destroy enemy elements that may have penetrated its position; and

7. It can support the counterattack by friendly second echelons and reserves.

The batteries of the infantry-support group should occupy firing positions that are not accessible to tanks, and if there are no natural antitank obstacles, artificial obstacles such as ditches, snow banks, mine fields, etc., should be constructed. The batteries should have, in addition to their main firing positions, at least two alternate firing positions for each gun, taking into consideration direct fire against tanks and positions for roving guns.

Tanks are used mainly as a mobile striking force for counterblows against the enemy infantry. Counterattack routes should be carefully reconnoitered and prepared. If the snow cover is deep, tanks should operate along roads that have been prepared for the counterattack and are widely used for stationary fire from ambushes or cover. In all cases, measures must be taken so that the tank motors can be warmed up.

The basis of antitank defense, according to war experience, was made up of antitank strong points; the infantry fire system (as in the case of the Twenty-ninth Army) was laid out to reinforce these centers. Antitank defense was on an all-around basis, and the antitank centers had interlocking fire. The troops took readings of the depth of the snow, determined the most likely approaches for tank attacks, and erected antitank obstacles and defenses along roads.

On the basis of experience, the following essential measures stand out:

1. Engineer antitank obstacles must be built in relation to the overall system of defense, and they must be covered by fire. The 275th Rifle Division did not observe this requirement while defending the eastern bank of Morkaya Sura River; the escarpments and ditches of the division's defensive system did not correspond to the tactical situation, and they were not covered by friendly fire. As a result, the enemy was able to use them as cover when he was assembling for the attack.

2. Antitank reserves and attached tanks should be used to cover the most important sectors and approaches under winter conditions. The sappers in the antitank reserve should be given skis, and the guns should be mounted on runners.

Since darkness, snowfall, and storms greatly diminish observation, which can give timely warning of an enemy attack, it is necessary to

- keep weapons in a constant state of readiness and be prepared to use them under conditions of limited visibility;

Characteristics of Defensive Combat

- increase the number of observers at infantry and artillery observation points;
- increase the number of patrols for reconnaissance and for security of intervals between positions;
- set up listening posts and trip devices near barbed wire obstacles;
- increase the alertness of combat security and to have commands of small units make more frequent inspections of their defensive areas;
- check the functioning and the state of the communications system and to organize a warning system that will give timely notification of the enemy's approach;
- clear snow out of trenches and communication trenches;
- maintain fields of visibility and of fire as unobstructed as possible during and after snowstorms; and
- keep ready all skis to use immediately.

The defense of a populated place should be set up on an all-around basis. No matter how deep the snow cover, a village can be attacked from any direction of the 360 degrees (as for example the attack of the 249th Rifle Division on Toropa on 21 January 1942). The defense of a populated place is organized and conducted in coordination with the troops that are operating nearby but outside the place itself.

In defensive combat, it is desirable to
- Make the enemy leave the roads as early as possible and deploy his main force across country in deep snow by air strikes and by the fire of long-range artillery and by the actions of the forward elements of the defense;
- deny the enemy the possibility of finding warm places for his troops to rest and get warm in villages, woods, or in folds in the terrain by destroying populated places and other sorts of cover and by the use of obstacles and air strikes;
- exhaust the enemy and cause him heavy losses and then destroy him by counterattacks and by superior fire systems. It is also useful to force enemy personnel to spend a long time held down by our fire while he gets colder in the snow in open terrain; and
- carry out counterattacks in previously prepared directions, striving by blows on his flanks and against his rear to cut his units off and destroy them piecemeal. Thus, the 270th Rifle Division in the defense along the Northern Donets River was able by small-element attacks to cause the enemy heavy losses and take Chervony Shakhter.

If the enemy succeeds in penetrating deeply into our defensive position, he should not be given the opportunity to fortify populated places, individual buildings, woods, or groves. It is necessary to have fire prepared beforehand that can cover such places.

If the defense has insufficient strength and materiel, then it should concentrate on stubborn defense along roads mainly and against the enemy's ski detachments that are off the roads. For this, it is necessary to

• occupy and hold as stubbornly as possible all the most accessible roads and directions;
• set up a defense consisting of separate strong points and centers of resistance covering the directions most likely to be threatened;
• have reserves and second echelons consisting of ski troops; and
• clear the roads of snow and make ski paths along the directions of one's own counterattacks and make wide use of antipersonnel and antitank obstacles.

Intervals between strong points should be secured by clearing good fields of vision, by covering them with artillery and machine gun fire, by designating ski patrols to cover them, by having small bodies of submachine gunners and riflemen in them, and by constructing antitank and antipersonnel obstacles.

In withdrawing from action in winter, it is necessary to take into consideration the more than normal slowness with which the troops are able to break contact, unless they are mounted on skis; the difficulty in bringing back materiel; and the action of enemy aviation on our troops. Breaking off contact should be accomplished at night if possible, and if it must be done by day, it should be under cover of smoke. In the withdrawal, there should be reserves of ski troops and mobile elements to deal with the enemy ski troops that are seeking to press forward.

Characteristics of Marches in Winter

In organizing a march in winter, it is necessary to take into consideration the following:
• roads that are passable under normal conditions may be covered with a heavy blanket of snow, and great effort may be necessary to clear them;
• streams, rivers, and lakes should not be considered as obstacles, but they may be used as convenient routes for clearing winter roads;
• swamps usually freeze over, but if there has been a heavy snowfall before the deep frost sets in, swamps may remain frozen for a long time;
• a snow cover of over 30 centimeters slows down the movement of foot soldiers and rapidly exhausts their strength, if it is deeper than 75 centimeters, it will prohibit the movement of tanks except along roads;
• the long nights increase the importance of night marches; they facilitate secrecy in regrouping; and they reduce the likelihood of enemy aviation being able to operate effectively against our forces;
• the necessity arises on the march as well as during halts — especially in bivouac—of taking measures to prevent frostbite of individuals and freezing of vehicle radiators, etc.

Particular attention must be paid to preliminary training and exercises for the troops in winter marches. They should be gradually accustomed to road marches, to being out in the cold for long periods, and to spending the night out of doors in winter. Artillery, mortars, heavy machine guns should be

Characteristics of Defensive Combat

mounted on runners or sled-like devices. Radio facilities normally mounted on trucks should be remounted on sleds.

In roadless terrain and with deep snow, it is possible to move not only small detachments or reconnaissance and security groups but also units and even whole divisions.

In moving along roads, the speed of movement may be diminished by about one-third, and across country by a good half.

In January 1942, in the offensive of the troops of the Fourth Army against Toropets, movement was accomplished for the most part without roads, and two or three divisions used a single road. The 360th Division moved some 200 kilometers without roads and made 16 to 20 kilometers a day. The 249th Division, moving by night marches from Velizh toward Vitebsk, made more than 80 kilometers in two days. The remaining divisions of the army marched an average of 15 to 25 kilometers each day.

Movement along narrow winter roads (two abreast usually; more rarely, three abreast) nearly doubles the length of a unit column and consequently the length of time for a unit to clear a place and to close on a new concentration area. At the same time, the maneuverability of troops and the problem of control become more difficult; deployment is slowed down; and columns become more vulnerable. Therefore, it is essential to try to draw groups closer together and to try to reduce the length of columns, mainly by using all available routes, including cross-country trails.

In march formations, it is desirable to use units and detachments on skis for cross-country movement; and at the same time, these elements can serve as mobile security detachments. The leading elements and units should frequently be relieved. With the aim of conserving strength and attaining greater speed in movement along roads, sleighs belonging to the local inhabitants can be used for the rapid displacement of reconnaissance elements and for the movements of security screening forces. As soon as an action begins, troops on the sleighs leave them to fight dismounted, and the sleighs are gathered to the column in the rear of the unit.

In order to avoid the artillery following too far behind the rest of the column on the march (as happened, for example, with the Third and Fourth Armies, where the artillery followed one or two days' marches and sometimes even further behind) it is desirable to attach part of it to the rifle elements. In order to help the artillery along difficult sectors of the road, details of riflemen and sappers should be designated to move with it and manhandle it if necessary. Heavy artillery moves in a separate column, following the infantry. In order to protect it against raids by enemy ski units, it also should have infantry security detachments detailed to move with it.

If the snow cover is not too deep, tanks move independently or in route column. If the cover is deeper, it is best to have tanks move in groups interspersed between the echelons of the infantry column.

In movement over roadless terrain (or on roads after a heavy snowfall and especially in blizzards or at night) or through heavy woods, it is necessary to designate a particularly experienced officer as commander of the point or to detail an officer from the staff to move with the point to ensure that the correct route is followed.

During short halts, especially at night, personnel should not be permitted to lie down in the snow and go to sleep. For longer halts, overnight halts, or temporary bivouacs, a place must be chosen that will make it possible for the soldiers to get warm, or at least to get a measure of shelter against the wind (villages, woods, ravines, etc.).

On terrain with few roads and heavy snow cover, flank protection can be carried out by small detachments of ordinary (not mobile) infantry that block lateral roads; close-in flank security is ensured by small ski patrols.

Communication on the march is maintained by means of skiers, mounted messengers, liaison aircraft, motorsleds, liaison officers on skis, and radio.

In weather preventing reasonable visibility (blizzards, heavy snowfall, fog, low clouds), the infantry must usually go to its own antiaircraft protection, since fighter aviation cannot operate effectively under such conditions.

In movements by truck, particular attention is paid to the clearing of the roads; for this purpose, all the local population capable of working as well as all available rear-services elements are employed. In late December 1941, the motor movement of four divisions from the Moscow area to the Northwestern Front took fifteen days instead of the planned four days because of poor traffic control and road service.

If a single road is to be used by several formations in a movement, then the commander of one of the formations is designated as the officer responsible for traffic control on the road and for keeping it in good repair. To help him in this task, he must be given extra detachments of sappers and traffic-control personnel.

Conclusion

The second winter campaign now faces the Red Army. We enter this campaign enriched by the combat and operational experience of last winter, when we dealt the enemy a series of telling defeats and brought his troops on various sectors to the brink of full disaster.

Before us is an enemy who is cunning, stubborn, and desperate. He has studied the lessons of last winter from the tactical-operational point of view as well as from the logistical and winter-warfare point of view. The German forces are extremely well commanded.

The winter victories we shall gain will depend on a decisive improvement in the quality of our combat and operational leadership.

In discussing the Soviet offensive tactics, it seems that Hitler's decision to hold on to fortified areas—the so-called "island" defense—was basically correct. These strong points delayed the Russian advance, allowing for orderly withdrawal and for time to create defensive lines. There is also an admission of superiority of German weapons: the Germans had automatic weapons, while the Red Army infantry still relied on rifles. The study also points out a major German weakness during the battle of Moscow: the poor clothing for the troops resulted in more casualties from frostbite than from enemy action—Ed.

3

Characteristics of Offensive Combat in Winter

THE experience of the offensive operations of the Red Army in the winter campaign of 1941–42 is particularly worthy of study. Below are set forth briefly some conclusions concerning the organization and conduct of the offensive under winter conditions. These conclusions, which are by no means complete, point out only the basic and typical characteristics of winter warfare that all commanders and staffs of combined arms formations should know.

The snow lying on the ground, the frost, the short daylight, and the uncertain weather—these factors complicate the organization and conduct of the offensive in winter through their influence on the terrain as well as on the activities of the troops. In view of this, in past wars winter offensive operations did not occur on any significant scale. Prolonged offensive operations on an army or army-group scale have proved to be within the capabilities only of the Red Army.

The offensive operations of the winter campaign of 1941–42 were carried out by the forces of the Red Army in the field under complex and difficult circumstances, the substance of which included a particularly severe winter; the necessity of carrying out offensive operations on all sectors; a great variance in climatic and terrain conditions; and, finally, a stubborn and well-organized enemy defense.

The Germans, when they went over to the defense along the entire front, set up deeply echeloned defensive lines, and they made wide use of forced labor of our people in the areas they occupied and also of the local resources they found at hand.

Having a limited number of personnel available to them, the Germans were not able to set up a solid and continuous defense line. As a rule, their defense consisted of strong points joined together into centers of resistance. This gave the German defensive system an island-like character. The intervals between the islands or strong points were under the frequent observation of infantry patrols and roaming tanks and could be covered by fire from the strong points.

The island nature, or intermittent character, of the enemy defense made it relatively easy to break through the enemy line (taken as a whole) and to isolate enemy centers of resistance and then to destroy them one by one. If one strong point could be taken, the enemy defense system was disrupted, and the penetration of the tactical depth of the enemy front could be achieved.

The German defense was not stereotyped; it was laid out to take advantage of the particular terrain and the local situation. As a rule, the German defensive lines ran through villages and along heights and included groves and woods. In order to determine the system and layout of such a defense, it was necessary usually to use carefully organized reconnaissance and to employ dense networks of observation points.

The defense included antitank and antipersonnel features; it made wide use of obstacles including mines, wire, antitank ditches, snowbanks, etc. The defensive installations were generally of the field type and were always heated. Our artillery caused the enemy heavy losses and provided constant support to our infantry and tanks.

The German defense was based on the integration of fire and counterattacks. Its combat formations were organized into fire groups and maneuver groups. The maneuver groups, with the support of tanks, carried out small counterattacks on the first day of our offensive operation. For stronger counterattacks, the Germans gathered reserves from farther to the rear and from neighboring sectors; therefore, sizable counterattacks usually did not occur until the second day of the breakthrough operation. This made it possible for out attacking troops to consolidate the lines they had seized and prepare to repulse the counterattacks.

The Germans had many automatic weapons. The massed fire of their artillery and mortars was prepared and registered beforehand and could be called on signal. With the neutralization of individual strong points, our troops were able to open lanes between the enemy defensive center and the enemy's fire system and to penetrate to the flanks and the rear of the enemy centers of resistance. Therefore, in the offensive, the coordination of the actions of the infantry, tanks, and artillery became particularly important.

The German defense was stubborn. In order to shore up the resistance of its armies, which had been shaken by the blows of the Red Army, the German command resorted to a series of extraordinary measures: penal and disciplinary units were formed: Special units were formed to maintain straggler lines behind the battle lines, and these units fired on any soldier attempting to withdraw; individual soldiers were asked to sign statements that they would not leave their assigned positions; and there were even cases of men being chained to their machine guns. By such Draconian measures did the German command seek to strengthen its defense.

It is necessary also to point out that the enemy fought stubbornly even when he was totally encircled; there were numerous examples of this during the winter campaign of 1941-42.

The severe winter found the German command unprepared. The German soldier was poorly clad for winter operations, and he sat most of the time in warmed shelters or in buildings prepared for defense; he preferred to die in warmth than to die in the cold.

Preparations for Winter Offensive Operations

The winter that has passed showed that the transition to winter operations must be prepared long in advance, during the summer. The situation as it unfolded on the front before the winter of 1941-42 did not give us adequate time to prepare our troops fully for winter combat.

The troops of the field armies had to reorganize and prepare for winter actions at a time of active operations along the entire front. The foresight of the High Command made it possible to furnish the troops with warm clothing and with special mounts for their heavy weapons and equipment and to form ski units.

At the same time that the active units of the army were reorganizing and reequipping for the transition from general operations to winter operations as fast as possible, an intolerable indifference and lack of initiative were evident in some of the interior military districts and in some of the reserve armies; they did not use what local resources and leftover equipment that were available to prepare their troops, and it came to pass that some reserve and replacement units were sent to the front with neither the training nor the equipment necessary for winter operations. As a result, there were difficulties and hitches in carrying out plans for offensives. The units of the Third and Fourth Armies, for example, were changing their transportation from wheels to sleigh runners during the course of an offensive, which caused confusion and consequently slowed down the tempo of the offensive right at the beginning.

The supply elements must determine long before the onset of winter the requirements of the troops for winter equipment and supplies. They must determine precisely and accurately the level of supply of such stocks in their stores and depots and then must organize and carry out a concrete program to procure the items and quantities of materiel and supplies that are lacking. Our country is rich in local resources and in raw material. By timely organization of the necessary workshops and agencies, it is possible to prepare sleds and runners, special mounts for weapons, and skis and to repair and make ready winter uniforms and clothing.

Not just certain special units but the army as a whole must train for winter operations. All the offensive operations of 1941-42 in the winter—the counterblow at Moscow, the offensives at Tula, Kaluga, Itikhvin, Kalinin, Toropets, and a number of others—were carried out not by a few separate units but by whole armies and army groups. It simply would not have done to use in these operations a few well-trained and winter-equipped outfits. It was essential to teach entire armies how to attack in deep snow, without roads, at night, and in extreme cold. The troops had to be hardened to long exposure in winter weather. In the circumstances, units began their winter training while they were still in the rear, and they continued to improve their training and seasoning to winter warfare during the course of active operations.

In making ready for offensive operations in winter, the command of an organization has to take into account the snow cover, cold, short periods of daylight, and changeable weather. In this connection, it must be noted that—as opposed to the past when the command usually had adequate time to prepare for an offensive operation—in this past winter the same army was usually engaged in one offensive following directly after another, so that there was little or no lull during which the command could prepare without outside interruptions for a projected operation. For example, the Fourth Army had scarcely taken Andreapol when it launched an offensive for Toropets. The Kaluga operation took place with no real time for preparation, for it was a direct outgrowth of the Tula offensive.

The situation in the winter campaign meant that there were no operational pauses, yet the lack of time by no means meant that the command was freed from the responsibility of preparing meticulously for forthcoming offensives. In such circumstances, it was necessary to foresee accurately the way in which the operations currently underway were going to develop. It was necessary to orient the field commanders thoroughly concerning the overall plans of the High Command, and offensive operations had to be carried out in a manner that, when an operation came to an end, the troops were deployed in such a way as to be ready with a minimum of regrouping for the beginning of the subsequent offensive. The preparation for each offensive had to be carried out at the same time that the offensive just preceding it was under way. This made the preparation for winter operations most complex and caused additional difficulties in direction and leadership.

Preparation for offensive action in winter involves the usual series of things to be done, but each must be considered in the light of special measures and peculiarities caused by winter conditions.

Reconnaissance and security elements should be mounted on skis. On sectors having a heavy snow cover, wide use is made of ski battalions, and if there are no ski battalions, units and detachments of the ordinary troops on such sectors are issued skis.

Snow, frost, and short daylight make it particularly difficult to reconnoiter and discover the strength of the defense, the system of its strong points, the intervals between them, and the dispositions and nature of obstacles. Frequent snowfalls cover antitank obstacles and mine fields, so that reconnaissance of the battlefield in order to discover the antitank obstacles system takes on special importance.

Notwithstanding the difficulties surrounding reconnaissance in winter, there is no excuse for leaving any sector of the front unreconnoitered. In front of the right wing of the Northwestern Front, the reconnaissance section of the staff did not organize an adequate reconnaissance of a swampy forest area without roads and heavily covered with snow. As a result of this faulty reconnaissance, the command was given incorrect reports concerning enemy strength in the area, and this in turn led to an incorrect organization of an offensive operation in the area.

In choosing the direction of the main effort in winter offensive operations, the following factors must be considered:

- the depth of the snow;
- the road network;
- the presence and location of villages and towns;
- the amount of materiel with which the troops are equipped;
- the degree of training and seasoning of the troops for winter actions; and
- the degree of ski training the troops have had and the scale to which they are equipped with skis.

A deep snow cover makes movement difficult. In woods and swamps, it was found frequently that snow covered over unfrozen bogs, so that if units advanced into such terrain without its having been well reconnoitered, troops of such units fell through the snow and found themselves up to their waists in half-frozen mud and cold water, and in addition, tanks, guns, and other materiel got bogged down and could be extricated only with the greatest difficulty.

In choosing the direction of the main effort, reconnaissance and determining the depth of the snow cover are of capital importance. Thus, for example, in the Toropets operation, the 171st Tank Battalion was attached to the 360th Rifle Division, which was in action on the right flank of the army. But in this division's sector there was a snow cover some 80 to 90 centimeters deep, in swampy roadless terrain partly covered with forest. The division expended great effort to clear a way for itself. And the 171st Tank Battalion, following after the infantry columns all the way, took no part whatever in the operation. Obviously, if there had been proper reconnaissance of the terrain in which the division was operating, it could have been discovered that the terrain was not suitable for tank action, and the tank battalion would not have been attached to the 360th Division.

Often offensive operations led to the breaking up of the enemy defense into a number of small groups isolated from each other. The task of command in such a situation consists in directing the main forces against the most vulnerable sector, where such fractionalization of the enemy is most likely to succeed, having in mind at the same time which sector is the most important for the overall success of the action.

The basic aim of maneuver in the offensive operations of the winter of 1941-42 was the encirclement and destruction of the enemy. Since the enemy defense system was composed of a number of separate centers of resistance, there were numerous opportunities for undertaking such forms of maneuver; flanking, deep envelopment, and encirclement were possible not only during the phase of combat deep in the enemy position but also even during the penetration of the forward defensive position.

Flanking movements and envelopments made it possible to strike the enemy at places where he did not expect to be hit. In the Toropets operation, in spite of bad weather and the deep snow, the troops of the Fourth Army took the most populated places by bold employment of envelopment, flanking, and encirclement maneuvers.

Deep echelonment of combat formations gives greater steadiness and strength in combat. In most of the operations of the past winter, the combat formations of our troops were organized into two echelons plus reserves. Echelonments in this manner enabled the troops of the first echelon to push rapidly forward, avoiding being drawn into combat with difficult strong points and not fearing for their flank security. Flanks were secured by ski battalions or by detachments of the units themselves mounted on skis.

In winter, one is forced to use mechanized equipment only on terrain where the snow cover is not very deep. A deep snow cover cuts down the effectiveness of tanks markedly, while a cover deeper than 75 centimeters makes it impossible to use tanks.

To make possible a rapid rate of advance for troops moving through swamps and forests, through roadless terrain, or over country covered with deep snow, engineer elements should be attached to the column, and the infantry should be equipped with engineer tools, particularly snow shovels, cables, ropes, and such items.

In all cases, provisions should be made for the infantry to help artillery, tanks, and other elements with heavy equipment. For example, the 360th Rifle Division was able to advance some 135 kilometers in twelve days as a result of carefully planned and executed arrangements. It advanced through almost virgin forest, through marshy terrain with a snow cover of 90 centimeters' depth. The infantry cut out a path through the dense forest; it packed down the deep snow to make a path; it strengthened the ice on a lake to make it strong enough to support the advancing column; and much of the time it manhandled the heavy equipment forward—and in spite of such difficult conditions the division advanced at a relatively good rate—some 11 kilometers per day.

Ski battalions carried out various types of missions: they conducted tactical and operational reconnaissance; they acted as security forces on flanks and in intervals between units; they disrupted enemy communications; they set up ambushes, destroyed enemy rear installations, wiped out small enemy garrisons; and raided and destroyed headquarters in the enemy rear.

In cooperation with attacking friendly units, ski battalions were used to complete the encirclement of enemy forces.

Ski battalions successfully took part in the pursuit of withdrawing enemy forces. After the defeat of the enemy, the 155th Ski Battalion inflicted heavy losses on the retreating enemy and captured much materiel.

Ski battalions are highly maneuverable. Held at the disposal of the army or army group, they can be quickly concentrated where they are needed for an attack. Thus, for example, the 78th Ski Battalion, which had been in reserve near Andreevskoya, attacked the flank of a battalion of the German 386th Regiment and inflicted some 150 casualties.

And finally, ski battalions were an indispensable means of communication. In the offensive of the Fourth Army toward Toropets, ski battalions at times were the only available means of communication.

Winter slows down the tempo of operations. The scale and tempo of each operation depends on the actual course of events and on the particular situation. The task of the command and of staffs is to examine carefully the situation so that they can determine the correct tempo of a projected operation and then use this tempo as a basis for planning battles and planning the entire operation.

It is absolutely incorrect to set impossible goals and tempos of action in an effort to cause the troops to give their maximum energy. If this is done, then the effect will be quite the opposite of what is desired; day after day the troops will fail to achieve their assigned tasks, will begin to lose faith in their own capabilities and respect for the orders given them, and will perform only indifferently.

It is essential always to keep in mind that one of the basic principles of leadership is to set tasks for the troops that are within their capabilities and then to insist unconditionally that these tasks be accomplished.

In working out an offensive plan under winter conditions, it is necessary to see to the preparation of the departure position for the offensive (construction of shelters and snow trenches; and if the offensive is to take place in wooded terrain, then to set up shelters made of boughs for the protection of personnel and materiel); the cutting through of trenches leading to the enemy's forward edge if our position abuts his; and the clearing of roads and airfields.

Special attention must be paid to the care of equipment and the conservation of the energy of personnel. The troops must be furnished snowshoes, skis, and warm clothing; they must be given special sled-mounts for equipment, heating equipment, antifreeze mixtures, etc. The troops of the Fourth Army in the Toropets operation had good winter clothing and were well trained for lengthy winter operations. As a result they sustained virtually no frostbite casualties.

Winter Offensives

In winter offensive operations, the actions of the troops had certain well-defined characteristics. Artillery and machine guns were emplaced on the day preceding the attack, while it was still light. To conceal regrouping and occupation of the departure position by the troops that were to take part in the attack, combat security and reconnaissance were carried out by elements of the units that were already in contact with the enemy.

The infantry occupied the departure position by night, not long before the time for the launching of the attack. In order to reduce the danger of frostbite, it is essential to reduce as much as possible the time that personnel must remain in the departure position.

It is best to launch the assault in the dark or in snow storms; daytime assaults should be begun in the predawn darkness in order to have as much daylight possible later for the conduct of battle. The wide use of night attacks during the past winter as a rule proved favorable for our forces, even when the relationship of strength between us and the enemy was not in our favor. In places where daytime combat actions failed to produce substantial results, whole formations were able to achieve great success in night action, as in the case of the Fourth Army.

Offensives were launched from positions in immediate contact with the enemy. After the necessary artillery preparations had worked over the enemy defensive positions, our forward echelons surged forward on foot without skis, but with the necessary artillery and mortar support, and wedged their way into the intervals between the enemy defensive strong points and broke through to the enemy rear in order to cut his communications.

The first echelons of an attacking force should not permit themselves to become involved in heavy combat for defended populated places. Thus, for example, the 334th Rifle Division of the Fourth Army from 9 to 14 January 1942 was involved in a savage action aimed at taking from the enemy some strong points on the southwest bank of Lake Volgo. Lacking experience in combat in builtup areas and villages, the division suffered heavy losses from enemy fire and small-scale counterattacks during its effort to take the strong points. The army commander ordered the division commander not to get himself bogged down in such actions but to bypass the strong points. Their reduction would be left to the succeeding echelons that followed the 334th Division. As a result of this, the division began to achieve more success, and it was able to advance again.

The second echelons, pressing close behind the first echelon, thrust into

Characteristics of Offensive Combat in Winter

gaps already existing or created by the first echelons attacking unit and envelop resisting strong points in order to attack them from the rear. Reserves may be used in the same manner.

Artillery conducts its action in its customary combat formations, but if there is deep snow, the artillery often falls behind the infantry. In such a case, it is desirable to order separate batteries or even individual pieces to operate within the combat formations of the infantry. These artillery elements have to be manhandled in order to advance together with the infantry; the infantry furnishes the manpower for this, and in turn benefits, sometimes decisively, from the presence of this direct and immediate fire support.

Tanks operated in cooperation with infantry in terrain passable for tanks. In cases when the terrain had not been adequately reconnoitered and tank units ran into terrain they could not negotiate, the tanks got bogged down through mechanical failure in great numbers; they fell behind the infantry, got stuck in the snow, and were unable to take part in the operation or to influence its outcome.

The following movement factors for tanks were proven during the past winter campaign:

Type of Tank	Depth of snow that could be negotiated (in meters)	Thickness of ice that could support tanks (in meters)
KV-1	0.50–0.80	1.0
T-34	0.70–0.80	0.6
T-40 & T-50	0.40–0.45	0.3
Mk-3	0.40	0.4
Mk-2	0.35	0.3

Tanks and artillery separated from the infantry were roadbound. In roadless terrain covered by deep snow, they were not only of no help to the infantry, they were actually a hindrance by being in the way. For example, the artillery of the 334th Rifle Division in the actions around Nelidovo on 24 January 1942 fell behind, and with the exception of the infantry regimental pieces and one gun of the 270th Artillery Regiment, the division's artillery took no part in the actions at all.

Lack of roads, deep snow drifts, and lack of fuel and supplies led to the army artillery in the Toropets operation falling some 70 kilometers behind the line troops, with the result that it was impossible to organize an artillery offensive.

In infiltrating the enemy defense, it is essential to make wide use of flanking movements, envelopments, and encirclement maneuvers. In the Toropets, Kaluga, and other operations, when our troops came out in the enemy rear, cut his communications, and showed up in places where he was not expecting, the results were stunning; the enemy was obliged to commit his reserves in small packages in various directions, and by throwing his immediate reserves into combat little by little, he suffered the full impact of our blows. Thus, for example, the penetration of the 1191th Rifle Regiment to the enemy rear near

Selizharovsk (Northwestern Front) made it necessary for the enemy to abandon a strongly fortified line and undertake a withdrawal from Nelidovo under unfavorable conditions.

In this same operation, elements of three rifle divisions of the Fourth Army carried out an enveloping movement over roadless terrain and in deep snow; when they launched simultaneous attacks against Andreapol and Velichkov, taking these places and destroying the enemy's immediate reserves.

Making skillful use of flanking and enveloping maneuvers in December 1941, the troops commanded by General Boldin flanked Kaluga, defeated the enemy, and seized the town.

In the Toropets operation, in twenty-one days the Fourth Army under difficult winter conditions, advanced some 250 to 260 kilometers, gaining an average of 12 kilometers a day. Such a rate of advance, one must admit, is relatively rapid, but even so it should not be considered as a maximum or even exceptional. As has already been said, the tempo and scale of every winter operation must depend on the particular concrete circumstances and will correspond with the actual situation.

The fact that substantial gaps exist between enemy defensive strong points often made it possible for our command to launch a simultaneous attack throughout the entire *depth* of the enemy position, as in the case of the Toropets operation. In the context, ski battalions played a particularly important role; they penetrated the enemy rear areas at the same time that the frontal assault began and struck at the principal enemy centers of resistance from the rear. They cut the enemy communications and routes of withdrawal, disrupted his signal system, threatened his staffs and command posts, and brought about a thorough demoralization in his system of defense.

Direction and Control

Winter conditions slow down the rate of repair and restoration work on ground facilities; they cut down the speed at which signal systems can be installed; they reduce the speed of liaison traffic; and they reduce the usability of road systems. Aircraft can be used for liaison purposes only in good weather and where landing fields or strips have been prepared. Machinery often fails to function. Therefore, particular attention must be given to the organization and execution of direction and control of troops on a continual and uninterrupted basis during a winter offensive. Preparations should be made beforehand to depend principally on radio communication when that becomes necessary. Liaison officers should be prepared to move on sleds and skis; command-liaison officers must be ready to move on skis. The time for movement of command posts and plans for keeping them as close to the advancing troops as possible must be firmly set. All of these plans and precautions should be done ahead of time; preparations should be made on the terrain wherever possible, so that the appropriate action can be undertaken at

Characteristics of Offensive Combat in Winter

once when the command is given. In winter, no fewer than three or four duplicative communications systems should be provided, including radio, wire, runners, etc.

Supply and evacuation become more difficult in winter because of frequent blocking of roads by snowdrifts and because of deep snow and freezing.

In organizing the supply of troops in the offensive operations, it is often impossible, because of winter conditions, to use motor transport. Therefore, it is desirable in the case of units operating in roadless terrain to move supplies by horse-drawn sleds. The supply of the 360th Rifle Division during the Toropets operation was not organized with a recognition of winter conditions, so the division, being unable to use its ordinary transport for some days, was left without even rations and fodder.

In other cases, the movement of supplies to troops operating where they could not be served by the main lines of communication was organized along detour routes using pack transport and horse-drawn sleds; units were given extra reserves to carry with them before setting out, and the soldiers carried emergency dry rations with them. In urgent situations, the army maintained a reserve of transport aircraft prepared on immediate notice to undertake supply flights wherever needed.

So that personnel could periodically escape from the cold weather, get warm, and receive a warm meal along the routes of supply and evacuation, warming points and hot-meal points were set up. Medical evacuation rations were closely spaced along evacuation routes.

The offensive operations of the field armies of the Red Army during the winter of 1941–42 have provided a vast experience, which must be thoroughly studied and digested for the forthcoming winter campaign of 1942–43.

This experience should be of value to the Red Army in its future campaigns against the German invaders under winter conditions. The mistakes revealed in an examination of last winter's campaign must be examined and corrected.

The central directorates of the Peoples Commissariat of Defense, the military academies, and the scientific research institutes must all collect, study, and evaluate information concerning last winter's campaign so that they can prepare thoroughly for this winter's operations.

Commands at all levels must organize training programs for commanders and staff officers and troops in winter combat. In this connection, there must be a thorough study and consideration of the many climatic and other factors our wide theaters of operations involve.

Everything that can be learned from our 1941–42 winter campaign experience must be thoroughly studied and then appropriately applied in combat. The results of such studies should also be included in the appropriate manuals and regulations of the armed forces and services.

The following is a discussion of deployment of ski battalions in winter combat. Actually the lessons in this area were already learned, at great cost, during the winter war against Finland where the Finns made masterful use of ski troops. Some of the suggestions such as deploying troops from colder parts of Russia in ski battalions seem self-evident, but this was exactly the type of lesson that should have been learned from the winter war where ill-trained, ill-clad, and ill-equipped troops from the southern part of Russia were deployed in wintery conditions with predictable results—Ed.

4

Combat Employment of Ski Units

THE winter campaign of 1941–42 on the northern and northwestern sectors of the front has provided a wide body of experience concerning the employment of ski units.

The experience available in this respect provides practical answers to the following problems:
- the organization, armament, and equipment of ski units;
- the selection of personnel and training of such units; and
- the combat employment of ski units in various circumstances.

There follow brief conclusions based on the accumulated data relating to the experience in the use of ski units on those fronts where ski units contributed most significantly to the course of operations.

Organization, Armament, and Equipment of Ski Units

The basic organizational form for ski units employed by the Red Army during the winter of 1941–42 was the separate ski battalion, consisting of three companies and one mortar company with fifteen 50-millimeter and 82-millimeter mortars.

On some fronts (the Leningrad Front, for example), ski battalions were grouped together to form ski regiments.

The separate ski battalion proved itself as an organizational-tactical unit, but as a result of weak rear services and a lack of special ski and sled mounts, when the battalion advanced some 30 to 35 kilometers from its base it began to suffer from irregular and inadequate flow of supplies. In view of this, the actions of ski battalions in the operational depth of the enemy defenses were limited, and air supply, which might have partly corrected this weakness, was not employed. The supply operations of separate ski battalions must be critically examined, and some changes must be introduced.

1. In a ski platoon, eight to ten arctic sleds must be included for the movement of rations and supplies and for the evacuation of wounded. In place of such sleds, there can be specially built sled mounts or other appropriate sleighs for the movement of goods over snow.

2. The number of automatic weapons in the battalion should be increased, and the number of carbines correspondingly reduced. All the heavy weapons including machine guns should be transported on sleds. Ski battalions operating in areas with deep snow cover should be armed with 82-millimeter mortars, since the 50-millimeter mortar round has virtually no effect in deep snow.

3. The ski troopers' uniforms should include cotton-batting britches, a heavy jacket (or cotton-batting pants and coat), woollen underwear, a white camouflage suit, mittens, and a cap.

The ski bindings should have a soft cover to avoid chafing the skier's instep.

In addition to ski battalions for the forthcoming 1942–43 winter campaign, we must also have ski brigades or regiments consisting of three or four ski battalions, for actions in the operational depth of the enemy defense. The rear services of such regiments or brigades should be sufficiently strong to support actions up to a radius of 100 kilometers, and there should be provisions for air supply of ski units.

The basic signal resources of ski units should be radio, fast-moving liaison personnel, and visual signals.

Thus, for the forthcoming 1942–43 winter campaign we must have ski brigades or regiments for actions in the operational depth of the enemy defense; and separate ski battalions for actions in the tactical rear of the enemy defense, against the enemy flanks, and for reconnaissance and other shallow combat missions.

Selection of Personnel and Training of Ski Units

The personnel assigned to ski units in the winter of 1941–42 often came from southern districts where they would have had no chance to become accustomed to the use of skis.

The Leningrad Front approached the problem best of all; there, both command and enlisted personnel chosen for duty with ski battalions were selected on the basis of previous experience and skill in the use of skis.

In the view of the very short time available, the program of training of ski units was carried out extremely well, although there were some exceptions. But in some units, there was no training program whatsoever. The troops and even the commanders had only the sketchiest notion of how to use skis and sleds, and they were particularly unprepared for long marches on skis, for moving over rough terrain, and for using skis to move rapidly down slopes.

In training skiers, insufficient attention was paid to the proper adjustment of skis; as a result, many skiers set out on marches with improperly adjusted skis, which chafed their feet, and a good number of the men had to fall out of formation on the march.

The training of the individual soldier in firing and in tactics was not good. Small units tended to straggle and spread out, and combat security, movement under cover, deployment and the choice of combat formations, and the conduct of battle on skis all tended to be insufficiently worked out.

Commanders did poorly at orienting themselves on the terrain, particularly at night; and most of them were not able to lead their units by azimuth.

In most cases, newly arrived ski battalions were at once thrown into combat by the army commander without any preparatory training or orientation; this led to failures and unnecessary losses.

During lulls in the fighting, there was no systematic training program for most ski battalions.

In view of these shortcomings, it is essential in the selection of personnel for ski battalions and in their training to do the following:

1. Personnel should be chosen from troops originating in regions where there are long snowy winters, and these personnel should whenever possible already know how to ski. Personnel should by physically fit, energetic and resourceful; the maximum age for enlisted men should be 25, and for officers, 30.

2. The training of ski units should begin a good two months before snowfall; it should include mainly the normal training program for ordinary rifle units plus some extra physical training and training aimed at making the ski troops ready for ski work (including long runs, jumps, negotiating of rough terrain, and overcoming obstacles). When the snow begins to fall, the ski troops in training will have completed their preparatory work and can spend all of their time in training on skis.

3. In training the individual soldier, emphasis should be placed on his learning to do jumps, crawl, and sprint on skis; he should be taught to shoot and throw grenades on skis and to do so on all kinds of terrain. The soldier should be trained to make long marches on skis over difficult terrain.

4. In training small units (companies and platoons), the main objectives should be to achieve skill in speed and secrecy of movement, speed of

deployment for combat, surprise and rapidity in assaulting the enemy and in seizing favorable lines from which to take the withdrawing enemy under fire.

5. One or two platoons of each ski battalion should be trained in the use of explosives.

Combat Utilization of Ski Units

Ski battalions during the winter campaign of 1941-42 carried out varied types of missions, including cooperation with infantry and cavalry formations.

While operating independently, ski battalions carried out some of the following tasks.

Reconnaissance, Security of Flanks and Intervals between Units

The Guards Rifle Corps in the area of its offensive used for reconnaissance two ski battalions that through their skillful actions secured for the corps commander full and detailed intelligence information concerning the enemy.

The Eleventh Army on the east bank of Lake Ilmen had the 212th and 213th Ski Battalions, each of which, through patrolling, was able to cover a defensive front of some 10 to 15 kilometers' width. The 205th Ski Battalion firmly secured the left flank of the attacking 11th Guard Rifle Corps in the direction of Ramushevo.

In the Seventh Independent Army during the period of the April 1942 offensive, the 191st and 192d Ski Battalions were successfully employed on the flanks of the 114th Rifle Division for surprise blows against the enemy. The 111th Ski Battalion, securing the gap between the 272d and 368th Rifle Divisions, by its skillful attacks inflicted heavy losses on the enemy, who was attempting to penetrate the gap. The 119th Ski Battalion, together with an air-sled battalion, over a protracted period carried out the mission of defending a sector on the shore of Lake Ladoga and ensured the security of the left flank of the Seventh Independent Army.

Cutting of Communications, Destruction of Command Posts and Enemy Rear Installations

The 61st Ski Battalion (Northwestern Front) penetrated 35 kilometers into the enemy position and cut the road leading to Khodunovo. Ski battalions of the Eleventh Army, at the time of its offensive at Staraya Russya, cut all the enemy communications leading to Kholm.

The fact that the front is not continuous and that the Germans tend to organize their defense into separate strong points makes it particularly favorable for ski units to infiltrate enemy positions for actions in the enemy's tactical and operational rear.

Raids by ski units and formations in the enemy operational rear can be coordinated with actions by partisan groups operating in the same area.

Good results can be achieved by the skillful use of ambushes on the part of ski units operating in the enemy rear. Thus, the 254th Ski Battalion successfully organized an ambush on the road near Demidovo, causing heavy losses to the enemy.

The most important objectives for small ski units operating in the enemy rear are communications centers and rear-area installations.

Defeat of Enemy Reserves

In order to carry out this type of mission, a raid by a large ski formation must be carefully coordinated with combat aviation and with local partisan detachments, if they are available in the area of the raid. Thorough air and ground reconnaissance should precede such actions.

Parallel Pursuit

The 155th Ski Battalion, after the defeat of the enemy at Novaya Russa, pursued the enemy and by skillful maneuvering, the battalion inflicted heavy losses on the enemy and captured much equipment.

Joint Actions

Combat actions carried out by ski units in close coordination with ordinary infantry units and formations led to success in flanking and enveloping maneuvers; the ski units covered flanks and intervals between attacking forces and on occasion served as the mobile reserve of the combined-arms commander. Ski units were particularly useful in spoiling counterattacks by enemy ski troops. The result attained in the use of ski troops in these types of actions was in direct proportion to the care and skill with which the action was planned and organized. In cases where cooperation was clear-cut and well organized and where the ski units could be given some support in the form of motor transportation, the ski units showed up to the best advantage and demonstrated their strong points, namely, mobility and the sudden application of firepower.

There were also cases in which ski units were given the mission of assaulting well-prepared and strongly held positions. Not having any artillery, ski units as a rule took heavy losses in such attacks without achieving any worthwhile success.

Blocking Strong Points

The strong point Glukhoye-Demidovo was attacked by the 155th, 156th, and 259th Ski Battalions (Group Ksenofontov). The three ski battalions took heavy losses in personnel but did not succeed in taking the strong point.

The 256th Ski Battalion of Group Ksenofontov was committed against the strong point Sebezh; it was pinned to the ground and took heavy losses from enemy mortar and automatic weapons fire. The battalion finally had to withdraw.

The blocking and repeated assault of the strong point Vershina by several ski battalions also failed. The enemy beat off all our assaults and took a heavy toll; the strong point held out until later the enemy abandoned it of his own will.

There were rare occasions when ski battalions were used as ordinary line elements of regiments. This is absolutely wrong; ski battalions must be used only for the types of action for which they are best suited—blows against the enemy flank, in his rear, and in other actions where they can make fullest use of their mobility.

Conclusions

The combat experience of the 1941-42 winter campaign shows that the correct use of ski battalions must take into account their organization, their armament, and their tactical characteristics.

On the basis of the tactical-technical characteristics of ski units (principally mobility and cross-country ease of movement), the following are the missions suitable for them:

1. carrying out operational reconnaissance up to a depth of 100 kilometers, over a lengthy period of time;

2. ensuring the security of flanks and intervals between units, both by means of patrolling and by acting as mobile reserves;

3. combat against enemy air-dropped groups, against enemy saboteurs in our rear, and as security elements to protect our lines of communication;

4. actions in the enemy rear against command post message centers, various rear installations and bases, and airfields; the destruction of small enemy garrisons in the enemy rear; and the cutting of enemy communication;

5. pinning down reserves in the enemy immediate rear; actions against enemy troops on the march or while halted for rest periods; destruction of enemy stationary or mobile security detachments;

6. joint actions of ski regiments or brigades with cavalry or tanks in the operational depth of the defense for the purpose of exploiting success in the direction of the main effort; and

7. pursuit of the withdrawing enemy.

This list by no means exhausts the possibilities for the use of ski units. The great variety of situations that arise under winter combat conditions will always lay upon the commander who is organizing the battle the decision regarding the best employment of ski units available to him.

But in all cases in which ski units are used in combat, it is essential that their basic tactical characteristics of speed and maneuverability be made full use of.

It is wrong to use ski units for the assault of well-organized enemy strong points.

The conclusions concerning the combat employment of ski units must be studied by army-group, army, corps, and divisional commanders. In the forthcoming winter campaign of 1942–43, the mistakes that have been made in the past cannot be tolerated.

A discussion of the work of artillery during the Battle of Moscow shows that this branch of the Red Army surprisingly did not acquit itself well despite the fact that the Russian artillery, except in the case of the German 88 AA-AT gun, was usually superior. The experience of the winter campaign, which here includes areas other than Moscow, played a major part in artillery development during the remainder of the war by giving rise to, among other things, not only better equipment but also to independent rocket artillery divisions to soften the enemy positions. For further details in this area, see also Chris Bellamy, Red God of War *(London: Brassey's Defence Publishers, 1986)—Ed.*

5

Combat Work of the Artillery in the Winter of 1942

IN February and March of 1942, the officers of the staff of the Main Directorate of the Chief of Artillery of the Red Army conducted a survey of the work of artillery staffs and of the combat activity of the artillery of the Western, Leningrad, Kalinin, and Southwestern fronts.

The combat activity of the artillery during February and March took place at the time of a number of offensive operations on various fronts. In addition, this two-month period was characterized by the winter conditions typical for the northern fronts and by the spring mud that is particularly bad at this time in the area of the southern fronts.

We here set forth a brief résumé based mainly on the actual survey conducted on the artillery activity of fronts and armies. At the same time, we reproduce the opinions and conclusions that were transmitted to the staff of the Main Directorate of the Chief of Artillery.

The aim of this report is to gather in brief form some fundamental observations concerning the work of artillery under winter conditions for the attention of combined-arms commanders and artillery commanders and also to bring to the attention of such commanders certain shortcomings observed in the work of artillery so that measures can be taken to correct them in our further operations against the German invaders.

Enemy Artillery Activity

During February and March, the enemy continued to organize his defense around a system of strong points and centers; he fought stubbornly in defense and went over to counterattack on certain sectors of the front.

During this period, the enemy artillery was seen to make wide use of smoke shells as a device for designating targets. This method of target designation was used especially when the enemy artillery and air force were working in cooperation.

The enemy used night firing a great deal. There were cases when the enemy employed night fire to achieve surprise. After satisfactory registration had been made, the enemy would not immediately open fire for effect but would wait several hours or even a day or two; in this way he almost always achieved surprise with good results—for him.

For fire control, the enemy used individual officers and NCOs as observers; they were sent out forward into their operational line area, and they reported back by radio.

The Preparation for an Operation

From the materials gathered during the survey, it was discovered that the work of artillery staffs at the front in preparing for an operation suffers from numerous defects.

Thus for example, the artillery staff of the Fifth Army in preparing for the March offensive had far from adequate information concerning the enemy. Only the enemy's fire system had been reconnoitered; the tactical depth of the enemy defense had not been examined at all by our reconnaissance elements. Lack of full data concerning the enemy made it impossible for the army artillery staff to make the right decisions about grouping its artillery resources, the expected rate of ammunition consumption, and artillery targets and missions at the various phases of the offensive. In the divisions, artillery was grouped in a haphazard manner.

The army artillery offensive plan was worked out in abstract generalizations; it failed to coordinate the fire resources of the divisions; and in the divisions in turn, the plans for the artillery offensive did not take into account the full firepower of divisional and regimental artillery.

The plans for the subordination of artillery units consisted of nothing more than copies or extracts from the plans transmitted down from higher artillery headquarters. The plans failed to provide for the accomplishment of artillery missions in the tactical depth of the defense and along boundaries between divisions in any way that would be useful in the overall context of the army's offensive plan. Furthermore, the plan of the army artillery staff provided for the artillery of the 331st Rifle Division to fire for neutralization first against targets on the division's right flank, while the overall offensive plan provided for this same division's leading off on its left flank for its main effort.

The combat formations of artillery tended to be bunched up, and they lagged unconscionably far behind the advancing infantry.

Plans were not made for the use of roving guns, sections, and batteries. The logistical support and supply of operations was not well thought out; the rates of ammunition expenditure provided for in the various phases of an operation did not in any way correspond to the actual rates required by the missions assigned to the artillery during these phases. The artillery staff of the Western Front did not know that the Fifth Army was preparing for an offensive operation, so it was unable to provide the necessary supervision and control of the work of the artillery staff of the Fifth Army, not could it provide the practical assistance the latter needed.

In preparing for the Kharkov offensive operation, the following matters were not fully worked out by the artillery staffs of two armies of the Southwestern Front:

1. Coordination of artillery, mortar, and infantry gun fires was not carefully provided for.

2. There was no uniform system of target designation between artillery and tanks.

3. Divisions artillery staffs were weak in directing the fires of regimental artillery and mortars. In combat, divisional artillery chiefs and commanders of infantry support groups did not get sufficiently concrete directions and guidance from combined-arms commanders and their staffs; they did not get precise guidance on tasks for regimental guns and mortars; and they did not arrange to get help from the infantry when it came time to move the artillery forward so that it might keep up with the advancing infantry.

4. Measures to facilitate the advance of artillery by preparing roads were always undertaken too late on the muddy sectors so that the regrouping of artillery was slowed down, reinforcement artillery regiments could not rapidly be detached and moved, and the bringing up of ammunition, fuel, and rations was made difficult.

5. Not nearly enough use was made of the daylight hours for terrain reconnaissance and working out cooperation between rifle and artillery regiments and battalions. As a result, often the combined-arms commander simply assigned the artillery commander his missions on the map, rather than on the terrain itself.

The artillery staff of the Fifty-sixth Army of the Southern Front during the preparation for the Taganrog operation did not provide for the necessary grouping of its artillery in the direction of the main effort. The artillery was strung out along a 28-kilometer front. No effort was made to work out on the ground the problems involved in infantry-artillery-tank cooperation. During the operation itself, the light artillery and the regimental guns fell behind the advancing infantry.

Thus, on 8 March 1942, the 2d Guard Rifle Division forded the River Mius and wedged its way into the enemy position on the eastern bank, but the guns of its regimental artillery and of its antitank unit had fallen far behind. The enemy counterattacked with tanks, and the division, being without antitank guns or any other kind of artillery, had to retreat.

From numerous other cases the conclusion must be drawn that when direct artillery support is most needed by the infantry in the depth of the enemy positions, our staffs had made insufficient plans and preparations for infantry-artillery-tank cooperation. This is a common failing of our staffs.

As an example of good artillery staff work, we can cite the case of one of the armies of the Bryansk Front. In preparing the operation for the annihilation of the enemy Volkhovski grouping, a planned ten-day reconnaissance was carried out by our forces and commanders at all levels were given reconnaissance missions as part of the overall program. Every two or three days, division artillery commanders reported to the army artillery commander on the results of reconnaissance in their areas and their conclusions concerning the enemy positions. As a result of this thorough reconnaissance, the division artillery chiefs, the staffs of artillery groups, and the army staff all had a clear and accurate idea of the disposition of the enemy and his fire system.

The plans for the artillery offensive worked out by the artillery staffs of army, divisions, and regiments were precise and concrete: volleys were massed in the decisive directions, intervals between divisions were covered, and provisions were made beforehand for firings in the most likely directions of possible enemy counterattacks. Fire diagrams with tables of coordinates of targets that had been located by intersection were sent down in good time to the staffs of artillery groups. For the destruction of log-and-earthwork firing positions and bunkers, batteries were chosen that were known to be best prepared to fire precisely.

The plan provided for the use of mortars and of individual artillery pieces to deny the enemy the chance of rebuilding or reoccupying destroyed targets. The plan realistically provided for supply of the operation throughout its phases.

On the Crimean Front before the March operation a number of instructional exercises was held for commanders and staff officers. In the exercises, the organization of the artillery offensive was discussed, and questions of fire planning, the direction of massed fire against a given sector, and cooperation among infantry, artillery, and tanks were all dealt with.

In preparing for an operation in February, the artillery staff of one of the Western Front armies carried out a carefully planned and executed terrain reconnaissance together with the combined-arms commanders and the commanders of the artillery regiments. Combat documents were prepared and appropriate extracts were sent in good time to the staffs and commanders who would carry out the action provided for in them. The army artillery staff did all its work on planning the artillery part of the operation at night, and in daytime, the officers of the army staff visited artillery battalions and groups to help and supervise them in the detailed planning of their fire; furthermore, they saw to it that appropriate extracts were conveyed to battery commanders and that the latter understood them fully. The artillery supply elements of the army got as much transport of all kinds from the divisions as possible so that the supply of ammunition during the operation would be adequate. The army artillery staff arranged with the army engineer directorate for the clearing of the basic roads that would be used to move the artillery and the artillery rear services.

In written orders, the staff of the army provided for
- the establishing of artillery battalions and batteries in the infantry battalion and company areas;
- movement by night of the artillery to its firing positions;
- registration over a period of two days, and with a limited number of pieces, to prevent the enemy from getting an idea of our basic artillery dispositions;
- fire by specially designated pieces exclusively from reserve or false firing positions; and
- designation of certain regimental artillery pieces, and even some 107-millimeter guns for direct fire missions.

The order of displacement of batteries and battalions, their occupation of the correct firing positions, and the camouflage and engineer preparation of firing positions were all checked by the headquarter troops and the traffic control troops. This traffic control and guide work was done by officers who were briefed by the division artillery chiefs. This procedure made it possible for the firing positions to be occupied in complete secrecy, with no confusion or mistakes.

The Grouping and the Direction of Artillery

The grouping of artillery in the operations carried out in February and March corresponds in most cases with the requirements set forth in the letter directive No.03 of the Supreme High Command.

The density of artillery on various fronts can be seen on the following page.

The concentration of the basic artillery mass in the direction of the main effort of the operations carried out during February–March 1942 was achieved on all fronts and army sectors. This was done through the activities of artillery from the reserve of the High Command and through the temporary shifting of artillery from units (division armies) on secondary sectors and away from divisions that were in the rear refitting and resting or in reserve.

Front	Army	Average density of artillery pieces per km		Ratio: Soviet to German	Remarks
		Soviet	German		
		(in the direction of main effort)			
Western	5th	24.0	4.0	6.0:1	The enemy's
Southwest	38th	14.0	2.0	7.0:1	superiority
Crimean	51st	29.0	10.0	3.0:1	in mortars
Crimean	44th	26.0	9.0	3.0:1	amounted on
Leningrad	42nd	19.0	5.0	4.0:1	an overall
Leningrad	55th	13.3	5.3	2.5:1	basis to 25%.
		(on secondary sectors)			
Leningrad	23rd	3.4	1.6	2.0:1	
Leningrad	8th	5.5	3.4	1.5:1	
Bryansk		3.1	1.7	1.5:1	
Western		5.8	5.9	1.0:1	

In the armies, the practice was widely used of setting up army long-range artillery groups, directly subordinated to the army artillery chief. Thus, for example, in the Fifth Army the long-range group included one gun regiment of the reserve and one regiment of 155-caliber guns. On the Southern Front in one of the armies a long-range artillery group was set up consisting of three artillery regiments with 48 guns.

The experience in the use of such long-range artillery groups, directed immediately under the command of the army chief of artillery, proved their value. This arrangement is the most convenient for the employment of long-range heavy artillery in offensive operations. Thus, for example, during the offensive at Slavyansk, the army long-range artillery group consisting of 48 guns struck heavy blows against the principal enemy centers of resistance and neutralized nearly all the enemy batteries that were located in the direction of the main effort of our offensive.

On 20 March 1942 on the sector of our Fifty-first Army in the Crimea, the enemy's 22d Panzer Division unexpectedly struck our lines. Its forward elements penetrated 2 or 3 kilometers into the lines of our infantry positions; in some places, they came upon our artillery's firing positions. It was only thanks to the fact that the army artillery chief had at his disposal a powerful artillery group prepared to carry out certain fire missions and an efficient communications system that we were able to fend off not only the first enemy tank attack but also two succeeding ones involving tanks and infantry. The enemy suffered heavy losses. Some 48 enemy tanks were evacuated from the field of battle, 12 of them completely knocked out and abandoned by their crews.

On the Crimean Front, army mortar groups were often formed by taking the medium and heavy mortars of the divisions; this practice paid off handsomely, especially in the first phase of the artillery offensive. A mortar group under army control of some 100 mortars was able to bring down such heavy massed fires on enemy personnel and firing points on the forward edge of his defense that it achieved very successful results in the preparation of the assault. The principal shortcoming in the use of such groups was the inability to organize their maneuver on the field of battle.

The centralized direction of the massed fire of the artillery in armies was achieved through divisional artillery chiefs assigning the firing missions (including the covering of gaps between divisions that were related to the overall army objectives). But on the other hand, in actual practice there were many instances in which the army artillery chief devoted all his attention to a single narrow sector of the front, with the result that, in solving a single important problem, he left numerous other significant targets unpoached.

Artillery Reconnaissance

The actual procedures in assigning reconnaissance missions by many artillery staffs and in many artillery units still fall far short of a thorough reconnaissance of the fire system of the enemy defense, particularly in the depth of the defense. Furthermore, the reconnaissance data received are not studied in detail, and all too frequently, they are simply transmitted without analysis to the next higher headquarters.

Ground artillery reconnaissance of the enemy was carried out by means of
- the organization of basic operational points and the sending forward of artillery officers and reconnaissance personnel to the infantry positions;
- sending out artillery reconnaissance personnel together with infantry reconnaissance patrols;
- sending out artillery reconnaissance groups (of six to ten men) and individual artillery reconnaissance men into enemy territory, with the object of determining precisely the enemy defensive system, learning the enemy fire system in detail, and sometimes with the objective also of correcting our fire; and
- the organization of observation posts for accurate intersection of enemy targets, which was more widely employed in High Command reserve units than in divisional artillery.

Sending artillery officers and reconnaissance personnel out with the combat formations of infantry and, most particularly, the organization of active artillery reconnaissance groups gave good results. There are numerous examples showing how these forms of artillery reconnaissance aided in facilitating the neutralization or destruction by fire of objectives that were interfering with the advance of the infantry.

Sound fire direction instruments were effectively used in several fronts. Thus, for example, the instruments of the 2d Artillery Regiment from 16 through 26 March 1942 were able to locate thirty-two enemy artillery pieces in action. The instruments of the 320th Red Banner artillery regiment worked particularly efficiently. This regiment, with the help of its instruments, was able to knock out three enemy batteries, as was confirmed by the stories of enemy POWs local inhabitants, and personal examination of the position of these batteries after they were occupied by our troops.

There were shortcomings in the use of artillery instrumental fire control. In the first place, instrumental reconnaissance units generally served only their own parent units, which were subordinated to armies. The coordinates of targets pinpointed by this means were sometimes incorrectly transmitted; and systematic errors were not eliminated. Often artillery instrumental reconnaissance units were deployed so far behind the lines that they were not able to pick up the points of impact of our artillery rounds.

Air reconnaissance and air photo reconnaissance were poorly used in all army groups. The artillery staffs of the Leningrad and Western fronts have begun to make some improvements in the use of these forms of artillery reconnaissance, but there still is a decided weakness in linking up the results through air reconnaissance with those achieved through ground reconnaissance.

In artillery reconnaissance, there must be further improvement in the following respects:

- the organization of systematic observation from operational points of the field of battle;
- organization of command reconnaissance;
- the use of intersecting observation on a broader scale than heretofore, particulary in the division artillery regiments;
- the working out of efficient systems for the exchange of information between the reconnaissance elements of artillery staffs and those of combined-arms staffs and air reconnaissance;
- direction, planning, and detailed analysis of the reconnaissance data obtained by artillery staffs at all levels;
- the organization of cooperation between optical artillery reconnaissance resources and artillery sound resources, in order especially to eliminate systematic errors; and
- the organization of cooperation between optical and sound reconnaissance and artillery units in the interests of being able to open fire as soon as possible against enemy targets that have already been located by reconnaissance as soon as these targets reveal their location by opening fire (in other words, denying to enemy firing points the possibility of conducting undisturbed fire against our troops).

Cooperation between Artillery and Other Arms

The basic question involved in the coordination between artillery staffs and staffs of combined-arms formations is the joint working out of the preparations preceding operations. For the most part, army artillery staffs and combined-arms staffs have gotten together quite well in coordinating their preparations for projected combat actions and operations, but there are cases in which this sort of coordination has been less than adequate.

The following are the principal shortcomings in this respect:

1. Many divisional and regimental commanders still assign artillery fire missions on the map rather than on the terrain.

2. Tanks and infantry are not trained to follow closely behind the artillery bursts, while artillerymen, being afraid of hitting their own infantry, keep their barrages too far out in front of the advancing infantry (lifts of 500 or 600 meters at a time).

3. The infantry occupies a departure position for the assault too far (500 to 600 meters and sometimes even farther) from the enemy forward edge, and with the lifting of the artillery to the next line deeper in the enemy defense instead of energetically pushing forward, the infantry advances by short and timid bounds, which eventually makes it necessary for the artillery to repeat its initial fire preparation.

4. Insufficient attention is paid to the location of enemy antitank weapons and to the probable directions of enemy infantry and tank counterattacks.

5. Uniform fire-designation systems are not generally used, nor is there a generally accepted system, in a given action, of uniform designation of terrain features and of basic repair points.

6. Infantry often is late in launching its assault, which leads to a general breakdown of planned coordination.

7. Coordination between artillery, mortars, infantry guns, and bomber aircraft is weak in both defense and offense.

8. Coordination in combat is usually lost from the moment the infantry assault begins.

9. Artillerymen still have not learned to accompany the infantry with fire and maneuver throughout the entire depth of the enemy defense.

10. There is insufficient coordination between artillery and infantry in the defense and consolidation of lines taken and of populated places.

11. Many artillery and infantry commanders believe that they are fully discharging their responsibility for mutual cooperation simply by being together in the same observation point during battle.

12. Infantry is often left without support either from its own artillery or the supporting artillery.

As a result of inadequate cooperation among the artillery, the infantry, and the tanks, there were occasions in which there were unnecessarily large losses in artillery materiel. In the 20th Tank Brigade on 4 March 1942, nine tanks were knocked out because the tanks had failed to give the artillery the agreed signal indicating the direction from which they were receiving antitank fire from enemy guns.

An operation carried out by one of the armies of the Southern Front can serve as an example of poor coordination. The offensive by the army's shock group was begun at 1700 on 8 March 1942. Several units of the army succeeded in forging the River Mius, but as a result of weak artillery support and a lack of support from ground-support aviation, when counterattacked by enemy infantry, these units and their tanks were forced to withdraw to their original departure positions. During three days the enemy continued to beat back all efforts to set the offensive in motion again; and by the third day, the offensive had made no gains, while the units involved had taken extremely heavy losses.

The principal shortcomings in the grouping and direction of the artillery lay in the fact that the army artillery chief did not have at his disposal artillery to make its weight felt in the decisive direction. Though he did have at his disposal 12 long-range artillery pieces, the limited observation afforded by the terrain made it impossible for him to use these weapons to advantage.

Infantry regimental guns and antitank artillery had been ordered by the army chief to advance in the combat formations of the infantry and to support the infantry by fire and movement, but this failed to happen. The artillery fell behind the infantry; it fired from cover, using indirect fire. As a result, the infantry elements that reached the opposite bank of the river were totally without accompanying guns, and this was brought home when the enemy counterattacked with tanks and infantry. The infantry was forced to withdraw with heavy losses simply because there had been no preplanned coordination with the artillery and the tanks.

Artillery Combat Formations

The following basic comments should be made:

1. Artillery of all types began as a regular practice to occupy firing positions at night.

2. Firing positions and observation points began to be prepared much more satisfactorily from an engineering point of view.

3. The practice of preparing reserve, false, and temporary firing positions is becoming much more common.

4. Artillery is showing more energy in advancing close together with the infantry.

5. Traffic control and housekeeping arrangements have been improving.

6. Regimental and divisional artillery pieces are being more effectively used for direct fire.

Artillery actions from temporary, reserve, and false positions in a number of cases have produced excellent results. Thus, the artillery of the armies of the Southwestern Front in a defensive operation as a regular practice conducted all their fire from temporary firing positions and, after firing the batteries, moved back to their primary firing position. As a result, the enemy, in returning our fire, struck at our temporary positions, thus wasting a considerable quantity of ammunition.

Night firing by our 178th Artillery Regiment from temporary positions was picked up by the enemy by flash-ranging. On the following day, the enemy shot some 80 rounds on these temporary positions and even used aircraft to help with fire correction.

Nevertheless, there are still instances in which the firing positions of artillery, particularly regimental and divisional artillery, are set up far from the enemy forward edge so that the artillery cannot provide support for the infantry throughout the depth of the enemy positions without displacing.

The antitank defense of artillery positions is not thoroughly thought out in all cases.

Artillery Fire: Preparation and Conduct

In army artillery regiments, actual firing is usually preceded by topographic preparation, by sound reconnaissance, and by intersection of the targets through observation. The artillery survey battalion carries out these tasks. In artillery regiments, less attention is paid to topographic (survey) work. In rifle division artillery, bilateral observation (intersection) is used very little; division artillery commanders excuse this shortcoming on their part by pointing out that they do not have necessary equipment to do the job properly, and they make do with what they have at hand.

Topographic platoons were hardly ever used for their own kind of specialized work. On the Volkhov Front, topographic platoons were used for ordinary observation point work. The platoon commanders, who had had specialized training in peacetime for topographical work, were for the most part wasted on other tasks.

The combat formations of divisional artillery were taken up casually and either without an effort at planning or else planned in a most amateurish manner. Commonly, firing positions were assigned on the map in general terms or else in an offhand way by relating them approximately to some local landmark. The basic firing data were usually prepared from the map, or by visual estimation, without correction for wind or temperature.

The preparation of basic firing data through the use of the plane table was far less common in division artillery than it was in the regional artillery regiments. Precise methods of target designation and correction were used rarely in divisional artillery; for the most part, the method of correction was simply to depend on the estimates of people watching the bursts. Fires were lifted and shifted by very approximate methods. Even in army artillery regiments and in long-range artillery units, most of the preparation for firing was done by map; the plane table was not used often, and survey computations were rarely made.

Direct fire and firing from open positions were used often, particularly on the Western Front. This sort of fire gives good results in combat against enemy tasks and infantry. Good results were also obtained by using illuminating shells and shrapnel for night firing, and shrapnel and rounds together for day firing against enemy personnel.

Counterbattery work had good results, mainly through well-organized artillery reconnaissance. On the Leningrad Front, one of the armies was able to locate nearly all the enemy batteries in its sector that were firing against the city; then, as a result of our counterbattery fire, the enemy artillery was obliged to redeploy in greater depth, in an effort to get out of range of our fire.

The following principal shortcomings were observed in artillery firing:

1. Our artillery has not been quick in perfecting its ability to fire shrapnel rounds effectively; too many rounds are expended in registration, and registration itself takes too long;

2. Ricochet fire is not used enough; only occasional army artillery regiments use this method;

3. Many battery and battalion commanders are not able to conduct neutralization fire effectively;

4. Firing regulations are not sufficiently studied; the excuse is used that there are not enough manuals available;

5. Many battalion commanders are really inexperienced in directing fire, and they are not learning how to do so quickly;

6. Artillery battalion staffs all too often do not play a sufficiently active and decisive role in the direction of the battalion firings.

Employment of Artillery Fire

There are still instances of combined-arms commanders making incorrect use of artillery fire. for example, in one of the armies of the Southern Front, the commander of the 15th Guard Rifle Division ordered an artillery battalion to fire a four-hour artillery preparation involving the expenditure of some 1,500 rounds to support two 30-man reconnaissance patrols that were going to try to take some prisoners.

And again, the fact that artillery resources of rifle regiments are not considered by combined-arms commanders as fully capable of breaking up enemy attacks is an indication that these combined-arms commanders do not fully understand and make use of the capabilities of artillery.

In the armies of the Southern and Southwestern fronts, proper use is not made of the available heavy artillery, and at the same time that heavy artillery is being used for light tasks, insufficient use is made of the fire resources of the infantry—the light artillery, 50-millimeter mortars, machine guns, and even rifles.

Mortar units are awkwardly used in massed-fire tasks, and the artillery chiefs lack skill in directing massed mortar fires.

Conclusions

The combat actions of Red Army artillery during February and March of 1942 constitute the basis for the following conclusions:

1. The requirements set forth in letter directive No.03 of the Supreme Command concerning the artillery offensive are being widely circulated, but

not all of the artillery units at the front have fully mastered them. The massing of artillery resources at the point of main effort is understood as a principle, and in the main, this is being done correctly. The grouping of artillery in general corresponds to the tasks set by the combined-arms commanders.

2. The Red Army artillery each day is gathering more and more valuable combat experience; it is perfecting its combat procedures, and it is conducting training for its personnel.

3. In training and practice, shrapnel is not given the importance it merits, and various advanced firing methods prescribed in the firing regulations are not used as much as they should be.

4. The experience of a number of offensive operations makes abundantly clear the value and effectiveness of direct fire, using pieces up to and including 152-millimeter caliber.

5. Often massed artillery fire is interpreted as meaning piling a very large number of artillery pieces up in a small space without taking into proper consideration the amount of ammunition they will be able to expend effectively. This simply causes a waste of ammunition in registration and involves the commitment of more pieces than can be supplied with ammunition. It would be preferable to use fewer pieces (thereby revealing less to the enemy of our artillery order of battle) and to ensure that they get as much ammunition as they effectively need and, in terms of the mission, can expend.

6. The organization of artillery groups directed by army artillery chiefs proved thoroughly worthwhile in the actual experience of the winter offensives just past.

This part of the report is highly critical of the Red Army's reconnaissance operations, which were poorly coordinated and carried out in piecemeal fashion resulting not only in losses but in poor intelligence. This was not only true in Moscow but also in other sections of the front such as Crimea. The report once again urges careful planning and use of well-trained troops that should not be squandered in reckless operations. Also discussed here are deployment of "hunter groups" for capturing worthwhile prisoners and reconnaissance operations at night—Ed.

6
Reconnaissance

THE lack of control and direction over the reconnaissance work and reconnaissance organs can create a false intelligence picture—one full of error. This was frequently the case in units of the Forty-eighth Army of the Bryansk Front. Patrols, often when they had reached the enemy wire, would simply take cover and stay put; then shortly before dawn they would return and report "no results." Lack of direction in reconnaissance encourages this sort of laxness and does not create the will to overcome difficulties and accomplish the mission on the part of the patrols that are actually sent out to do the job.

It is not only the fault of the commanders of reconnaissance units that reconnaissance in general until now had been rather inefficient; it is also the fault of the commanders and chiefs of staffs of the combined-arms units and formations of which the reconnaissance units form a part. They, and the intelligence officers of their staffs, should exercise firm control, particularly since many of the reconnaissance unit commanders lack experience themselves.

The role of army-group and army staffs in reconnaissance has often been limited simply to drawing up and distributing plans and directives; there are too few cases in which reconnaissance training for patrol and platoon commanders has been organized. There should be short courses of instruction in the field for small-unit reconnaissance commanders, local gatherings of reconnaissance men, and the exploits of outstanding men could be popular-

Reconnaissance 57

ized in unit newspapers, etc. It is rare that practical exercises or rehearsals precede the execution of reconnaissance missions.

The sooner commanders and staffs of formations at all levels get away from directing reconnaissance by paper and by remote control and get down to direct personal contact with the men who are going to do the job on the ground, the sooner we shall get good results.

Reconnaissance Planning

Reconnaissance should be fitted into a well-integrated plan, and it should be active and continuous. These things are basic in reconnaissance planning. The chief of the intelligence section in accordance with orders from the commander and chief of staff works out his reconnaissance plan, which is his working document; and on the basis of this document, subordinate staffs are assigned specific missions, in accordance with the concrete situation, to utilize their reconnaissance resources in obtaining specifically needed information concerning the enemy.

But in practice, things do not often work this way. Some divisional staffs and even some regimental staffs, instead of working out their reconnaissance plan based on the actual situation, simply copy the orders and even the reconnaissance plans they have received from higher headquarters and then send them on to their subordinate units.

Even worse, we sometimes find staffs that do not plan reconnaissance at all. Thus, in the 143d Division of the Bryansk Front, reconnaissance orders were given only orally and in the most general terms. In the 6th Rifle Division of the same army group, the reconnaissance order was given without any indication as to *when* the reconnaissance data were to be reported. And on the other hand, some army intelligence sections planned everything in such minute detail that they robbed the divisional intelligence sections of any initiative. In some divisional staffs the same thing happened, and in others the chief of the intelligence section—with no one directing or checking his work—worked out his intelligence plan and issued his orders to the reconnaissance elements two weeks ahead of time, not stopping to realize that the situation might change radically during such a period.

Actual experience shows that in a relatively stabilized situation, the intelligence staff of an army group can plan generally the intelligence work of the subordinate armies for no more than two weeks; if the situation is more fluid, the army group intelligence staff should not plan more than six to eight days ahead. A division or brigade receives from the army (or corps) staff its general reconnaissance mission covering a period of eight to ten days if the situation is stabilized, while it plans the reconnaissance missions of its regiments for a period of no more than three days in an unstabilized situation.

If reconnaissance missions are properly planned and passed to the actual reconnaissance elements that will carry them out soon enough for the reconnaissance elements to prepare for their missions, there will be good results. In order to prepare for a reconnaissance mission properly, even an experienced reconnaissance man or a well-trained patrol needs a minimum of six to eight hours of daylight. If a reconnaissance mission is not properly planned, its results will be negligible.

The reconnaissance platoon of the 140th Rifle Regiment (Northwestern Front) on 31 January 1942 was given the mission of seizing a prisoner near "N." No time was given for preparation, despite the fact that the terrain had not been studied. The platoon wandered about all night until finally it ran into the reconnaissance company of the 122d Rifle Division; neither group knew that the other was operating in the area. It turned out that both reconnaissance outfits, without adequate preparation, had been sent out at about the same time and into the same area with the same mission, unbeknownst to each other!

In the staff of the 82d Motorized Rifle Division of the Western Front, the following incident occurred: The chief of the intelligence section of the division in December 1941 gave the 210th Motorized Rifle Regiment the mission of penetrating the enemy combat security and seizing a prisoner. The order included tables showing who would support the reconnaissance mission, the time table, and the signals to be used. But after a careful study of these documents in the regiment, it was discovered that the area that the order proposed to send the reconnaissance into (and where the enemy security positions were supposed to be) had already been taken by our own troops several days earlier.

These examples illustrate clearly how harmful inaccuracy in reconnaissance planning can be in a combat situation.

Reconnaissance men often fail to understand, and their leaders do not explain to them, that a reconnaissance plan is a working document; that it develops and changes as the actual combat situation develops and changes. But even in a stable situation, the size of the units involved, the terrain conditions, the enemy dispositions, and the strength and resources at hand always determine the character of the reconnaissance mission and the way in which it will be carried out.

In staffs where inexperienced reconnaissance men themselves are incapable of planning reconnaissance, it is up to the chief of staff and the commander to provide personal guidance and direction.

Combat experience fully confirms the validity of the requirement laid down in the *Field Service Regulations for Staffs* that the commander himself or his chief of staff should personally prepare the reconnaissance order. It is absolutely inexcusable to delegate this function to an insufficiently trained or inexperienced person.

Conduct of Combat Reconnaissance

Information concerning the enemy can be obtained in various ways. The type of information needed and the particular situation together determine the method of reconnaissance to be used in each case. Combat reconnaissance provides the fullest detail concerning the enemy. It helps to reveal the enemy's positions, his fire system, and the system of his defensive works. In addition, in some cases, it can reveal hidden arrangements or measures taken by the enemy for the defense of a given line. Well-organized combat reconnaissance will always give exhaustive details concerning the enemy, particularly if during the reconnaissance it is possible to take prisoners and documents as well.

Combat reconnaissance is used to discover or clarify the true location of the forward edge of the enemy defense; the system of defensive installations and engineer works (antitank and antipersonnel) on the enemy's forward edge and especially in the depth of his position; the enemy systems of infantry, mortar, and artillery fire; the location of second-echelon and reserve troops; the location of command posts, communications centers, and gaps between enemy units; and the numerical designations of the units in the enemy defense.

Combat reconnaissance requires the assignment of sufficient forces and resources (mortars, artillery, tanks, engineers) and particularly careful organization and preparation. Each commander and each soldier must know in full detail the *who, what, where, and how* of the planned reconnaissance mission he is to take part in. *Combat reconnaissance will succeed only when the enemy believes that an offensive and not a demonstration is being launched on his sector.*

A combat episode that occurred on the Kalinin front is characteristic. A strong point was occupied and strongly fortified by the enemy, who had developed a system of timber-earthworks firing points and open firing points as well. One of the rifle divisions preparing to attack in this sector had tried numerous times to find out the fire system of the enemy defense in these woods, but all efforts by small reconnaissance elements to reach the enemy forward edge were caught in heavy cross fire from enemy automatic weapons.

The divisional commander decided to conduct a combat reconnaissance in force. The motorized infantry reconnaissance company supported by one battery of the divisional artillery regiment and a battery of 82-millimeter mortars was ordered to carry out a demonstration simulating an offensive and to penetrate the enemy security and determine the precise location of the enemy firing points and defensive installations on the eastern fringe of Round Woods.

The company commander carefully prepared his outfit; all those who were to take part in the reconnaissance knew precisely their own missions as well as that of the company as a whole. Cooperation with the artillery and mortars was organized with extreme accuracy, and the necessary signals were worked out and verified. Only after all the preparations had been made and checked did the company commander deploy his platoons in combat formation. After penetrating the enemy front line as had been planned, the platoons came up to the edge of the woods and opened strong fire from machine guns and rifles. At the same time, on signal from the company commander, artillery and mortar fire was opened up on the enemy forward edge.

The strong artillery fire, and the lively mortar fire as well as the fire from infantry automatic weapons, and the continued advance of the platoons gave the enemy the impression that a serious offensive was in progress, so he opened fire on the advancing infantry and the supporting weapons not only with weapons sited along the forward edge of his defense but also with ones in the depth of his defense. After the enemy firing positions on the forward edge and particularly in the depth of the position had been carefully observed, and accurately located, by the company and platoon commanders, the reconnaissance company withdrew to its departure position.

Combat reconnaissance as a rule should precede every offensive against a strongly fortified position or a fortified area, as well as against a defended village or the edge of a wood. And at the same time, there should be continuous observation by combined-arms commanders, staff, and specialists.

An example of badly organized reconnaissance occurred in the 390th Rifle Division of the Northwestern Front. A reinforced platoon under the command of a lieutenant was to conduct a combat reconnaissance supported by the fire of four mortars. Firing signals had been arranged. The platoon commander ordered the mortarmen to draw 117 rounds, but he did not check to see that his order had been carried out. When they had advanced a bare 700 meters, the mortar crews on their own initiative opened fire from all four mortars, and they used up the 40 rounds that they had brought with them instead of the 117 they were supposed to bring. Later, at the decisive moment, when the commander called for mortar fire, there were no rounds left. It became necessary to withdraw, and the mission was not accomplished.

In the Arzhukhova–Vyazovka area on the Kalinin Front, a combat reconnaissance produced great success because of good preparation. A 113-man reconnaissance company took the village of Arzhukhova, and it destroyed 25 enemy personnel and took a prisoner who provided valuable information. In addition, booty was captured.

For five days before the reconnaissance mission began, Arzhukhova and its environs were continuously under observation. On 22 April 1942 the regimental commander personally went over the following points with the command group that was to lead the reconnaissance: a careful terrain reconnaissance; a preliminary reconnaissance of the enemy position; a reconnaissance of the routes of advance; and a review of the objectives of the projected combat reconnaissance. In addition, the reconnaissance group's departure was accurately fixed, a plan and table of coordination was drawn up, signals were agreed, artillery support was worked out, and a withdrawal plan prepared for use in case of necessity.

The carefully worked-out plan succeeded. The enemy, under the impression that a powerful force was attacking, withdrew from Vyazovka. The village of Arzhukhova was taken by the reconnaissance company. The success was facilitated by the constant observation and the carefully worked-out coordination among the groups that were to participate in or support the reconnaissance before the action was launched.

But in addition to clear-cut organization, a thoroughly detailed plan, and careful preparation, combat reconnaissance depends for success on competent direction on the part of senior commanders. Commanders who organize combat reconnaissance should be particularly on the alert to determine when the mission has accomplished its purpose (or as much of it as is practicable) in the circumstances. This is especially important in cases when a combat reconnaissance does not produce immediate success. For sometimes, when enemy opposition is energetic and immediate, it is preferable to cease the action as soon as convenient rather than to reinforce it (to throw good money after bad) with additional forces and run the likely risk of taking additional losses. In such cases, it is more advantageous to organize the reconnaissance along different lines after having determined through further observation that another sector may promise greater success.

In one of the regiments of the 63rd Motorized Rifle Division (Crimean Front) in a March 1942 combat reconnaissance northwest of Feodosia, as a result of bad organization and direction, nearly half the regiment was fed piecemeal into the action. Enormous quantities of ammunition were expended, and heavy losses taken, yet the original mission remained unaccomplished.

On the same front in February 1942, units of the Fifty-first Army conducted a badly organized combat reconnaissance west of the Akmonaisk position; several battalions were eventually drawn into the battle, but the mission was not accomplished even though losses were heavy, and the entire force that had become involved in what started as a reconnaissance was obliged to withdraw to the departure position.

Night Raids

This is a useful form of reconnaissance, but its success depends especially on the amount of time allowed for preparation, on the amount of careful planning and thought put into it and, finally, on the general fitness and suitability of the men assigned to this type of mission. In order to be sure of success, the commander who is designated to carry out a night raid must do a great many things as soon as he has received his order. He must:

1. Choose the objective he will attack, if it is not already designated in his order.

2. Study the objective in detail, the approaches to it, and the enemy firing points that may interfere with his task. The objective must be studied and observed over a considerable period (one or more days), and this observation must be very carefully organized. Sometimes it is desirable to send out small

groups or even individual scouts (including engineers) to reconnoiter the mine fields, signal lines, the depth and width of water obstacles, etc.

3. Draw up a plan of action in which he prescribes how his forces and resources will be divided between the main body and the security element, what the tasks of the supporting artillery will be, what is expected of the mortars, how the action will be timed, how the group will withdraw after the task has been accomplished, and what the signals will be both within the group and between the group and the elements that will be in support.

4. On the basis of the plan, after it has been agreed to, he must assign missions to his subordinates, actually on the ground, and this must be done in sufficient time so that each subordinate leader can fully brief his subordinates in turn so that every man will be thoroughly oriented on the ground and will understand the mission.

5. Personally check to see that all men understand the mission and are fully prepared for their part in it.

An example of a well-organized night raid is that carried out by a regiment of the 334th Rifle Division (Kalinin Front) on 8 June 1942 near Skubyatino.

Information concerning the strength of the enemy garrison at Skubyatino, the enemy firing points and field works, the procedure and routine of his sentries, the layout of the approach routes to the village, etc., was collected through systematic observation, questioning of local inhabitants, reconnaissance patrols, and listening posts. After a careful study of the enemy situation, it was decided to overwhelm the relatively small enemy garrison and seize prisoners and documents.

In preparing the raid, three main groups were set up: one to make a demonstration and two for the actual attack. In addition, smaller groups were set up specifically to seize prisoners, to collect documents from the enemy dead, and to gather enemy weapons and equipment.

Carefully observing security discipline, the reconnaissance men approached Skubyatino—thanks to systematic observation they knew the routine of the enemy sentries—they silently seized an enemy guard and then suddenly burst into the enemy position that was built around a timber-and-earthworks firing position and a nearby house in which the bulk of the enemy troops were resting with a false sense of security. Ten enemy soldiers were killed, and prisoners and documents were seized. The reconnaissance group suffered no losses.

The reconnaissance unit of the 371st Rifle Division was given the mission of seizing a prisoner, but all efforts to do so proved in vain. The situation obviously was one that called for careful preparation. So this was done. For five or six days, officer observers conducted continuous observations; they studied the layout of the enemy combat security and searched for covered approaches. Finally, scouts who had penetrated one night into the enemy security area found a place between two enemy emplacements where a German observer and his assistant met when one was to relieve the other.

The following night, Senior Sgt. Semidovsky and two scouts moved up to this spot along a previously reconnoitered approach and seized a corporal of the 11th Motorized Regiment of the 14th Motorized Division; the prisoner gave valuable information about the disposition of the division, its strength, armament, dumps, and rear area. Our group of three scouts returned safely to our lines with the prisoner and suffered no losses.

A night raid to seize prisoners as a rule should be covered by previously prepared firings that in case of failure can be called down to protect the raiding party in its withdrawal. There should be more than one type of signal provided in case fire must be called for.

In many of the frontline units of the Southern Front, night raids were poorly organized, and not enough time was given for preparation. The terrain was not studied sufficiently, the enemy fire systems were not observed enough to be thoroughly understood, and in the conduct of the raids themselves, discipline was sloppy with the result that members of the raiding parties often opened fire unnecessarily. Then, the enemy, being forewarned, met the raiders with strong fire, and the raid failed. In the 349th Rifle Division, for example, the wrong use of signals caused the failure of a raid.

An action that took place on the 56th Army sector (southern front) in the Taganrog operation can serve as an example of a well-prepared night raid. On various sectors of the front, numerous efforts to carry out combat reconnaissance in force had failed. During the preparatory period before the offensive, night raids and ambushes on the sector from Ryazhenaya to Solyony Hill were organized with the object of taking prisoners for interrogation. Though these raids themselves did not produce the desired results, they did make it possible to plot the enemy position fairly well so a later raid could be successfully organized.

After the responsibilities in connection with the organization of the raid had been assigned, the exact location of the raid was chosen during a terrain reconnaissance in which the intelligence chief took part. From forward observation points, the objective of the raid was precisely defined, and round-the-clock observation was provided for in order to learn the enemy fire system, the enemy's habits, and also in order to determine the best approach route to the objective and the return route the raiding party would take. Then the procedure to be followed in the raid was decided on, and the strength of the actual raiding party and of the group to support it were decided. The men to take part in the raid were chosen, and the armament, ammunition, and equipment they were to employ was decided, then issued to them, and finally checked.

A detailed plan was worked out on the basis of the data obtained through observation and later coordinated with the covering and security groups. In an appropriate area behind the line, chosen because it was like that in which the actual raid was to be carried out, rehearsals of the raid were carried out, with particular emphasis on the movement of the raiding party from its departure position to the area of the raid.

The work of the officer who was to lead the raid and the intelligence officer who had ordered it—and the work was done for the most part at the actual departure position—included the following:

- Ensuring that each participant in the projected raid personally observed the terrain and the objective, so that each could be sure of the approach route, the nature of the enemy defense, and the repair points;
- Assigning the tasks to each of the groups (raiding, security, covering) and to each individual soldier, so as to ensure cooperation between and within the groups and so that everyone would know the who, what, when, how, where, and why of the projected action and all its phases;
- Working out and checking with all concerning the system of signals for coordination and direction, designation of passwords, and assignment of alternates for all tasks;
- Working out of the possible reactions of the enemy during the course of the projected action; and
- Checking to see that each man knew his tasks thoroughly.

The experience gained from the actions of a number of patrols in night raids indicates that anywhere from eight to ten hours to several days of daylight are necessary for the satisfactory preparation of such a raid.

Hunter Groups

The seizure of combat documents and really worthwhile prisoners (officers and signalmen) in order to determine the enemy's order of battle and his plans is one of the difficult and responsible jobs of combat reconnaissance. This type of mission is carried out by experienced reconnaissance men, by "hunters." Before a hunter group is sent out, there must be a careful study of the enemy's dispositions, of the locations of his command post and staffs, of his communications centers, and of his roads, paths, and communication trenches. It is especially important to know the enemy's routine—when and where in the area of the projected action his sentries are relieved, when the enemy troops receive their meals, and how their rest schedule is organized.

In actions in the enemy rear, reconnaissance groups should always be assigned purposeful missions that are within their capabilities to execute. Hunter-reconnaissance groups should not be lured away from their mission by attempts to destroy enemy elements they may meet. For them, destruction of enemy personnel is a useless activity if in so doing they fail to accomplish their basic reconnaissance mission.

An episode that occurred in the sector of one of the divisions of the Kalinin Front can serve as an example of an irresponsible approach to the matter of assigning missions to hunter groups. This group of four men was ordered to accomplish the following: locate the enemy's left flank; establish contact with the 188th Rifle Division; and infiltrate the enemy position and seize prisoners. However clever and capable the four men chosen for the patrol might have been, with such an all-inclusive mission, it is clear that they were bound to fail.

The depth to which hunter groups may infiltrate the enemy position depends on the location of their objective and on the nature of the terrain. But in any case, it should not exceed 10 to 15 kilometers, and normally it will be between 3 and 6 kilometers. Such a group may remain in the enemy area several days. The length of time hunter groups remain behind the enemy lines depends on how well and thoroughly the objective has been "cased," how far the objective is from the front line, and how well the group is prepared to carry out its mission in the enemy rear.

A hunter group normally has from six to twelve reconnaissance men in it. Two or three of them should be sappers (combat engineers). Those chosen for the group should be volunteers, and they should be officers and men with good nerves and demonstrated resourcefulness. Such groups are organized usually at divisional level and form part of the divisional reconnaissance company.

Hunter groups are given their mission personally by the divisional commander or his intelligence officer. Hunters are armed with submachine guns, hand grenades, and knives. Their armament, equipment, and clothing will depend on the weather, but it should be as light as possible in any case. Hunters should as a matter of course have camouflage suits, and they should be given extra rations.

Hunter groups can be used in any type of combat, but they are particularly useful in the defense in wooded, swampy terrain in summer, or in rough terrain in winter, and occasionally in open terrain, if they can be mounted on skis.

The Organization of Ambushes

The methods of obtaining prisoners are extremely varied, and they depend on terrain, on the concrete situation, on the nature of the mission, and on the time allotted for the accomplishment of the mission. One way of obtaining prisoners is through ambushes. An ambush will succeed if it is carefully prepared, if it is well planned, and if those who execute it are resourceful and have steady nerves.

An ambush may be set up on a regular enemy patrol route that has been thoroughly observed, or it may be set up along an enemy communications trench, or even sometimes directly at places where enemy listening posts, observers, or reconnaissance personnel are located.

On a certain sector of the front, a covered communication trench was discovered through observation that obviously connected two enemy detachments occupying the enemy forward edge on that sector. Two reconnaissance men secretly moved up to the communication trench and organized an ambush. Five reconnaissance men armed with submachine guns covered them from nearby.

Exercising great restraint, the men constituting the ambush waited until they had the chance to fall upon two enemy soldiers moving along the communication trench. One they took alive; they disarmed him, and in order to make him stop resisting, they poked him lightly with a bayonet. Then they returned to our lines, fording a stream that dividing our position from the enemy's and dragging their prisoner along with them.

The total number of men involved in an ambush should not exceed twelve. Of these, only three or four should be directly in the ambush while the others should remain in a position from which they can observe the men constituting the ambush itself (as well as the enemy) and from which they can be ready to support the ambush if necessary.

In organizing an ambush, the actual locale is studied very carefully. The most favorable approach routes are chosen, and the enemy's sentry locations and patrol routes are identified exactly. The observation necessary to determine all these things is carried out over a period of several days by the leader-designate of the ambush group and also by the men who will take part in the action.

The commander must study every aspect of the situation in fullest detail. Any effort to simplify matters is liable to lead to lack of success or even to outright trouble during the ambush.

On open terrain the place for an ambush is chosen along a path or between two enemy installations. It must be approachable under cover, preferably where there are some slight terrain features at least, or shell holes. In forests, an ambush should be laid along a road or path passing through specially thick underbrush. The men taking part in an ambush should be appropriately clothed for the season but, in any case, as lightly as possible. They should be armed with automatic weapons. Each man should also have two grenades, a Finnish knife, a gag, some rope, and a signal pistol.

The fire support should be armed entirely with automatic weapons, and it should be located where it can readily cover the ambush area with its fire.

The men who are going to form the actual ambush group should be chosen for their steadiness, ability to act coolly under pressure, and resourcefulness, and they should be able to orient themselves readily into a situation. Courage, self-restraint, precision, exceptional discipline, and strong sense of mutual support—these are the essential qualities in a reconnaissance man chosen to take part in an ambush.

The objectives of an ambush should be individual enemy soldiers, small groups, patrols, enemy listening posts, and patrolling sentries.

The commander who sends out an ambush group should give it explicit orders concerning what it should do in case it runs into a sizable enemy patrol. In sending out an ambush group, the commander must provide for fire support of the group, so that the fire-support element will be ready on call to open fire immediately. For this purpose, a system of signals must be carefully worked out beforehand.

Reconnaissance

In planning the actions of an ambush, due consideration must be given to the route and method of withdrawal of the men taking part. It is always possible that the ambush may not have the chance to take prisoners on the planned night. In such a case, the ambush patrol must withdraw without giving itself away before dawn and then repeat the sortie on the following night.

The example described below of an ambush designed to seize a prisoner for interrogation gives an indication of the various ways in which this particular form of reconnaissance can be carried out. In the example cited, the commander was thoroughly successful in choosing the time for seizing his prisoner, and he made the right decision about whether or not to destroy an enemy firing point.

The staff of one of the Kalinin Front divisions learned that there had been a regrouping in the opposing enemy sector and that new enemy formations had been brought up. To learn the identity of the new enemy units and how many of them there were, it was essential to procure a suitable prisoner for interrogation.

The commander of the reconnaissance company decided to set up an ambush on a road leading to a forest to get the needed prisoner. The mission was assigned to a group of six volunteers.

After first studying the situation in detail on the map and then conducting a thorough observation of the area itself, the group waited for a dark and foggy night, on which as soon as darkness began to fall it went into action.

There was a light snowfall. The wind came from the direction of the enemy. The reconnaissance group moved by way of wooded areas and along the shoulder of the road. The group infiltrated the enemy security outposts and came upon a machine gun. Having in mind that this area had been recently under fire from our artillery, the leader of the group decided to knock out the machine gun with a grenade, since the sound of its detonation would likely be taken for the impact of an artillery round. In this way, the sound of the detonation would be unlikely to alert either the security outposts or the nearby garrison.

It began to get light. Two soldiers came into sight, coming along the road carrying a thermos containing breakfast for the combat security outposts. The commander of the group decided that it would be better to go into action when the two soldiers returned, after they had delivered the rations to the security outpost. He figured that if he were to try to capture them on the way to the outpost, the men at the outpost would become suspicious if their rations failed to arrive on schedule, and in addition, the slight noise the action was bound to cause would add to their suspicions. His reasoning was sound.

So he let the soldiers pass through without revealing the presence of his group. A couple of hours later they came back, serene and unconcerned, with the empty thermos. Suddenly, the group struck the Germans from behind, and a scuffle broke out. One of the Germans was knocked down by a rifle butt and gagged and tied. The other tried to resist, so he was killed. Then the group returned to its own lines by a different route, moving parallel to the road but some 40 meters off it. There were no losses. The prisoner turned out to be a twice-decorated soldier of the Special SS Brigade who gave much valuable data during his interrogation.

Training and Employment of Reconnaissance Small Units

Important questions in relation to the combat activity of reconnaissance elements concern their training and the manner in which they are employed. Generally, reconnaissance is efficient in cases where key personnel have been carefully and conscientiously trained. It is not enough to find brave and devoted men; they must be well trained, and they must acquire almost as second nature the skills and the feel for reconnaissance. Only in such a case, with team training, and much practical work carried out in exercises in the rear area, can reconnaissance units achieve the capability to accomplish their mission without unacceptable losses.

But in fact such training of reconnaissance personnel is not being carried out in all units. There are cases where not only the enlisted personnel but even the officers of reconnaissance units do not know the enemy organizations, the insignia and distinguishing symbols, the indications to look for in searching out the enemy deployment and combat formation on the ground. A good reconnaissance man must not only know these basic facts, but he must also have a thorough grasp of enemy tactics and of the basic enemy procedures and ways of operating in combat, including enemy reconnaissance techniques.

At present as a rule in almost all army groups, officer reconnaissance training takes the form of courses, organized on an army-group level, for junior lieutenants chosen by the army group or army. About two-thirds of the time is taken up in training on the basic subjects, and the remaining time is devoted to reconnaissance problems entirely, with instruction taking the form mainly of practical fieldwork under the direction of experienced reconnaissance officers.

The training provided in these courses for army and army-group junior lieutenants provides a contingent of reconnaissance officers with fairly good basic knowledge; it makes them ready for assignment as regimental reconnaissance platoon commanders.

But these graduates still need a good deal of serious additional training before they can qualify as reconnaissance company commanders or for comparable reconnaissance or intelligence assignments. In this connection it must be mentioned that there are quite a few reconnaissance commanders who have had only the most elementary training; a substantial proportion of them have had no specialized training, though they have a certain amount of practical experience.

Reconnaissance

The brief meetings held between regiment and division staffs and reconnaissance outfit commanders during quiet periods at the front make it possible for these commanders to get a certain amount of practical advice in matters having to do with the planning, organization, and conduct of reconnaissance.

Training of ranks takes place in reserve regiments. The quality of this training is something less than satisfactory. The way the course is organized, the abstractness of the instruction, the relative lack of practical exercises, and the poor quality of the instructors themselves all contribute to producing troops who have only the vaguest notion of what they will actually be up against.

Thus, both officers and ranks who are assigned to reconnaissance units are in direct need of serious instruction and training. It must be noted that in the reconnaissance units themselves both officers and ranks do receive some basic training and that this training is more carefully planned and applied right down in the units than it is in the courses devised by the higher-level echelons. In this connection, of course, much of the training of the reconnaissance troops takes place during the preparation for actual reconnaissance missions.

A serious and continuing problem is the employment of reconnaissance officers and units for inappropriate tasks. Commanders and staffs realize for the most part how harmful and wasteful this can be, yet still this situation is fairly widespread, as the examples cited below will indicate.

Very often, faced with shortages in combat personnel, commanders will use reconnaissance units as ordinary line companies. The reconnaissance unit of one of the armies of the Northwestern Front carried out two reconnaissance missions in the enemy rear and lost only 9 men. This same recon outfit was used as a line outfit shortly thereafter and lost 118 men in two actions.

The reconnaissance company of the 57th Rifle Brigade (Volkhov Front) was ordered to block an enemy timber-and-earthworks firing point. In doing so it lost some 80 percent of its personnel. The reconnaissance company of the 26th Rifle Brigade was sent into the assault as a line company several times and ended up with 90 percent of its personnel as casualties. The reconnaissance company of the 310st Rifle Division was assigned to see to the security of the divisional combat point. The reconnaissance 288th Rifle Division from 15 January through May 1942 was used as a security detachment for the divisional combat point; it was used on various other working details, and in combat on April 30, it was attached to the 1014th Rifle Regiment as the regimental reserve.

From January to March, the divisional G-2s of one of the armies designated as assault armies were relieved on an average of two or three times, mostly as a result of wounds. Thus, for example, the G-2 of the 327th Rifle Division was wounded while taking part in the blocking of an enemy timber-earthworks firing point. The deputy G-2 of the same division was killed while on a detail to gather German dead from the field. Several divisional G-2s were wounded while carrying out liaison officer functions.

Divisional commanders and chiefs of staff sometimes use their G-2s for inappropriate tasks. Thus in combat on 28 April 1942 the divisional commander of the 310th Rifle Division (Volkhov Front) ordered his G-2 to act as a morale officer; as a result, the G-2 was not able during the whole period of this particular battle to perform his normal recon duties.

On the Southwestern Front in the 393d and 411th Divisions the reconnaissance units were used as ordinary rifle units in both the offense and the defense instead of conducting reconnaissance as they should have.

In the 379th Rifle Division, the G-2 was actually assigned billeting-officer duties. The chief of the intelligence reports section of an army was used as the headquarters administrative and military police officer. Similar situations were encountered on the western, Bryansk, and other fronts.

These examples show very clearly what can happen to intelligence and reconnaissance personnel if they are not used for their own types of work.

This type of misuse of specially trained personnel and units cannot be tolerated, for it can lead to a failure of reconnaissance, which is a very important element in the security of commands at all levels.

Conclusions

1. The experience of the war shows that in actions against such an active, resourceful, persevering, and stubborn force as the fascist German army, combat reconnaissance must be exceptionally active, subtle in its methods, deceptive, bold, and daring.

Formalized procedures, carelessness, and indifference are not worthy of a good reconnaissance man. He is a hunter. The fascist is the beast he is stalking. He must learn the habits of the beast, so that he can kill him or take him alive.

Reconnaissance men should be trained with perseverance and continually; they should be carefully chosen from among the troops for bravery, boldness, and innate qualities; and their heroism, self-control, and resourcefulness should be cultivated. These are the priority tasks of unit and formation commanders and of party and Komsomol organizations.

2. Reconnaissance personnel are precious and must not be squandered. However difficult the situation, no commander must throw his reconnaissance unit into the attack or use it for a task other than that for which it is intended. It is not easy to train a reconnaissance unit quickly. A good reconnaisance man is the result of careful selection, much training, and careful instruction.

Reconnaissance men must be given regular training exercises, and these exercises must be run by thoroughly experienced officers. All the skills and knacks of military deception and cunning—those acquired as a result of combat experience as well as those that result from the initiative and creative talent of the reconnaissance men themselves—must be studied and applied as appropriate in the training and development of combat reconnaissance personnel.

The outstanding reconnaissance men and recon units should be given rewards: they should have special privileges and the best armament, and they should receive extra rations, distinctive insignia or uniforms, and extra leave or rest periods. They must be given the feeling that they are appreciated, and that the army wants to help and encourage them. The honorable and difficult work of the Soviet reconnaissance men must be given due recognition.

3. Experience shows that in units where the commander and the chief of staff devote proper attention to the choice, instruction, and training of reconnaissance personnel, the reconnaissance elements of those units will really be capable of carrying out any reconnaissance mission. Insufficient personal attention on the part of the commander and chief of staff to these matters will produce the opposite results.

4. Commanders, chiefs of staff, and intelligence officers of armies and divisions and regiments must develop in themselves the habit of skillful direction of reconnaissance, including:

- The discipline of never dissipating or squandering their reconnaissance resources;
- Rapid and precise reactions to changes in the situation, involving the dispatch of missions and patrols to sectors that have gained in importance;
- Continuous attention to keeping in touch with reconnaissance elements and getting from them as quickly as possible the information gathered by them;
- The continuous maintenance of reconnaissance reserves;
- Absolute refusal to accept temporary lapses (and all the more so lengthy lapses) in the flow of information concerning the enemy and the terrain; and
- An equally absolute refusal to put up with any slovenliness, inaccuracy of reporting, imaginary reporting, or off-the-cuff reporting by reconnaissance agencies, and stern and swift punishment of any such shortcomings.

5. The uninterrupted conduct of combat reconnaissance demands a continuous, day-to-day, persevering, and personal study of the situation by the commander and concrete guidance on his part and on that of the chief of staff of the work of intelligence staff elements and reconnaissance organs.

The continuous conduct of combat reconnaissance involves skillful and competent direction; it requires well-organized coordination with other forms of intelligence and reconnaissance. Only if these conditions are met will it be possible to obtain the data necessary for a commander to make a decision, and only then will it be possible to be sure that one can protect one's troops from the various unexpected surprises that are likely to develop during the course of a battle.

6. Reconnaissance can be conducted in a logical and planned manner only when the chief of staff and the G-2 of a formation study all changes in the enemy groupings, make appropriate and correct deductions therefrom, and take appropriate action involving the reconnaissance resources at their disposal.

There can only be a realistic reconnaissance plan where combat reconnaissance is skillfully and adroitly directed, where the commander himself studies reports concerning the enemy, where he personally interrogates the most important and knowledgeable prisoners, and where he also personally examines the most important captured documents.

On the other hand, when the commander depends entirely on staff documents, estimates, and conclusions presented to him by his chief of staff and his intelligence officer, then there is a virtual certainty that reconnaissance direction will fall into formalistic and bureaucratic stereotypes.

7. The reconnaissance plan under any conditions should be a true working document; it should reflect the entire process of change and development in the combat situation and should itself change accordingly from phase to phase.

The reconnaissance plan, once it has been accepted by the chief of staff, should not be given wide distribution. The practice of sending one's plan to the next higher headquarters and of copying out details of the plans of lower units for incorporation into one's own is a carry-over from the paper-pushing methods of direction and control.

Staffs at all levels have the responsibility of working out dependable systems for keeping higher headquarters and neighboring units informed concerning the reconnaissance missions they have sent out and their missions, as is stated on p. 195 of *Field Service Regulations for Staffs*.

8. Adequate preparations before the undertaking of each reconnaissance mission should always be uppermost in the minds of commanders and staffs. Every reconnaissance raid, ambush, or patrol must be meticulously prepared, and neither time nor energy should be spared in this. An essential part of such preparation is always the organization of a well thought-out observation system, supported by a dependable signals system.

Missions should as a rule be assigned to reconnaissance organs on the terrain rather than by map, and at the same time provisions should be made, on the terrain, for the setting up of fire support from automatic weapons, mortars, and artillery.

Staffs should not limit their interest in reconnaissance simply to drawing up plans and issuing orders; they must also organize systematic checking and control of the reconnaissance agencies under their command, and they must also help these reconnaissance agencies by making known and popularizing their achievements and by giving them a deserved sense of value and appreciation.

9. Staffs at all levels must in the light of the experience of the Patriotic War, observe the requirements of our manuals and regulations concerning the necessity of *coordination between all forms of reconnaissance and observation*.

Commanders of staffs, and reconnaissance men particularly, must:

- Know how to organize clear cooperation between the various forms of reconnaissance, in the interests of the combined-arms commander;

- Quickly assemble the results of the various forms of reconnaissance into an integrated picture; and
- Provide the combined-arms commander with a timely resume and summary of the information concerning the enemy obtained from all sources.

10. In organizing an offensive, the army staff must distribute down to subordinate units (down to and including battalion), no later than two days before the offensive, thoroughly detailed maps or overlays showing in detail all the available data concerning the enemy. The maps should be on as large a scale as practicable.

During the course of the offensive, special reconnaissance groups should be attached to the forward units; their mission is to infiltrate into the enemy defense positions and discover the system and layout of the defense, in depth.

The net of observers organized during the preparation for the offensive should move out with the attacking troops following closely; these observers continue to watch the enemy, his observation and firing points, tanks, and reserves, etc.

Reconnaissance groups should have adequate signal resources for quick reporting, including radios, telephones, and pyrotechnic equipment.

The reconnaissance and intelligence chiefs should take measures to ensure the quickest possible reporting of information obtained.

The report shows that emotional and bureaucratic attachment to the cavalry overcame what should have been a more critical evaluation of its use, and in fact, the failure of cavalry is blamed on winter conditions. Other Soviet commanders such as Marshal R. Ia. Malinovskii had a much more critical view of the deployment of cavalry, which they felt was outdated and of little value in the age of mechanized warfare. The Red Army, as this report indicates, felt there was still a place for the cavalry and continued to deploy cavalry and cavalry-mechanized groups until the very end of the war—Ed.

7

Combat Employment of Large Cavalry Formations

THE inspectorate of cavalry of the Red Army has studied and drawn general conclusions from the sum of experience involving the actions of large cavalry formations in army-group operations during the Patriotic War so far. Below, in the form of brief statements, illustrated by combat examples, are set forth the basic principles that should govern the employment of cavalry on a strategic scale in the Patriotic War.

These principles and conclusions must be brought to the attention of cavalry chiefs, staffs of formations of the various arms, and combined-arms commanders so that they can be studied and confirmed or modified as a result of experience obtained in the course of future military operations against the German invaders.

Cavalry Possesses High Operational and Tactical Mobility

Cavalry is able to carry out combat tasks in cooperation with other arms. Cavalry is less dependent than other arms on the time of year, the time of day, weather, and the condition of roads.

Cavalry formations constitute a resource of the Supreme Command or of army-group commands. In cooperation with other arms, cavalry takes part in decisive force to strike a decisive blow at an army group's point of main effort or to exploit success achieved by other elements. Cavalry formations should be used in directions leading, if possible, to open flanks of the enemy and opening up possibilities of wide maneuver.

In an offensive against enemy fortified positions, cavalry formations should be used to exploit the breakthrough and then to operate in the enemy rear, engaging his operational reserves and coordinating its own action with those of the Soviet armies attacking or advancing frontally.

Cavalry formations are also used to cover the concentration of one's own troops or their regrouping or withdrawal. Cavalry is also valuable in the pursuit.

Cavalry formations should not be tied down by boundaries or phase lines. Generally they should be given their mission or objective, the direction or axis along which generally they are to operate, and the time by which the mission must be accomplished.

A basic condition for the successful combat activity of cavalry on an operational scale is mass employment as an *important operational-strategic resource of an army group* command to be used in cooperation with the basic striking force of the army group.

This strategic cavalry force of an army group is organized as a *cavalry corps of not less than three divisions.*

Directive No.005698 of 14 December 1941 of the Supreme Commander Comrade Stalin states in clear and positive terms that *cavalry corps are to be subordinated to army groups, not armies.* This puts into clear perspective the place and role of strategic cavalry in large operations.

A cavalry corps should have not less than one rifle division attached to it. In summer the division should be motorized; in winter equipped with sled, runner, and sleigh transport, and the personnel on skis. Without an infantry force at his disposal, the cavalry corps commander, if he runs into opposition from a few enemy battalions with artillery, will have to tie up part of one of his cavalry divisions wastefully. As a result, the cavalry will get involved in a local action of purely tactical significance and will lose its freedom for strategic maneuver. It will in effect be no different from an ordinary rifle formation. But if the cavalry corps commander has attached infantry, he will be able to deal with the enemy by using his infantry, while the mass of his cavalry and ranks can be employed for a decisive blow against the enemy flanks and rear.

Thus, in the strike by the 1st Guard Cavalry Corps against Venev and Stalinogorsk and in the pursuit of the panzer army of General Guderian during 1–17 December 1941, the 173d and 322d Rifle Divisions, which were attached to the corps, played an important role in keeping the corps groups mobile and moving in a position to realize the full value of its maneuverability. The two rifle divisions engaged the enemy frontally on several occasions while the basic mass of the corps was employed for a wide envelopment.

The attachment to the commander of the 11th Cavalry Corps of the 2d Guard Motorized Rifle Division while the corps was operating on the motor road between Moscow and Minsk during the period January to March 1942 was of great value. The rifle division's firepower greatly augmented that of the corps and made it possible for the corps commander to retain an entire cavalry division as a mobile reserve in spite of the fact that the corps front extended for a length of some 60 kilometers.

On the other hand, the failure of the commander of the Sixth Army to detach the 411th Rifle Division to operate with the 6th Cavalry Corps at the time the latter was committed in the 23–26 January breakthrough led to bad results. The cavalry corps became involved in a drawn-out action on a tactical line and thereby lost its operational mobility. When finally on 2 February 1942 the Sixth Army commander did release the division for attachment to the 6th Cavalry Corps, this shift had no value, because by then the enemy, having been able to tie down the cavalry corps, had been able to bring up sizable reserves.

The inclusion in the cavalry corps of the tank brigade has proven in practice to be one of the essential prerequisites for operational success on the part of cavalry corps. In a number of cases it has been found necessary to reinforce cavalry corps with heavy KV tanks.

In offensive operations involving the commitment of cavalry corps against enemy flanks (and sometimes when the corps is thrown into the breakthrough as well), the cavalry often must be reinforced with reserve artillery, mortars, and rocket-launcher units.

The attachment to the group of General Kamkov (which consisted of the 3d and 14th Cavalry Divisions, the 3d and 142d Tank Brigades, the 34th Motorized Rifle Brigade, and the 297th, 81st, and 212th Rifle Divisions) of the 4th Guard Rocket Launcher Group made it possible for Group Kamkov to hold a 130-kilometer sector of the front during eleven days in October 1941 against overwhelming enemy forces and in a situation where the front was poorly drawn with both flanks pushed far back behind the center.

Cavalry formations should be employed against operationally important objectives on the enemy flanks and in his rear.

In such tasks the cavalry should have an opportunity for freedom of maneuver, and it should not be called upon to undertake frontal attacks against fortified lines or fortified areas with its own forces.

In this connection, the example of the employment of cavalry by the command of the southwestern theater in the Yeletakoye operation in December 1941 is interesting. The 5th Cavalry Corps (with the 3d, 14th, and 32d Cavalry Divisions and the 129th Tank Brigade) under General Kriuchenkin was given the mission of operating against withdrawal routes of the enemy Yelets Group. It was able to retain its capability for rapid maneuver, and in an engagement with the 95th German Infantry Division on December 6, it was able to strike a powerful blow against that division as a result of its advantage of greater mobility. Later, by cutting the communications of the enemy 45th Division, the 5th Corps completed the encirclement of the enemy groupings and met up with elements (the 52d and 55th Cavalry Divisions) of another Soviet cavalry corps near Rossosh. Then—together with these cavalry elements, elements of the 34th Motorized Rifle Brigade, and the 1st Guard Rifle Division—the 5th Cavalry Corps defeated the 34th Army Corps of the enemy, which included the 95th, 45th, and 134th Infantry Divisions.

The successful direction and guidance of the command of the southern front of the 5th Cavalry Corps including the 34th, 60th, and 79th Cavalry Divisions and the 12th Tank Brigade, under command of General Grechko against Barvenkovo in January 1942 made it possible for this cavalry formation to come out in the rear of the enemy Seventeenth Army and to seize Losovaya and Barvenkovo stations in conjunction with the flank divisions of the Soviet Sixth and Fifty-seventh Armies. Very large quantities of enemy stores and materiel were taken in this action.[1]

Firm and adequate coverage for cavalry corps against air attack is an absolute prerequisite for success in cavalry operations on a corps scale. Such cover must be provided by fighter aircraft and antiaircraft artillery supplied by the army and army group during the period preceding the operation and throughout the entire duration of the operation itself.

No fewer than one or two battalions of light antiaircraft artillery from the army-groups reserve should be attached to a cavalry corps during the course of an operation in which the corps is involved.

If there are firm and uninterrupted signal communications among the army group and headquarters and the headquarters of the cavalry corps during the operation, then air cover for the corps can be furnished by army and army-group air units according to a plan worked out by the army-group staff and in consonance with the requests sent in by the corps headquarters. But if such uninterrupted communications cannot be anticipated for sure, then it is preferable to subordinate directly to the corps headquarters an air formation (brigade or division) to provide air cover. In such a case, a liaison officer from the air formation in question must be with the corps headquarters throughout the operation, and he must have liaison aircraft, automobiles, and radio facilities, all of which are supplied by the air formation in question.

In view of the relatively small organic antiaircraft elements of the cavalry corps, the army-group headquarters must pay particular attention to the problem of reinforcing the antiaircraft protection of cavalry operations with the army group.

Supply and logistical support of cavalry operations throughout their entire depth by resources of army and army group-transportation are of the highest importance under present-day conditions of cavalry operations.

The experience of the Red Army's offensive operations during the winter and spring of 1942 has shown conclusively that figuring on supplying rations by means of local foraging, requisitions, etc.—after the fashion of the Hitlerite armies—is not sound. Cavalry, in addition to all its normal rations and fodder needs, will need an extra amount of fodder if a good part of its horses are being used for foraging side trips and raids. In any case, if it attempts to depend on local resources for rations and fodder, it will to a significant degree lose its most valuable characteristic—mobility.

It is essential to provide periods of rest and refit for cavalry at more or less regular intervals, particularly so that the horses can be seen to, rested, and put into good shape for the next operation. As a rule, when cavalry is fighting as infantry, the horses are left behind in the immediate rear, under the guardianship of a few caretakers. In such a case, both the horses and men of the cavalry suffer; the horses tend to be less well looked after than when they are with the units, and the number of horse nonbattle casualties increases. This in turn means that a fair number of men must be detailed to convoy the sick horses to the rear, to the detriment of the combat strength of the cavalry formation.

During January and February 1942 the 2d Guard Cavalry Corps (on the front of the Twentieth Army) and the 6th Cavalry Corps (on the front of the Sixth Army) were both involved in lengthy combat actions as infantry combat formations against fortified positions occupied by the Germans. The horses had to be left behind in some villages that had been half destroyed by the Germans before they abandoned them. There they were subjected to a highly irregular regime; enemy air activity interrupted supplies to the point where even the water supply was not assured on a regular basis and not enough fodder could be brought up. As a result, there were serious losses of horses, and it was not possible to provide replacements to make good these losses.

The length of rest periods will depend on various factors: on the overall situation, on the state of the cavalry formation after the operation it has just concluded, on the degree of urgency of the next operation it is to carry out, etc. But in any case, there should be enough time to bring up from the rear areas the men and horses of the formation that had been gathering there for one reason or another during the course of the operation; to receive and integrate personnel, horses, and materiel replacement; to shoe the horses, etc.

On the average, a cavalry corps should be given a rest period of eight to ten days after it has closed on the area where it is going to rest and refit.

Characteristics of Combat Actions of the Cavalry in the Patriotic War

During the first period of the Patriotic War, while the Red Army was fighting as it withdrew eastward in order to gain time for the mobilization and concentration of the main armed forces of the USSR, elements of our strategic cavalry were fighting under extremely unfavorable conditions.

Because of the surprise of its first strikes and because of a substantial numerical superiority, the German air force was able for the time being to gain air superiority for the Germans. Our cavalry formations during this first period sustained heavy losses as a result of enemy air action, and their operational mobility was markedly reduced.

The sudden invasion of our territory by the German armies led to meeting engagements, and then to defensive engagements in which our cavalry was pitted against powerful enemy motorized formations.

Using the good roads of the western part of the USSR, and having the advantage of the dry summer season, these motorized enemy formations had in fact more operational and tactical mobility than our cavalry, so that they were able by envelopments and flanking movements to get the best of our not very numerous cavalry.

In the first period of the war our cavalry had entirely insufficient support in the form of tanks, since the enemy had a great numerical superiority over us as a whole in this form of weapon. Here again, the superiority was quantitative; the quality of our new tank models (T-34 and KV) was incomparably better than anything the Germans had.

Though our army had the advantage over the Germans in both quantity and quality of its artillery, we were inferior to the Germans in mortars (especially heavy mortars), and we had fewer automatic small arms and antitank weapons. This meant that in the mobile kind of warfare of the period the enemy had a clear-cut advantage over us in readily available and highly mobile firepower.

The Red Army's offensive operations of the winter of 1941–42 took place in conditions that were not favorable for cavalry actions. The winter that year was especially long and severe, and the snowfall was exceptional. As a result, our cavalry was largely tied to the few routes of communication in the country where it was fighting, for it could not maneuver off the roads due to the exceptionally deep snow cover. So the operational mobility of our cavalry was very reduced, though experience showed that, even so, its mobility was proportionately reduced no more—and in some cases less—than that of mechanized formations, and it was, if anything, somewhat less tied to the roads than these later.

Cavalry actions, especially on terrain without forest cover, were extremely hard to conceal from enemy air reconnaissance. Many cavalry units suffered heavy losses from enemy air attacks; if they were not to be vulnerable to such attacks, they had to have powerful antiaircraft artillery and fighter protection.

The lack of fodder available straight from the fields (the snow cover was too deep) and the irregularity of fodder supply brought up from the rear caused heavy casualties in horses in nearly all cavalry units.

As far as combined-arms commanders were concerned, particularly when cavalry corps were subordinated to army commanders, there have been many mistakes and inadequacies in the operational employment of cavalry formations throughout the whole war so far. As a result of these mistakes, cavalry has not always produced the results it is capable of if it is employed properly.

The following examples will illustrate this.

1. Combined-arms commanders have ignored the principle of mass employment of cavalry, and they have permitted cavalry formations to be weakened and frittered away. Corps have been split up when subordinated to army commands, and regiments and even divisions of cavalry corps have been detached, under army command, for various inappropriate tasks. Thus, at the time of the breakthrough by an enemy mobile group in the vicinity of Pervomaisk on 4 August 1941, the 2d Cavalry Corps (5th and 9th Cavalry Divisions), which had been put under operational subordination of the Eighteenth Army, was broken up, and one division covered the left flank. This order caused the 9th Cavalry Division to move to the area of Voznesensk, while the 5th Cavalry Division remained near Balta, covering the left flank of the army. The corps, as a result of this arrangement, ceased to exist as an operational formation, for all practical purposes.

During the period from 8 through 15 August 1941, the command of the Twenty-sixth Army detached from the 5th Cavalry Corps for special missions the antiaircraft battalions and the engineer squadrons of the 3d and 14th Cavalry Divisions and the armored squadron of the 34th Cavalry Division. As a result, when the 5th Cavalry Corps was assigned a very important mission involving a strike at the rear of the First Panzer Army of General Kleist, it was virtually without antiaircraft and pontoon resources.

On 13 February 1942, the commander of the Sixth Army sent the 6th Cavalry Corps (26th, 28th, and 49th Cavalry Divisions and the 5th Guard Tank Brigade) back to rest and refit. But in the process, the 5th Guard Tank Brigade was detached by the army command from the 6th Cavalry Corps and attached to the 411th Rifle Division. And two or three days later the army command ordered the 28th Cavalry Division of the 6th Cavalry Corps to return to the line but not as part of the corps. As a result, when the 6th Cavalry Corps was given the important task of striking a counterblow against the 113th German and 1st Rumanian Infantry Divisions—which had broken through between Lozovaya and Barvenkovo—the corps moved out on 17 February 1942 with only two still-understrength divisions and no tanks. When it attacked, it was able to achieve no significant results.

2. When cavalry corps were subordinated to army commands, they were often used for missions of significance only to that particular army. This in turn often led to cavalry corps being ordered to assault heavily fortified enemy areas or lines, which was wasteful and ineffectual in many cases due to the small amount of organic artillery and mortars the newly formed cavalry corps had at that time. And such employment also deprived the cavalry of its operational mobility.

On 27 January 1942 the 6th Cavalry Corps was subordinated by order of the headquarters of the Southwestern Command to the Sixth Army. Then, instead of continuing to carry out the orders of the Supreme Command to continue and develop further the cavalry offensive toward Krasnograd, the corps was ordered by the Sixth Army to assault the fortified line of Verkh Bishkin-Bereka, in spite of the fact that the strong artillery of the 411th Division was on the sector and not otherwise engaged. As a result, the 6th Cavalry Corps, tied down in this action and thereby losing its operational mobility, lost more than 1,800 men, or some 30 percent of its combat personnel in the course of 15 days of stubborn battle against an enemy who was constantly being reinforced. And no significant gains were made, notwithstanding the heavy losses.

The commander of the Twentieth Army during the period from 13 January to 15 February 1942 employed the 2d Guard Cavalry Corps (3d and 4th Guard Cavalry Divisions and 22d Tank Brigade) for the assault of several strongly organized enemy strong points, such as Chukhalovo, and Bykovo. Instead of defeating the Rumanian division, it was able only to detain it.

3. Along the entire front it was relatively rare that cavalry corps were reinforced with rifle divisions. Army staffs preferred merely to organize cooperation between cavalry and infantry rather than actually attach rifle divisions to cavalry formations. But in practice, army headquarters usually found themselves far removed from the actual battle. They were usually unable to bring about such cooperation, so they often were obliged after all to order the subordination of rifle divisions to cavalry corps. The trouble then was that in the majority of cases it was not possible to bring about such attachments until it was too late to bring about the desired results.

In the plan of operations for the Sixth and the Thirty-eighth Armies in January and February 1942, it was intended to commit the 6th Cavalry Corps (26th, 28th, 49th Cavalry Divisions and 5th Guard Tank Brigade) at the breakthrough point on the front of the Sixth Army. This corps was supposed to be reinforced by a rifle division, which was to be furnished by the Sixth Army. The commander of the 6th Cavalry Corps assigned to the rifle division expected to cover the crossing of the North Donets River at Balakleya, Andreyevka, and Liman. But the commander of the Sixth Army did not carry out his agreement; he attached the 411th Rifle Division to the 6th Cavalry Corps but merely ordered it to "cooperate with the cavalry corps" and to follow along after it. As a result, the right bank of the river (the western bank) was not secured, and the enemy retained a bridgehead on the left bank in the vicinity of Shebelinka and Glazunovka that constituted a serious threat to the communications of the 6th Cavalry Corps and to the whole right flank of the Sixth Army.

4. Virtually no attention was paid to the problem of ensuring an adequate flow of supplies to cavalry formations by way of the army rear services apparatus. Cavalry formations in many cases found themselves 120 or 150 kilometers ahead of their supply stations, which meant that at the most critical moment in their operations they ran out of rounds of ammunition and even of

rations and fodder, for their own organic transportation facilities were extremely limited and could not cope with a logistical problem of this magnitude.

The Use of Large Cavalry Formations in Army Group Offensive Operations

In general offensive operations on an army-group scale, large cavalry formations can be employed for the following missions.

A Flank Attack in Coordination with a Frontal Attack

In such an operation, it is desirable first to tie down the enemy by strong frontal attacks with infantry and tanks to deprive him of capabilities for operational maneuver and also to discover the enemy grouping and give the enemy the impression that the whole force of our offensive is being devoted to the frontal attack.

Then cavalry formations (a cavalry corps reinforced with rifle divisions and artillery and mortars from the reserve) move under cover, mainly by night marches to a location from which they will be in a position to strike a powerful blow against the flank of the main enemy grouping.

It is most desirable to bring up the cavalry formations on the side of our own most advanced flank, so that in cooperation with the formations that make up that flank they can strike a powerful blow at the enemy flank, seeking to penetrate to the tactical-operational depth of the enemy position in overall coordination with the combined-arms infantry and tank formations that are attacking frontally.

In this connection, the actions of the 1st Guard Cavalry Corps in December 1941, which contributed to the defeat of the Germans at Moscow, are well worth studying.

When the forces of the Western Front counterattacked against the elements of the German Second Panzer Army of General Guderian—which had broken through northeast of Tula and were threatening to seize Kashira and Ryazan and thereby to envelop Moscow from the south and southeast—the main counteroffensive role fell to the 1st Guard Cavalry Corps (1st and 2d Guards Cavalry Divisions, 9th Tank Brigade and 273d Rifle Division). This corps under General Belov fended off all the blows of Guderian's panzers against Kashira and struck against the flank of the enemy grouping at Venev that was trying to advance in the direction of Serpukhov and Kashira.

From the right the tank and infantry forces of the Fiftieth Army, which while defending Tula, went over to the offensive; from the left some units of the Tenth Army were operating against the enemy, though they were not in touch with the 1st Guard Cavalry Corps.

Throwing back the motorized columns of Guderian's army, the 1st Guard Cavalry Corps beginning on 5 December 1941 went over to the counterattack. The 173d Rifle Division attacked from the vicinity of Gritcho while the remaining elements of the corps struck from the Pryakhino area. Near the latter area 12 guns, 40 personnel carriers, and some 300 enemy soldiers were put out of action. Elements of the enemy 17th Panzer Division and 70th Motorized Division withdrew southward along the Kashira–Stalinogorsk rail line, while the 18th Panzer Division was concentrating in the vicinity of Mikhailov.

During the period from 6 through 8 December, elements of the 1st Guard Cavalry Corps continued to exert strong pressure against the enemy tanks and motorized infantry; they seized the railroad station of Mordves and the fortified village of Tyunezh and continued their offensive toward the south.

On 9 December Venev was seized, and the enemy left there over 2,000 dead and enormous quantities of equipment. On the following day, the 2d Guard Cavalry Division, together with some attached tanks, broke into Stalinogorsk as it continued the pursuit of the rapidly retreating enemy.

On 11 and 12 December, the remnants of the German garrison at Stalinogorsk were liquidated; and the cavalry guardsmen took over 50 tanks, 42 guns, over 2,000 trucks and cars, some 100 motorcycles, and great quantities of other booty.

At the same time, the 322d Rifle Division of the Fiftieth Army pushed forward to the vicinity of Sergievo and Vykova. It was put under the operational control of the 1st Guard Cavalry Corps and continued its advance in a southwesterly direction.

Meanwhile, elements of the corps continued their pursuit of the enemy; on 13 December they seized the Uzlovaya railroad station, and on 14 December they reached Khomyakova, while advance detachments had advanced as far as the Kryukovka area.

On 17 December the cavalry had reached the Tula–Orel highway and had finally and for all time thrown the enemy back from the wedge Guderian's troops had driven into our position in November.

As a result of the operation of the 1st Guard Cavalry Corps, the 17th Panzer Division, the 20th and 70th Motorized Divisions, and the 167th Infantry Division of Guderian's Second Panzer Army were all badly mauled: they had to abandon nearly all of their materiel and motor transport, and they all suffered enormous losses in killed, wounded, and frostbite cases. Only ragged remnants of these formations were able to escape to the southwest.

Actions in the Operational-Tactical Depth of the Enemy Position, and Encirclement of the Enemy

Cavalry corps, when they are reinforced with tank and motorized rifle formations, have the capability of penetrating to the operational-tactical depth of the enemy position and cutting his communications. They are able by means of encirclement actions to cut off and destroy separate enemy groupings.

It is essential to point out in this connection that the most decisive effect can be achieved if the enemy front is broken through first by assault rifle formations, after which the cavalry formations are thrown into the breach so that they can come out on the enemy rear as rapidly as possible and thereby achieve the maximum surprise. This in turn requires strong and continuous air cover for the cavalry masses.

If an army-group command has two or more large cavalry formations at its disposal, it is often possible to employ them in cooperation with troops attacking frontally to achieve the total encirclement and destruction of the enemy.

As an example of this type of operation, we can cite the actions of the 5th Cavalry Corps and the Provisional Corps at Yelets in December 1941.

Toward the end of November 1941 the German command, having seized Yelets, was concentrating the 44th Army Corps near the town. This corps was to advance and seize the Gryazni-Voronezh area, cut the Moscow-Rostov railroad, and cut apart our Bryansk and southwestern fronts.

In order to defeat this German assault group, the command of the Southwestern theater brought together the special force under command of General Kostenko that included rifle and tank elements and also the 5th Cavalry Corps (3d, 14th, and 32d Cavalry Divisions and the 129th Tank Brigade) of General Kryuchenkin concentrated near Kastornoye and the Provisional Cavalry Corps (52d and 55th Cavalry Divisions) which was near Telegino and Ploskoye.

On 6 December 1941 the 5th Cavalry Corps, moving north along the flat lands near the Olym and Knesh rivers, came upon the German 95th Infantry Division in the vicinity of Alekseyevka, Volovo, and Zakharovka and engaged it in close combat. This German division had been covering the Yelets area from the south. It was forced back by the 5th Cavalry Corps, which energetically moved ahead to the northwest. To the right of the cavalry corps our 1st Guard Rifle Division and 34th Motorized Rifle Brigade were in action, while the 121st Rifle Division was attacking as the second echelon, following up the 5th Cavalry Corps.

During 8 and 9 December the corps continued to pursue the disorganized remnants of the German 95th Division, and December 10 it had reached the line Khukhlovo (3d Cavalry Division)–Prilepy (32d Cavalry Division)–Kozminka (14th Cavalry Division)–Khmelevaya (129th Tank Brigade). Meanwhile the 1st Guard Rifle Division had taken the Vyazovaya–Pokrovskoye area; and the 34th Motorized Rifle Brigade was engaged in combat along the line Svobodnaya Dubrovka–Kazanskoye; while the 121st Rifle Division had reached Krasny Lug and Aleksandrovka.

The enemy reacted to our threat against his rear and began to withdraw, breaking contact with our attacking infantry, which was driving toward Yelets from the east and northeast.

On 12 December, the 5th Cavalry Corps widened its offensive, aiming in the general direction of Verkhovya. The 3d Cavalry Division defeated a battalion of the 95th German Infantry Division, overran the divisional command post, seized Shatilovo, and engaged major elements of the German 45th Infantry Division that were attempting to get out of Malinovo and move westward. The 32d Cavalry Division together with the 129th Tank Brigade fought their way into Rossosh, where they took 215 cars and trucks and large stores of ammunition and rations. The 14th Cavalry Division took the Nikitino-Nikolskoye area.

From 13 through 15 December, having joined up with formations and units of the Provisional Cavalry Corps, which were attacking westward and northwestward from the Telegino-Ploskoye area, the 5th Cavalry Corps continued to strike and wear down the columns of the German 45th and the 134th Infantry Divisions, which were seeking to escape. On 15 December elements of the 14th Cavalry Division attacked and dispersed completely a German column consisting of more than a regiment of infantry together with artillery.

As a result of the blows struck by the two cavalry corps at the flank of the German grouping, and the blows of the cavalry actions in the tactical depth of the German formations, it was possible to carry out a complete encirclement of the 34th German Army Corps (consisting of the 45th, 95th, and 134th Divisions) and to smash the enemy with losses to him of over 12,000 men, 226 guns, 319 machine guns, 907 trucks and cars, 1,260 horses, and enormous quantities of individual weapons, supplies, and other equipment.

Entry into the Breakthrough, Actions to Exploit the Breakthrough, and Combat with the Enemy Operational Reserves

In the breakthrough of a prepared enemy defensive position or line, cavalry formations together with tank and motorized formations are the principal resource of the army-group command for the development of the breakthrough.

The basic task of the cavalry in operations to develop and exploit the breakthrough consists of defeating the enemy operational reserves in depth and destroying them by coordinated actions with air and airborne forces and with forces attacking frontally.

Cavalry formations in this phase of their operational activity should keep their attention focused on the principal operational objective within the framework of the overall army group mission and should not let themselves be sidetracked into actions that are of significance only to the mission of one of the individual armies of the army group.

The actions of cavalry in the depth of the breakthrough and cavalry combat with enemy operational reserves can succeed only when they are thoroughly coordinated with air, airborne, and frontal operations by other friendly forces; they will fail if they are attempted alone and without such close coordination.

The actions of the 6th Cavalry Corps in the exploitation of the breakthrough on the sector of the Sixth Army in January and February 1942 are worthy of examination.

The 6th Cavalry Corps (26th, 28th, 49th Cavalry Divisions) and the 5th Guard Tank Brigade of General Bychkovsky by 21 February 1942 was concentrated in the area of Kravtsovka. It had been given the task by the command of the Southwestern theater to follow the rifle divisions of the Sixth Army near Lageri-Volvenkovo, and then, develop a breakthrough, by attacking in the general direction of Alekseyevka. It was to take the Alekseyevka area, then take Likhachevo and Mironovka and subsequently operate toward Krasnograd. The corps was to be given a rifle division, detached from the Sixth Army.

With the seizure on 22 January 1942 by advancing units of the 393d Rifle Division of Volovenkovo and Lozovenka, the 6th Cavalry Corps on the night of 23 January forded the Severny Donets River and began on 23 February to carry out its immediate mission.

Mauling the enemy rear guard as it advanced, the corps had by 24 January reached the following positions: 28th Cavalry Division and 5th Guard Tank Brigade to Mikhailovka; the 26th Cavalry Division was closing on Mironovka; and the 49th Cavalry Division on Maksimovka.

The enemy meanwhile had held on to a bridgehead on the right bank of the Severny Donets River near Glazunovka. The bridgehead was held by a force of two or three battalions, with artillery and twelve tanks; it posed a threat to the right flank and rear of the 6th Cavalry Corps.

On 25 January 1942 the 28th Cavalry Division and the 5th Guard Tank Brigade attacked Alekseyevka. The dismounted 132d and 126th Cavalry Regiments attacked from the east while the mounted 137th Cavalry Regiments enveloped the town from the north. After the eastern half of the town had been taken our cavalrymen were obliged to withdraw some two to three kilometers to the east.

The 49th Cavalry Division, which was deployed to the left of the 29th Cavalry Division, attacked Sivash at 0800 on 25 January. This place was defended by a German battalion with artillery and mortars. After a stubborn battle, by 1900 hours the enemy resistance had been overcome, and both Sivash and Likhachevo Station had been taken.

The 26th Cavalry Division with two regiments also took part in the engagement at Sivash.

During the night preceding 26 January, the 411th Rifle Division acting under orders of the commander of the Sixth Army, began to move out from the Mikhailovka area toward the area of Mironovka and Nizh-Orel, thereby leaving the right flank of the 6th Cavalry Corps uncovered and bare. Therefore the 123d Cavalry Regiment of the 26th Cavalry Division had to be sent to the vicinity of Kiseli to cover the open flank.

During the day of 26 January, after a savage street battle, the 28th and 49th Cavalry Divisions and the 5th Guard Tank Brigade took Alekseyevka. The enemy abandoned some 300 dead, machine guns, 12 mortars, and many trucks and small arms.

On the night before 27 January, the 6th Cavalry Corps was operationally subordinated to the Sixth Army and was given the mission of taking the line Verkh-Bishkin–Bereka, to which the enemy 179th Infantry Regiment and 531st Road Construction Battalion had withdrawn and which these elements were fortifying with many artillery pieces and mortars. At the same time, the Cavalry Corps reconnaissance reported that fresh enemy forces were moving up along the road from Zmiyev toward Verkh-Bishkin and along the rail from Merefa toward Likhachevo.

On 27 and 28 January, the 28th and 49th Cavalry Divisions were engaged in stubborn actions with the enemy units that had occupied and prepared for defense a number of small populated places. The 125th Cavalry Regiment of the 26th Cavalry Division was taken out of these actions and put in corps reserve. The 130th Cavalry Regiment of the same division was sent in the direction of Krasnograd; it destroyed several small enemy garrisons and discovered a concentration in Krasnograd of some Rumanian ski troops and tanks.

Having also discovered a concentration of German and Rumanian troops at Efremovka and Semenovka, the commander of the 6th Cavalry Corps moved the 125th and 130th Cavalry Regiments of the 26th Cavalry Division up toward the Mironovka area, while the units of the 28th and 49th Cavalry Divisions and the 5th Guard Tank Brigade continued to carry out the mission that had been given by the commander of the Sixth Army. From 27 January through 1 February, these units repeatedly attacked Bereka and Verkh-Bishkin. They fought their way partway into these places and inflicted heavy losses on the enemy, but having only eight 82-millimeter mortars and 22 regimental guns for support, and being short of artillery and mortar rounds even for these few pieces, they were unable to overcome the stubborn enemy resistance.

On the night preceding 3 February, the army commander attached the 411th Rifle Division to the 6th Cavalry Corps. This division had been idle all the while, but it still was not able to complete its concentration in the Alekseyevka and Sivash area before 3 February.

From 4 through 7 February, the corps, together with the 411th Rifle Division, repeatedly attacked in the Shebelinka–Verkh-Bishkin–Bereka area; parts of these places were taken, but the enemy fire was so strong that each time the attacking forces were eventually forced to withdraw.

Meanwhile, the enemy, having tied down the 6th Cavalry Corps and deprived it of its maneuver capability in the actions along the fortified line, was able to concentrate along this line (Shebelinka, Glazunovka, Verkh-Bishkin, Bereka, Efremovka, Nizh-Orel) some 17 to 20 battalions with 20 tanks, 10 to 12 batteries of artillery and a great number of mortars. Beginning on 7 February, the enemy launched a series of attacks that, by 12 February, had forced back the 6th Cavalry Corps and the 411th Rifle Division to the line Alekseyevka–Sivash. There, on the night of 13 February, the 6th Cavalry Corps was taken out of the line and relieved by an infantry formation.

During the first phase of this operation, when the 6th Cavalry Corps was directly subordinate to the command of the Southwestern theater and had full freedom of operational maneuver, it achieved its immediate mission successfully. It drew the enemy operational reserves toward itself, thereby lightening the task of the rifle divisions of the Sixth Army engaged in the vicinity of Balakleya. And at the same time the corps destroyed about 1,000 enemy personnel and took 24 guns, 93 machine guns, over 150 cars and trucks, 8,000 rounds of ammunition, and much other materiel. During the second phase of the operation, after the corps had been subordinated to the Sixth Army, the cavalry was thrown into the assault of a fortified line. It lost its operational mobility and lost 1,823 dead and wounded or about 30 percent of its combat strength in 16 days of hard combat. Yet because of the weakness of its support weapons, it failed to gain even any tactical success.

The enemy, meanwhile tying down the cavalry in infantry-style actions, was able to bring up reserves and undo most of the initial gains the cavalry had made.

Operational Pursuit of the Withdrawing Enemy

The experience of the Patriotic War confirms that cavalry, when it is correctly employed and given adequate air support, possesses fully as much mobility as it ever has in the past.

In certain conditions—roadless terrain, mud, deep snow, for example—cavalry is even more mobile than mechanized forces, and in any case, it is no less mobile. Therefore, by taking advantage of local conditions, cavalry can be used successfully in pursuit.

Parallel pursuit produces the best results. In parallel pursuit, cavalry can make the most of its mobility, its independence of regular roads, its ability to overcome bad weather, and its ability to operate well in winter in order to overtake the withdrawing enemy and come out in front of his column, thereby bringing about his encirclement and total destruction.

An example of the operational pursuit can be seen in the actions of the 2d Guard Cavalry Corps in December 1941.

After defeating the German assault armies, which had the mission of seizing the capital of the Soviet Union, on the immediate approaches to Moscow, the forces of the Western Front went over to the counteroffensive on 6 December 1941.

The 2d Guard Cavalry Corps (3d and 4th Guard Cavalry Divisions, 20th

Cavalry Division and 22d Tank Brigade) had completed its concentration by 11 December in the area north of Kubinka. The corps had the mission of entering the breakthrough on the sector of the Fifth Army at Spalshchino and Zaovrazhye, moving by way of Pokrovskoye where it was to cut the route of withdrawal of the enemy to the west and then destroy the withdrawing enemy.

On 13 December elements of the 2d Guard Cavalry Corps, having annihilated the German garrison at Spalshchino, moved forward toward the north and seized Gorbovo.

When prisoners revealed that the 78th German Infantry Division had begun to retreat from the vicinity of Lokotnya toward Terekhovo, General Dovator, the commander of the 2d Guard Cavalry Corps, decided on a parallel pursuit to prevent the enemy from withdrawing to the west and to encircle and destroy him in the Zagorye–Safonikha area.

During 14 and 15 December, the enemy tried repeatedly to break out to the west, but he was unable to make any progress. Elements of the 20th Cavalry Division maintained a hot pursuit right on the rear of the German column, seizing much booty and mauling the enemy rear guard. At the same time, the left column of the 2d Guard Cavalry Corps was moving along forest paths to the west of and parallel to the enemy withdrawal route. It knocked out small enemy garrisons on the move and kept fending off all efforts on the part of the 78th Infantry Division to turn westward.

On 16 December, the 78th Infantry Division, moving in a column over six miles long, was finally encircled by our cavalry units on a stretch of road between Zagorye and Safonikha. General Dovator threw the 3d Guard Cavalry Division and the 22d Tank Brigade against the Germans in an attack from the west; the 20th Cavalry Division struck at the tail of the German column, while the 4th Guard Cavalry Division was held in reserve to the northwest, ready to go into action in case the enemy succeeded in breaking through north of Safonikha.

The German column, under the cavalry attack, was broken up into small groups, and most of it was destroyed. About a battalion and a half of Germans who were intercepted as they were moving from Safonikha toward Denisikha held out against the attack of our cavalry until the morning of 17 December, when they were finally overrun and dispersed.

The 78th Infantry Division was thoroughly trounced; only remnants were able to escape and take refuge in the woods. The cavalrymen of the 2d Guard Cavalry Corps took some 83 guns, 23 mortars, 143 machine guns, 23 tanks, 2 armored personnel carriers, 431 trucks and cars, 89 motorcycles, 381 bicycles, and enormous quantities of small arms, ammunition, and other supplies.

Conclusions

The experience of the war shows that in offensive operations large cavalry formations can constitute an important factor on an operational scale. However, to succeed, it is essential that

1. Reinforced cavalry corps be employed as army-group troops in the direction of the main effort and in close cooperation with the army operating in that direction;
2. Without fail cavalry corps be reinforced by rifle divisions, reserve artillery and rocket launchers, engineer and special troops;
3. Cavalry corps not be used by themselves for the assault of fortified positions or lines nor be used for actions that deprive them of their operational freedom of maneuver;
4. Large cavalry formations be given adequate air cover, not only during the time they are concentrating, but also throughout the period of their action against the enemy defense, right on through the depth of the latter. The army-group command has the basic responsibility to provide such air cover to its cavalry formations;
5. The theater command pay particular attention to the organization and uninterrupted functioning of the rear services of the cavalry and reinforce these rear services with its own ground and air transport facilities.

Use of Large Cavalry Formations in Army-Group Defensive Operations

In major army-group defensive operations, cavalry formations together with tank, motorized, and fighter formations as a rule constitute the maneuver reserve at the disposal of the army-group command. This maneuver reserve is employed for counterattacks against the main enemy grouping that is in action on strategic sectors and under conditions that will bring about the decisive defeat of the main enemy grouping and thereby bring about a favorable change in circumstances for the launching of an army-group-scale counteroffensive.

In addition, cavalry formations are capable of carrying out other tasks on an operational scale in the defense.

Mobile Defense on Operationally Important Lines. The Patriotic War has confirmed that major cavalry formations, with their considerable firepower and shock value and their high operational and tactical mobility, are capable of opposing even very large enemy's tank or infantry formations.

The operational measures characteristic of mobile defense are particularly appropriate for cavalry, since they enable it to make the most of its tactical mobility on the field of battle. By tying down the enemy in a frontal engagement with part of its strength and the greater part of its firepower, a reinforced cavalry corps can set up the conditions for the exploitation of its maneuver capabilities to strike with strong cavalry and tank elements against vulnerable points of the enemy and cause him serious losses.

The actions of the 2d Cavalry Corps in the Kishinev area in July 1941 are characteristic of the active mobile defensive use of cavalry against enemy motorized infantry.

On 29–30 June, strong German-Rumanian infantry and tank forces forded the River Pruth and began to launch an offensive in the gap between the 47th and 35th Rifle Corps of our Ninth Army. This offensive threatened to engulf Kishinev.

In order to hold the threatened front, the commander of the Ninth Army quickly brought up the 2d Cavalry Corps from the vicinity of Komrat. The corps was commanded by General Belov.

Having covered a distance of some 150 kilometers in three days by night marches in roadless terrain and with drenching mudmaking rains, the corps by 1 July had reached the Kishinev area and began to undertake the mission assigned it by the command of the Ninth Army—namely, to prevent an enemy breakthrough to Kishinev and to hold firmly the area around Strasheni.

By 8 July, the enemy, after suffering several checks in his effort to take Kishinev by frontal assault against the area held by the 2d Cavalry Corps, shifted his forces somewhat to the north and renewed the attack. This time the main effort was delivered by units of the 50th German Motorized Division from the area south of Beltsy against Kishinev. The Germans succeeded in forcing the 35th Rifle Corps back east of Beltsy.

On 9 July the commander of the 2d Cavalry Corps received the order to move by forced marches from the area of Strasheni to the vicinity of Orgeyev and then to move out westward from Orgeyev, and in cooperation with elements of the 35th Rifle Corps, to destroy the enemy in the Beltsy area.

The right column of the corps (5th Cavalry Division) moved along the Kishinev-Orgeyev highway and by 14 July had reached Orgeyev. The left column of the corps (9th Cavalry Division) had to move over poor mountain roads and trails, so that it was not until the morning of the 15th of July that it came to the flat lands near Lukashevka. On that same day its leading elements crossed the river and occupied Serateni, General Belov then decided to defend his westward flank with parts of the 9th Cavalry Division. General Bychkovsky employed the entire 5th Cavalry Division and the 72d Cavalry Regiment of the Cavalry Division for a blow against the left flank of the German 50th Motorized Division in the vicinity of Kukuruzeni.

On 16 and 17 July in actions on the Kukuruzeni-Serateni sector, the 2d Cavalry Corps carried out a series of stiff attacks against the 50th Motorized Division and forced it to break off its offensive actions and go over to the defense.

On 19 July, the 2d Cavalry Corps received the mission of covering the crossing by units of our 15th Motorized Rifle Division of the Pruth River along the Krioleni-Dubossary sector and to cover generally the withdrawal of the Ninth Army. Deploying in the vicinity of Okhrincha, the 5th Cavalry Division of General Baranov let the withdrawing 9th Cavalry Division pass through its defensive positions, and then, with its defensive fires and counterattacks, it threw back the pursuing Rumanian infantry.

On 19 and 20 July, the 2d Cavalry Corps, together with the 15th Motorized

Rifle Division, which had come up to reinforce it, threw back sharp attacks by the Germans and Rumanians and caused the enemy heavy losses; and then on the night preceding 21 July, on the orders of the commander of the Ninth Army, withdrew to the east bank of the Dniester River.

Counterattacks against Mobile Enemy Troops that Have Broken into Our Positions. One of the characteristics of the German army's tactics is to thrust deep armored and motorized wedges into our positions, with the subsequent mission of destroying our forces piecemeal. As they are pushing rapidly forward with the object of encircling groups of our forces, these enemy mobile groups themselves are vulnerable to blows against their flanks and rear.

Cavalry formations, using their great mobility, are entirely capable by rapid maneuver of gaining the enemy's flanks and even his rear, as he is thrusting into our positions, and then striking him hard with cavalry and tank attacks and with fire.

The counterblow struck by the 2d Cavalry Corps against an enemy mobile group that had broken through in July 1941 near Balta is an example of this type of action that is well worth studying.

When the armies of the Southern Front withdrew to the Dniester Line, a serious threat to the right flank of the Ninth Army became apparent. The Ninth Army's neighbor—the Eighteenth Army—under strong enemy pressure had withdrawn considerably farther to the east than the Ninth, leaving the latter's right flank exposed. The enemy pushed forward his mobile group, consisting of the 19th Motorized Division and the 293d and 297th Infantry Divisions, and seized Balta and threatened to come out at Pervomaisk and isolate the Ninth from the Eighteenth Army.

In order to liquidate this enemy breakthrough, the commander of the Ninth Army brought up the 2d Cavalry Corps from the Krioleni–Dubossary area and gave it the mission, in cooperation with the 47th Rifle Corps, of defeating the enemy breakthrough group and then covering the withdrawal of the Ninth Army to a new defense line farther to the east.

Having in two days covered a distance of some 100 kilometers over roadless terrain, the 2d Cavalry Corps on 24 July made contact with the enemy south of Balta and engaged him.

During four days, the cavalry fought a heavy battle along the line Balta–Yelenovka–Eftodiya; finally the enemy wavered and then began to withdraw. Then, the 160th Cavalry Regiment of the 5th Cavalry Division, with tanks operating within the cavalry formations, struck at the disorganized enemy infantry, cutting down many officers and men and seizing much materiel.

On 28 July, units of the 5th Cavalry Division together with the 72d Cavalry Regiment of the 9th Division drove the enemy out of Balta and eliminated the enemy salient. The units of the 19th Motorized Division and the 293d and 297th Infantry Divisions were badly mauled, and the Ninth Army had time to withdraw without being pressed by the enemy to a new line that linked up with that already occupied by the Eighteenth Army.

Protecting the Intervals between Combined-Arms Formations. The German Army's tactics involve frequent deep thrusts by tank and motorized formations into the gaps between our formations. This characteristic of the enemy tactics makes it essential for our commanders to make sure that gaps between formations are well secured, and cavalry formations are particularly capable of carrying out this important mission.

When they are under army-group command, cavalry formations in action in the intervals between armies can accomplish the following:

• Using the methods of mobile defense, they can defend operationally significant sectors when the interval between neighboring armies is dangerously wide;

• They can strike brief but sharp counterblows, using strong cavalry tank and air formations, against enemy groupings that are penetrating our position by thrusting between two armies.

In both of those types of actions, it is essential that the cavalry formation commander have at his disposal a strong mobile reserve.

An example of this type of action is the Shtepovski operation of the 2d Cavalry Corps.

Toward the end of September 1941, after having forded the Dnieper River near Krememchug, an enemy mobile group consisting of the 9th Panzer Division and the 16th and 25th Motorized Divisions threatened to break through between the Fortieth and Twenty-first Armies of the Southwestern Front that were occupying a defensive line running from Sumy to Akhtyrka.

The 2d Cavalry Corps of General Belov was brought into action by the front commander to defend the interval between the Fortieth and Twenty-first Armies. By 27 September, the 9th Cavalry Division had taken up the defense along the line Zelenkov–Kozelyonnoye, while the 5th Cavalry Division was at the line Khorol–Beyevo. Three or four enemy battalions of motorized infantry with tanks were in front of our cavalry.

On 28 September, units of the German 9th Panzer Division and 25th Motorized Division struck the defensive positions of the 2d Cavalry Corps, seeking to break through to the Sumy area. The enemy main attack, involving 52 tanks and a regiment of motorized infantry, was directed against the sector held by the 5th Cavalry Division. The Cavalry was forced back first to Vasilievka and then cut into two groups: the 11th and 96th Regiments withdrew to the southeast while the 131st and 160th Regiments withdrew toward Galushkin where they linked up with the 9th Division. The latter was under heavy attack and was half encircled, but it was able to fight free, and that night it withdrew to the Lutsinovka–Markovka area.

On 29 September the 1st Tank Brigade counterattacked the enemy who was widely deployed generally northeast of Podoprigory, Pavlenkovo, and Shtepovka and destroyed 17 tanks, knocked out over 100 personnel carriers loaded with infantry and supplies and took much booty.

Capitalizing on the success of the 1st Tank Brigade counterattack, the 2d Cavalry Corps on 30 September went over to the counteroffensive with the objective of defeating the enemy forces that had succeeded in wedging in between the Fortieth and Twenty-first Armies. After a hard-fought two-day battle, on 1 October the 9th Cavalry Division of General Bychkovsky, reinforced with tanks, took Shtepovka.

From 2 to 4 October, the 2d Cavalry Corps continued to pursue the defeated units of the 9th Panzer Division, the 25th Motorized Division and the 43d Infantry Division of the enemy. After eliminating the enemy threat to the interval between our two armies, on 5 October the 2d Cavalry Corps took up the defense on the line Shtepovka–Vasilievka, in order to protect the interval.

During the battles between 27 September and 4 October, the 2d Cavalry Corps took 2 tanks, 32 guns, over 500 trucks and personnel carriers, 250 motorcycles and much other materiel. The enemy lost over 2,000 dead and some 40 tanks and armored cars, while another 100 trucks were put out of action.

Covering the Withdrawal of Combined-Arms Formations. Large cavalry formations can also be used to cover the widthdrawal and disengagement (and also the regrouping) of rifle formations. Cavalry can carry out such missions in two ways:

- By holding the enemy (mainly by mobile defense actions) on a given line for a given period of time so that the rifle formations will have enough time to regroup or disengage.
- By striking short flanking counterblows against an enemy force that is already attacking our infantry, in order to attract the enemy's attention to the cavalry and then later, as the enemy prepares to deal with the cavalry, slipping away by usually mobile defense methods.

The actions of the 21st and 52d Cavalry Divisions near Roslavl in August 1941 are an example.

By the end of July, the German Second Panzer Army of General Guderian had taken the Krichev–Chausi area and was continuing its rapid eastward advance toward Roslavl, thereby threatening the route of withdrawal of the Twenty-eighth Army, which was defending a line north of Roslavl.

The commander of the Western Front ordered the 21st and 52d Cavalry Divisions, which were concentrated near Artemovka, to strike a counterblow against the right flank of the German shock group and thereby to frustrate its move to seize Roslavl; this would give the Twenty-eighth Army time to withdraw safely to a new defensive line.

On 1 and 2 August the cavalry, marching principally during the night between these two days, concentrated in the area of Starshavka and on 2 August struck at the enemy motorized columns.

As a result of the cavalry suddenly opening fire and of its also hitting the flank of the enemy column near Shumovka, the enemy lost some 30 tanks, over 50 trucks with personnel, and two mortar batteries. The enemy held up his advance toward Roslavl, and General Guderian diverted his main force to deal with the cavalry that had struck him from the south.

Using mobile defense techniques, the cavalry skillfully drew the Germans farther to the south and, at an opportune moment, disengaged. By then, the Twenty-eighth Army had had time to extricate itself from a bad situation and take up a new line farther to the east.

Conclusions

The experience of the war confirms the following basic principles concerning the employment of cavalry in defensive operations:

1. Cavalry formations in defensive situations constitute a mobile reserve of the army-group commander, together with tank, motorized, and fighter aircraft formations. They can be used for active and powerful counterblows against large enemy mobile and infantry groups that are seeking to break through, and they can also be used to protect the gaps between armies and to cover the withdrawal and regrouping of armies.

2. It is inappropriate to give cavalry formations missions of conducting stubborn positional defensive actions in line together with infantry formations. Cavalry in such actions loses its mobility; it has proportionately less firepower than infantry or combined-arms formations; and it will be obligated to earmark up to one-third of its strength to remain in the rear to look after the horses.

3. In mobile operations, cavalry formations can undertake the defense on operationally important lines, using the methods of mobile defense to wear down the attacking enemy and then strike him a crushing counterblow with the main force of cavalry and tanks.

4. In defensive operations, cavalry formations must be reinforced by artillery and mortars and by engineer units. The attachment of rifle formations enables the cavalry corps to use the infantry for frontal defense and to hold the main mass of cavalry and tanks in reserve for decisive counterblows, thereby greatly increasing the strength and effectiveness of cavalry formations in the defense.

Employment of Large Cavalry Formations in the Enemy Rear

Formations of strategic cavalry are ideally used in mobile warfare for actions in the enemy rear and against his lines of communication.

The characteristics of German tactics—rapid and energetic offensives that seek to exploit success to the utmost and stubborn defense of strong points and large hedgehog positions when they are forced into positional warfare—explain why there is no continuous front line. This circumstance to a significant degree facilitates the actions of cavalry formations in the enemy rear and along enemy lines of communication.

Cavalry actions in the enemy rear can influence the course of events on an operational scale under the following conditions:

- They should take the enemy by surprise, and the cavalry that is to be used against the enemy rear should be brought up to the front in secrecy; particularly, it should be concealed from enemy air observation;
- If it is necessary to break through the enemy front before the cavalry can gain the enemy rear, the breakthrough should be accomplished not by the cavalry but by line infantry formations;
- The cavalry should not go deeper into enemy-held territory than 50 to 60 kilometers from its own front lines, and it should not be called on to remain in the enemy rear longer than four or five days. Neither should it be tied down to a particular area; it must be given every opportunity to retain freedom of movement and maneuver;
- Continuous communication between the cavalry and the army-group command must be maintained, and the cavalry's actions should be closely coordinated with those of the troops operating frontally as well as with friendly air and airborne actions.

An example of action in the enemy rear is furnished by the operation carried out by the cavalry group of General Dovator (then Colonel Dovator) in August 1941.

Early in August the German forces, having reached the line of the Mezha River, halted in order to regroup for further actions farther to the east.

On 11 August the commander of the Western Front gave the cavalry group of Colonel Dovator (50th and 53d Cavalry Divisions) the mission of breaking through the enemy defense, and operating in his rear, to come out in the Demidovo–Dukhovshchina area and overrun enemy command posts and rear installations there.

By 15 August the cavalry group, with a strength of some 3,000 sabers but without artillery or trains (they did have mobile machine guns and light automatic weapons), overran small enemy defensive positions and reached the area of Rozhano, Fomino, and Budnitsa, where up to 22 August they remained in the forest, hidden from the enemy air, conducting reconnaissance of the enemy defensive installations.

Having determined that the sector Ustye–Podvyazie, which was occupied by two battalions of the German 450th Infantry Regiment with artillery, was the most favorable for a breakthrough, Colonel Dovator before dawn on 23 August formed up his two cavalry divisions each in two echelons with the second echelons in each case in cavalry-style deployment. Then, in a strong and rapid attack, the cavalry group broke through the enemy position and annihilated more than a battalion of the enemy infantry.

From 23 through 29 August the cavalry group operated in the enemy rear, smashing enemy garrisons, command posts, wagon trains, dumps, and cutting communications between German units. The group came out in the vicinity of Zhelyukhovo where it defeated the German 430th Infantry Regiment. The headquarters of the enemy Sixth Army, hearing of the exploits of Dovator's group, precipitously fled, and the German rear area echoed in panic the rumor that "a hundred thousand Red Cossacks have broken through."

On 29 August the cavalry group began to move back to its own lines. Notwithstanding the strong air forces, tanks, motorcycles and motorized infantry the Germans sent against it, the group successfully broke through the enemy line again and returned to Soviet lines.

As a result of actions behind their lines, the Germans lost over 2,500 men; two regimental command posts were overrun; the topographic section of the German Sixth Army was destroyed; and the following materiel was either destroyed or taken and turned over to strong partisan detachments operating behind the German lines: 200 trucks, 2 tanks, 4 armored cars, 4 guns, 6 mortars, 30 heavy machine guns, 65 light machine guns, 1,500 rifles, etc. The German command's confidence was shaken by this raid; it stopped its offensive on this sector, and on the front facing our Sixteenth Army, the enemy even withdrew in some places.

A characteristic example of the actions of cavalry in the enemy rear and against his lines of communication during an offensive by our forces is the operation carried out by the 2d Cavalry Corps along the Moscow-Minsk highway from January to March 1942.

The 2d Cavalry Corps (18th, 24th, and 82d Cavalry Divisions and 2d Guard Motorized Rifle Division) had the mission of moving out from behind the right flank of the Thirty-ninth Army in the general direction of the railroad station of Semlevo and cutting the highway and the rail line. On 26 January, having concentrated its main forces near Ostashkova, Yamnovo, and Gridino, the corps threw out advance detachments toward the highway.

The enemy had strong garrisons including armor at Gorodishche and Chepchugovo. At Vyazma there were large stores of motor vehicles and various other major rear installations.

During the period from 27 January through 8 February, elements of the 2d Cavalry Corps cut the highway at Barsukovo and Chernovo, but the enemy brought up the 208th Infantry Division (which had just been transferred from France) and in a series of infantry and tank attacks drove off our cavalry troops from the highway and obliged them to withdraw to the north.

The units of the corps continually sent out detachments that attacked the enemy convoys along the Moscow-Minsk highway, knocked out individual small garrisons, and generally disrupted movement in the German rear on that sector. At the same time, contact was made with the sizable partisan detachments operating in the area; these were armed, equipped, and supplied with the arms and materiel captured by the cavalry in its raids. A sizable area was completely cleared of Germans, and Soviet governmental authority was restored.

From 4 through 12 March, the enemy repeatedly attacked the corps positions; he used some six infantry and one tank regiments in these attacks. But the enemy was able to take only one place—Lysovo, and this only after an attack by two battalions of the 478th Infantry Regiment accomplished by three tanks; all his other attacks were beaten off, and the cavalry corps maintained its defensive position and continued its raids against the highway.

During the period from 26 January through 15 March, the 2d Cavalry Corps liberated over 150 populated places from the enemy, armed several thousand partisans with captured weapons, rescued some 250 of our wounded who had been taken by the enemy, having had to be left behind when the Red Army was retreating. Over 3,000 enemy personnel were put to flight, 426 trucks loaded with personnel or supplies were destroyed, as well as the following items: 19 tanks, 12 guns, 4 mortar batteries, 4 heavy machine guns, and 53 motorcycles. And 32 machine guns, 4 mortars, numerous rifles, and much ammunition and foodstuffs were captured.

The movement of enemy transport between Smolensk and Vyazma was to a large extent paralyzed during this period.

Note

1. The report fails to mention that the 5th Cavalry Corps was so badly mauled that it was never reformed.

The report leaves the Battle of Moscow to discuss the problems faced by the Red Army fighting the German-Finnish forces on the Karelian Front. Here is strong evidence that the Soviets had learned some very painful lessons from the winter war and finally managed to devise countermeasures against the Finns' tactics. Overall, this section of the front remained fairly quiet after the first months of the war, with both sides satisfied with tying up the enemy and preventing each other from sending reinforcement to the more active parts of the front. The situation was to change dramatically in 1944 when the Red Army—now considerably more experienced—launched the massive attacks that forced Finland out of the war—Ed.

8

Special Characteristics of Actions in the Karelo-Finnish Theater

THIS theater covers an enormous area, and in it there is nothing like a continuous front line. It is full of craggy hills in the north, and in the central and southern sectors its terrain is largely wooded and full of lakes and marshes. The road and rail net is rudimentary, and the whole area is very thinly populated. The climate is rugged; there is little daylight in winter and little warm weather in summer. All of these facts make this a particularly unique theater of military operations.

The limited population resources of Finland prevent the Finnish Command from gathering large reserves and oblige it to economize in the employment of personnel. The Finnish Command cannot undertake major offensive operations. In view of this, even in peacetime, the Finns concentrated on the training and formation of separate battalions as well-balanced, self-sufficient organizations, capable of operating independently in complex situations.

Not only the Finnish but also the German units have rear service organizations consisting of men who, in combat periods, are capable of forming provisional combat detachments consisting of drivers, administrative personnel, and other rear service personnel.

In some cases these provisional combat detachments have had a decisive influence on the course of events. This was the case in the April and May actions on the Murmansk and Kestenga sectors.

It is necessary to keep in mind that in the Karelian theater there are both Finnish and German troops, and their tactics differ considerably.

The German units are deployed on the northern operational sectors (Murmansk, Kandalaksha, Kestenga); while the Finns occupy all the front to the south. In addition, separate Finnish battalions are used on the northern (German) sectors of the front to cover the flanks of the German units.

The staff of the Karelian Front (army group) has undertaken to review and generalize the experience of operations in its theater. The examination and summarization of this work is not yet finished, but it is possible nevertheless to make some observations concerning the nature of military actions in the theater.

Reconnaissance

In the organization and conduct of reconnaissance on land, the Finns are outstanding for their skill and energy. The Germans are much weaker at reconnaissance and show no particular resourcefulness or energy.

In their reconnaissance the Finns usually use small groups of three to five men up to a platoon in size. They are armed with automatic weapons and carry a portable radio. The Finns use this sort of group for reconnaissance of our front lines and for reconnoitering our position in depth, but their procedure differs in the two cases.

For reconnoitering the front lines, the group makes the approach by covered routes, then opens fire with all its automatic weapons, and continues firing until our firing points are provoked into returning the fire and thereby revealing themselves. After this, the Finnish group withdraws. The procedure is repeated in neighboring sectors, until the Finns succeed in locating (through observing their fire) all of the firing points along our front line.

The actions of Finnish groups in reconnoitering the depth of our defensive positions is to cross into our area by way of unoccupied sectors of the front; unobserved, they advance into our rear where they conduct reconnaissance, mine roads and paths, carry out raids, and sometimes clear routes of advance for larger groups that are to follow them. If the group runs into organized resistance, it avoids becoming engaged; it withdraws along covered forest paths. Only in the event that the group has the chance to dig in and prepare a good position in our rear does it offer stubborn resistance.

A small group that has infiltrated into our rear, if it meets with good success,

Special Characteristics of Actions in the Karelo-Finnish Theater 101

is quickly reinforced by additional similar groups and by mortars as well. And supplies are also sent to sustain it. Sometimes such groups penetrate 40 to 60 kilometers into our rear areas. This was the case in 1942, when groups of 100 to 150 men moved into our rear areas and struck at army bases, hospitals, and dumps.

The withdrawal tactics employed by these groups is also of interest. A withdrawing group breaks up into several smaller groups that move by different routes, thus making pursuit difficult. Often these groups do not move in the direction of their own lines, but deeper into our territory, after which by a wide swing they move round and begin the trek back to their own lines. These small groups cross our lines at a number of points and do not go back by the same route by which they set out.

The staff of the Karelian Front (army group) recommends the following methods, proven valid by experience, of combatting enemy reconnaissance groups.

First there should be excellent fire discipline: fire should not be opened against small groups. The group should be let to pass through our line, after which it can be destroyed. This method, however, can be used only when it is clearly determined that there is not a larger enemy group following the initial small group. For in this case it is most risky to permit the enemy to reach our rear.

For repelling enemy groups of platoon and larger size there should be special, predesignated, firing positions that, after they have revealed themselves, should be abandoned and used as reserve firing points.

It is essential to organize active reconnaissance not only in front of the line and along the flanks but also in the rear. There must be covered observation posts, equipped with signal facilities, and places that seem most likely to be the scene of enemy reconnaissance group activity.

One method of observation in winter is to establish, along unoccupied sectors and in intervals between units, patrolled ski trails; these trails are covered by periodic patrols that will discover the intersecting trail of any enemy group that has penetrated into our rear. Picked hunter groups mounted on skis (in winter) should be formed to track down and destroy enemy groups that have infiltrated our rear. Ambushes should also be organized in the places enemy ski patrols are most likely to aim for, such as road junctions along paths, at the intersection of forest clearings, and the like.

On our side, the method of deep reconnaissance by small groups of up to battalion strength proved useful. These groups move around the enemy flanks and often penetrate up to 40 kilometers into enemy territory where they carry out raids, seize enemy signal personnel as prisoners, and capture enemy documents.

Experience has shown that combat reconnaissance carried out frontally does not yield worthwhile results. Usually heavy losses are sustained in reaching the enemy front line, and in the best circumstances, the group is not likely to take any prisoners except badly wounded ones who are likely to die before they can be interrogated.

In the Murmansk sector, the method of landing groups along the shore behind the enemy lines proved useful. Groups of 150 to 200 men were landed; they annihilated enemy groups deployed along the coast, destroyed their artillery, and seized prisoners. But it must be kept in mind that such raids cannot be repeated at exactly the same place. This is equally applicable to raiding groups operating entirely on land.

In summertime, with the long polar daylight, the work of reconnaissance groups is extremely difficult, and for this reason it was a fact that in the summer of 1942 there was a virtually complete stoppage of reconnaissance on both sides.

Air reconnaissance in wooded areas does not give useful results, for the woods effectively conceal all ground movements. The best results from air reconnaissance are obtained in winter when the trees have lost their leaves yet there is still daylight in which to carry out the observation.

Offensive Combat

Both the Germans and the Finns carefully prepare their offensive actions, and both make wide use of procedures intended to deceive the defense. For this purpose the main enemy assault group is usually concentrated opposite the defender's flanks, in order to envelop them, while holding groups engage the enemy frontally. Sometimes these holding groups, heavily armed with mortars and automatic weapons, are surprisingly small in numbers.

The offensive is preceded by reconnaissance of the defender's front line and of his rear area. Reconnaissance in our rear is accompanied by active raiding and sabotaging actions.

The enemy troops move out for the offensive along covered approaches at the same time that a heavy artillery and mortar preparation covers our front line and our immediate reserves.

The Germans commit tactical aircraft to support the offensive; the aircraft strike at regimental and divisional reserves with the object of pinning them down.

The combat formation of the attacking groups is of interest. In front, in extended order, go submachine gunners, who carry out area fire either from halts or on the move. The purpose of this is to cause our infantry to keep down in their trenches. Following the screen of submachine gunners come the shock groups whose mission is to develop the attack. These groups are deployed as skirmishers. The third echelon in the attack grouping is the support group, which is also responsible for the security of flanks against our counterattacks.

If our front line is breached the submachine gunners push forward, widening the breach and clearing the way for the shock group and protecting its flanks.

It often happened before an offensive that the enemy dropped soldiers in our rear who were in Red Army uniforms and spoke Russian. These men sought to provoke panic by various means, and they tried to give false orders designed to disrupt our lower command channels. Such enemy subterfuges call for strict checking of movement within our lines of individual soldiers and for the verification of orders.

In cases when the screen of submachine gunners moving ahead of the shock group was held up in front of our front line, the submachine gunners simply melt into the assault group and continue to move forward with it. But at the first opportunity they leave the shock group and infiltrate our positions, thrusting forward so that from the depth of our position they could cooperate with and facilitate the advance of the shock group.

If the attacking shock group, having penetrated our position, comes under a flanking counterattack by our forces, then the support group that follows it as the next echelon comes to its assistance by seeking in turn to strike at the flank of our forces that are counterattacking the shock group's flank.

The enemy acts in a somewhat predictable manner when the shock group and support group are isolated by our troops from each other and the shock group is encircled by us. In this case, the encircled group does not try to break its way out of encirclement and fight its way back, at least not immediately. It organizes all-round defense and defends itself with great stubbornness, trying to tie down as many of our troops as possible, to make it easier for the support group to break through the encirclement and relieve the surrounded shock group. The support group seeks to break through the ring of encirclement from outside and reach the shock group and then, together with the latter, to encircle a part of our blocking force.

This form of offensive is used quite regularly by the Germans and especially by the Finns. The Germans used it in the Murmansk direction at the time of their September 1941 offensive. The Finns have used it repeatedly, the last time quite successfully in their Medvezhegorsk operation in the winter of 1941 when they also employed tanks.

In order to oppose this type of offensive, the defender must plan the organization of "fire sacks" and switch positions in the probable direction of the main effort of the offensive. In the counterattack, it is essential to determine the number of echelons in the offensive force so that we can correspondingly echelon our own forces to have sufficient force to strike at the enemy shock group and also at his support group.

In the most probable directions of the enemy main effort, it is necessary beforehand to organize barrage fires, interdictory fires, and concentration fires along our front line as well as in the depth of our position. This form of opposition against the attacking enemy was used in the defensive operation in the Murmansk direction in September 1941 when the German 3d Alpine Division was defeated. The attacking enemy units were caught in a fire sack and after a thorough going-over by our artillery, they were attacked and for the most part annihilated. The Germans after that called the scene of this particular battle the "valley of death."

There is another form of maneuver that is characteristic of the Finns and that they began to use after the front had become more or less stabilized. They took advantage of the large gaps in the front and the wooded nature of the terrain, which make it possible for the attacker to send forces into the rear of the defender that can remain there unobserved for a fairly long period.

The enemy sought to reach our rear with forces of not more than battalion strength (reinforced with artillery and mortars) in order to interrupt the flow of supplies and to disrupt our command channels. Coming out in our rear, the enemy quickly organized an all-round defense, including wire and mine fields. Sometimes an enemy group that reaches our rear areas sets up a number of defensive positions, creating the illusion among our troops that they are encircled.

This maneuver is preceded by active reconnaissance of our flanks and of our rear area dispositions. This reconnaissance is begun with small patrols that probe our flanks and at the same time seek out and mark routes to be used in reaching our rear. The routes are generally marked by blazings on trees. Then larger groups move out along the already blazed routes and organize their defensive positions in our rear. As these groups move along the routes, they clear them so that supplies can be brought up along them. The Finns organize strong points along these routes or organize regular patrolling along them.

At the same time that he is carrying out this sort of enveloping action, the enemy activates combat actions along the front, increasing his artillery fire, his reconnaissance, and probes. If the enemy detachments that reach our rear succeed in digging in, the enemy reinforces them with new echelons and at the same time begins to attack frontally, trying generally to reach our flanks.

Appropriate counteraction against this type of enemy maneuver consists of strengthened security of the flanks of our positions and increased reconnaissance against the flanks and rear areas of the enemy. Ambushes and traps are set for the enemy along forest trails, roads, and paths that are likely to be used by the enemy.

Whenever our people discover forest paths used by the enemy, they must immediately set up ambushes along them and road blocks. It is desirable to set up road blocks that will channel the enemy into ambushes of ours. When the enemy sets up road blocks, we should arrange to intercept the routes used by the enemy to reach them.

Our combat formations should be organized in depth, and the commander should have mobile formations at his disposal as a reserve, so that they can liquidate any enemy groups that have succeeded in reaching our rear before they can set up a defensive position and dig in.

These reserves should be located to the rear of flanks that are likely to be exploited by the enemy, and they should be at a sufficient distance so that they will have freedom of maneuver in depth to be able to strike the flanks of the

Special Characteristics of Actions in the Karelo-Finnish Theater 105

enemy groups that seek to penetrate to our rear. Thus in the autumn of 1941 the enemy was able to come out in our rear on the Kestenga sector and organize a defensive position on the Lukhi–Kestenga road. But the enemy's success was short-lived. The battalion that had come out in our rear was surrounded and, after stubborn resistance, destroyed by our units, which had come up from the depth of our defensive position. In this case the enemy attempted in turn to encircle our counterattacking forces by committing new forces and seeking to envelop the flanks of our elements that were suppressing the initial enemy battalion penetration.

Defense

The barrenness and inability of the theater to support large forces make it both impossible and inadvisable to set up a continuous front line. Therefore, the defense in general is established only on short sectors that sometimes are hundreds of kilometers apart. These intervals, however, are by no means impassable. Therefore, both sides keep them under observation, mainly by sending out periodic reconnaissance patrols along them.

On some sectors, divisions acting independently may occupy a front of up to 30 kilometers. The defense, in such a situation, consists of a system of strong points and centers of resistance covering the most important approaches and sectors.

The enemy, and especially the Finns, organize their defense as a rule on an all-round basis, with two or three lines of trenches. Out in front and to the flanks regular observation is set up; often the observers take up concealed positions in trees. Roads and paths as a rule are mined, though not heavily. Along the front line as well as in the flanks, the enemy lays mine fields of antipersonnel mines. Both Germans and Finns hang a great many tin cans and booby traps on wires. At night the enemy illuminates the area in front of the front line with a great number of rockets.

The enemy digs in very quickly (the Germans love to accuse the Russians of the same vice) and builds first-rate underground shelters. The Germans on the Murmansk and Kandalaksha sectors build shelters of earth and stone and often use cement in their defensive works. Cement-and-rubble firing points are extremely sturdy, and heavy artillery is necessary for their destruction. On some sectors the Germans and Finns have built timber-and-earthen installations with two or three layers of horizontally laid logs as roofing.

The enemy leaves a certain number of machine guns on his front line and concentrates the main body of his infantry along his second line in underground shelters. It is necessary to point out that when he leaves a position, the enemy mines and booby-traps it—especially the shelters, as was the case in the spring of 1942 on the Murmansk sector. The personnel of attacking units must be particularly warned of this, and they should be prohibited from entering shelters abandoned by the enemy.

In order to strengthen the security of their front lines, the enemy employs watchdogs in addition to their other measures.

The enemy's fire system is very carefully organized. All intervals in a position are covered two or three ways by overlapping fire. The approaches to the front line are well covered by machine guns so that the enemy can effectively concentrate automatic weapons fire. Enemy snipers open fire on individual soldiers at a distance of up to 1,000 meters.

Artillery and mortars are ready beforehand to fire concentrations along the front line and within the depth of the position. Up to June 1942 both the Germans and the Finns used artillery fire not only against groups but even against individual soldiers and trucks. They were anything but economical of ammunition. They also fired area concentrations, often against vacant areas.

More recently, the enemy has become more economical with ammunition. Now he opens fire only against groups or against areas where he perceives that we are building or strengthening defensive works. The enemy also uses artillery and mortar fire against firing points that reveal themselves.

When we use artillery fire, the enemy seeks to withdraw or cover his personnel. The Germans draw back their personnel to the reverse slopes of hills or heights, and the Finns often generate smoke clouds, even in front of their front lines. Firing points often change their position in an effort to get out of the fire zone and usually have several reserve positions.

One further detail of the German defense: the German groupings except on the Murmansk sector usually have Finnish detachments of up to battalion size to cover their flanks.

Both the Germans and Finns defend with great stubbornness. Blocked strong points continue resistance right up until they are totally destroyed. In the spring operations on the Murmansk sector the enemy, whenever blocked or encircled, continued to resist until he was completely supressed by our fire. On the Kestenga sector one of the enemy strong points held out even after it had been blocked for several days and was far in the rear of our advancing units.

The enemy defends no less stubbornly on the front line; repeated efforts on the part of our attacking units to smash the enemy resistance failed even though we had clear numerical superiority. The stubborn resistance of the front line on the Kestenga sector continued even when our shock groups had carried out a wide envelopment of the enemy flank and threatened to come out on the single road, from Lukhi to Kestenga. This indicated that the enemy was prepared if necessary to continue fighting in encirclement.

As our offensive develops, the Finns try to send groups of submachine gunners against the flanks and rear of our attacking units. They often use explosive small-arms rounds, and some of their men hide in trees to shoot at us. If the submachine gunners are able to concentrate in some one place, they are reinforced with ordinary infantry and an attempt is made to cut off and encircle out attacking units. This took place during the January offensive of

Special Characteristics of Actions in the Karelo-Finnish Theater 107

our forces in the Medvezhegorsk direction, when several of our units were encircled by the enemy after they had broken into the enemy position.

When our units are able to drive a wedge into the enemy position, the enemy counterattacks energetically, with powerful artillery and mortar fire supporting his counterattacking elements. If the counterattack fails, the enemy steps up the intensity of his fire against the salient, keeping up this intense fire for several days if necessary and expending thousands of rounds daily on sectors as narrow as 1 to $1\frac{1}{2}$ kilometers, as was the case in our Medvezhegorsk offensive in September 1942.

In the offensive, it is necessary to count on having to use a very heavy volume of artillery and mortar fire in order to neutralize or destroy the enemy defensive installations. Therefore, it is preferable whenever possible to carry out the offensive by means of a wide envelopment of one or both enemy flanks with a view to cutting the enemy communications.

The very sparse road net and even their total absence in many sectors makes it necessary to plan on clearing roads and paths as quickly as possible on the heels of our advancing units and then constantly improving these routes. It is particularly important that the clearing of roads keep pace with the advance of our troops, for otherwise our artillery and our rear services may fall behind the front-line troops and not be able to provide adequate support.

Particular attention must be paid to covering the open flanks and communications routes of attacking units. For this purpose it is advisable to use ski battalions and brigades in winter and in summer to use light infantry brigades.

In making ready for the offensive, it is essential to provide free reserves that can be used to reinforce units that are meeting success in their attacks and to take the place of other units that are temporarily held up in blocking enemy positions.

To protect our attacking units against envelopment by enemy counterattacking units, it is essential to echelon the combat formation of the attacking army in great depth. When the second echelon of an attacking army is committed, a new second echelon must immediately be reconstituted out of first-echelon units that have been passed through or can otherwise be made available.

In divisions or brigades, special detachments should be formed that advance directly behind the combat formations of the regiments and battalions. Their task is to comb over the trenches, foxholes, and communications trenches abandoned by the enemy and clean out any remaining enemy submachine gunners or riflemen, some of whom may be playing dead. In order to clean forest roads of tree snipers who may have been left behind by the enemy, it is useful to spray the foliage of trees on both sides of the road with machine gun or automatic arms fire and also to have the regimental artillery rake them over with shrapnel.

The operational breakdown of an attacking army in this theater should include the following groupings: an envelopment group or groups; a group attacking frontally; a group operating in the secondary direction; and a second echelon, including armor and tank reserves.

The actions of the flanking or enveloping groups depend on the circumstances. They may take the form of attacking against the enemy rear or organizing a defensive position to block his withdrawal.

The group attacking frontally has the task of breaking through the enemy defense, breaking it up into smaller groups, and encircling these smaller groups in coordination with the flanking group.

To prevent the enemy from shifting forces from one sector of the front to another in order to oppose our flanking groups, our troops along the whole front should engage in active actions, and on several sectors these operations should actually be—or should appear to be—designed to achieve breakthroughs.

Taking into consideration that the enemy withdraws the bulk of his personnel from the front line during our artillery preparation and changes the position of his firing points, our artillery and mortars should carry out false lifts of fire. Artillery should be able to shift its fire quickly and accurately, and during the course of the preparation, artillery reconnaissance should be continuous, in order to discover as soon as possible any shifts in the location of firing points and enemy personnel.

Attacks in winter take place under polar night conditions or with extremely short daylight periods (from a few minutes to two or three hours). Therefore, all the provisions relating to night attacks should be applied to winter attacks in the far north.

Employment of Arms

Artillery

The character of the terrain makes artillery virtually road-bound and limits the maneuverability of artillery in changing firing positions. Therefore, alternate and reserve firing positions must be chosen ahead of time. Satisfactory routes or paths must also be cleared, so that the pieces can be quickly moved to these positions.

There should be no fire before the attack from the primary artillery firing positions; whatever firing is to be done should be conducted by specially designated pieces firing from temporary firing positions.

In wooded sectors, artillery fire must usually be conducted without the aid of observation points. Wooded terrain also reduces the availability of artillery. The disadvantage in observation can be partly overcome through the use of observation balloons, a procedure in which at present we have not had much experience.

The presence of a great number of covered approaches makes it possible for individual artillery pieces, even heavy-caliber ones, to be moved up close to the front line where they can fire for destruction against enemy defensive installations.

Special Characteristics of Actions in the Karelo-Finnish Theater 109

In the offensive over roadless terrain, artillery chiefs must provide for maneuver by fire to compensate for the difficulties in actual moving pieces. Also, they must provide for the bringing up of ammunition to artillery pieces accompanying the infantry. In roadless country, ammunition can sometimes be moved forward only by carriers. Therefore, it is essential to form provisional groups of ammunition carriers, using rear services personnel, gun crews who may be temporarily without guns, and in some cases, even infantry units.

Infantry commanders must help the artillery in every way possible, for otherwise the infantry may find itself without artillery support at a time when it most urgently needs it.

Tanks

Conditions on the Karelian Front are not favorable for the use of tanks on any wide scale, for only on a few sectors can tanks move freely off the roads.

Independent actions by tank formations should be considered an exception. Combat activity by tanks must take place in the closest coordination with infantry. On some sectors, particularly in the far north, tank activity may be so extremely difficult that tanks should be used not to lead the infantry in the attack but to follow it as a form of mobile fire support.

It is generally inadvisable to use tank-riding submachine gunners, for the branches of trees will often dislodge the tank-riding tommygunners, bruising and maiming them. Therefore, it is best for groups of submachine gunners not to ride on tanks but to move on foot close behind them. This is entirely practicable, for the tanks generally will not be able to move faster than the men.

In using tanks, generally it is best to use them in small groups—and often individually—cooperating closely with the infantry.

Communications and Control

One factor bearing on the control and direction of troops is the fact that runners and motorcycle messengers generally are road-bound. Therefore, it must be taken into consideration that a messenger may have to make a very long detour along roads to cover a very short distance as the crow flies.

Taking into consideration that the Finns excel at sending saboteurs and patrols into our rear areas and against our dumps, it is desirable to send out not individual motorcycle riders and messengers but pairs or even groups of them. They should not move bunched up but be strung out within visual distance of one another. Documents should not be carried by the lead man, but by the man following him, or—if there are several messengers and several documents—by several men.

Liaison officers in winter move on skis. In summer they must have motorcycles or cars. Very often it is necessary to provide them with security detachments as well.

The discussion of air power is one of the weakest parts of the report, and it reads more like propaganda than fact. The winning of air superiority during the Battle of Moscow and for the remainder of the war is debatable. Although one does not have to believe the exaggerated claims made by the German aces, it remains a fact they continued to be formidable opponents throughout the war. The Soviets never had the kind of air superiority that the West enjoyed in the campaigns of France and Germany, when daily movement by German troops in good weather was almost unthinkable. The report also fails to mention flying accidents, the bane of the Soviet air force throughout its history. Accidents quite possibly caused more losses than actual combat during the war—Ed.

9

The Struggle for Mastery of the Air on the Northwestern Front

Below is a résumé of the combat activity of one of the air armies in action on the Northwestern Front.

From this summary it is clear that the combat aviation of this army group, when it had parity of strength with the enemy, was able to seize the initiative.

The practical measures taken by the command of the air army and of the air formations to increase the effectiveness of the combat work of their fighters and bring about a decisive break in the course of air operations in our favor are worthy of careful study.

Combined-arms commanders and air commanders must study the experience of this air army and apply as fully as possible the lessons derived from it to improve, under their own local conditions, the quality of combat work of their fighter aviation.

The present war has shown how greatly the success and failure of ground forces depend on the degree of mastery of the air. The Germans undertake no major offensive operation without first assuring themselves that they will have air mastery.

To achieve decisive air mastery, the Germans do not hesitate to strip entire army-group sectors in secondary areas to build up overwhelming concentrations of air power at the point of main effort.

The basic consideration of every fighter-aviation commander should be to work toward bringing about the best possible conditions under which his fighter pilots can make the most effective use of their tools against the enemy. Combat experience has proven positively that in air combat only positive, aggressive actions can lead to decisive results and provide effective and real support to the ground forces, even under conditions of numerical inferiority in relation to the enemy air force.

On the Soviet-German front there was a period when the Germans had the initiative in the air. They were striking at us actively, and we had difficulty fending off their attacks and were just barely able to defend our ground troops. Although our airmen were working under the greatest pressure and were expending every ounce of effort, they were able to win only very modest successes. But we in due course changed our tactics and went over to the offensive in the air. The number of aircraft did not change, the pilots were the same men, yet now superiority in the air is firmly in our hands. We have full control of the air over our troops. Our fighters are able freely to fly over enemy territory, even as few as a couple at a time; they carry our aerial reconnaissance, they do fire-correction work for the artillery, and they divebomb and strafe enemy columns on the march. And those same German aces who not long ago were keeping some of our airfields out of action, who were flying solo missions over our troops and over our rear—these same aces are now either dead, or they have been shot down and taken prisoner. How has all this come to pass?

The Germans in the beginning sent against us a group of experienced and well-qualified fighter pilots, flying Me-109F and Me-109 aircraft. The bold and almost impudent tactics of the Germans were a deliberate device to create the impression that they had unquestioned air supremacy. Some of our commanders and flyers took the bait, and they adopted a purely defensive type of air action. They believed that against such "aces" it was necessary to fly only in large formations and that in air combat it was possible only to keep stricly on the defensive. This type of action was justified to a certain extent when the enemy had a clear-cut numerical superiority. In the confused and changing situation in the air, our fliers were able to go up and beat off some of the numerous enemy strikes successfully by working in close cooperation and by depending on each other's mutual support in flying close formations.

But with the appearance of new German fighters, these tactics did more harm than good.

Our fighters, flying in close formation, were at a disadvantage when a pair of

Messerschmitts came diving down on them, firing at the whole formation, obviously on the principle that they would be bound to hit something, then swerved off to the side and gained altitude for a repeat attack. At the same time, a pair of Messerschmitts would wait till some of our aircraft, running short of fuel, had to fall out of formation to go home. Then they would fall on these planes and knock them out singly. Every laggard and every badly handled plane of ours would be taken under fire by the enemy fighters and destroyed. Furthermore, by attracting the attention of one of our large formations of planes by engaging it with a couple of Messerschmitts, the enemy would gain the freedom to strike unopposed against our ground troops. The situation was clearly an impossible one, and it was evident that it would have to be corrected as quickly as possible.

In preparing our counterblow, which was to be coordinated with the actions of our ground forces, we began our work from the bottom up; we began with the individual pilot. Through training and simulated combat exercises we learned exactly what our strong points and weak points were. We became convinced that our pilots are first-rate and that our aircraft are excellent. Our system of organization was weak.

The experience of the war has shown that in present-day air combat the basic fighter entity is the "pair" (two fighter aircraft), consisting of the lead pilot and the wingman. The pair should be thoroughly integrated; it should constitute a unity. First of all, we concentrated on forming such pairs, consisting of the same two pilots and trying to pick men who were personal friends and whose combat experience would fit them to work well together.

Thus, for example, Senior Lieutenant Sharov loved to fly with Senior Lieutenant Korotkov as his No. 2 man. So it was ordered that they should constitute a pair and that they should always fly their airplanes together. They knew each other's idiosyncracies, and they trusted each other completely, so as a pair they were highly effective in combat. Subsequent experience showed that such measures greatly increased the fighting effectiveness of individual pilots and of pairs.

From among the best pairs we formed a group of fighter aces; others were formed later. Such groups were the leaders, the shock formations of our air force: theirs was the task of making the first breach in the enemy air formations in combat.

And here again, experience showed that such groups functioned better if they are made up of fliers from the same regiment rather than of men brought together from various regiments.

The next measure to improve the combat effectiveness of our air unit was the thorough training in dependable radio communications. We worked long and hard on this matter; we finally progressed to the point where we had two-way radio communication between each group on an air mission and the ground and also within the group.

We noticed that the wrong tactic of flying in very tight formation was the result of not making enough use of radio communication. After all, a commander who directs his pilots by hand gestures and wing waggles can scarcely hope to guide individual pilots to tasks on the flanks or in the rear of the formation.

But present-day air combat in high-speed aircraft involves open-formation tactics, and the victory goes to the side that can make the best and most effective use of space, to the one who uses the clouds to its advantage, to whomever makes passes from out of the sun, and to the air commander who runs his group like a well-coordinated football team.

Without radio communication, a pilot is half-blind. If we do not make use of a pilot's sense of hearing, and depend only on his sight and judgment, then we have taken away half the chance of success. Repeatedly we have seen examples of young pilots guided by radio who did a great deal better in combat than old experienced pilots who were guided in the old-fashioned manner.

Of course you cannot make fliers become entirely accustomed to the use of radio overnight. The thing cannot be done by a simple order; there must be a lot of hard nagging work before the pilot's natural aversion to having gear attached to his head and to the static and buzzing in the earphone can be overcome. We must demand of training regiments that they turn out pilots who are well trained in the use of radio.

In units were radio is effectively used, as a rule there are fewer losses, better success in combat, and a quicker integration of new replacement pilots.

The third measure that raised the combat capability and confidence of our pilots and the effectiveness of our air units was the establishment of forward control points (CPs) of fighter units. These forward CPs are set up in the areas of the ground battle where the most important air actions are anticipated. For some time now we have regularly set up such advance CPs equipped with radio and wire communications. They make it possible for the commanders of air units to direct precisely and accurately from the ground the course of air actions. Thanks to this arrangement, we have been able to economize in men and material; now we can send our aircraft exactly where they are needed to beat off the enemy attack and not send them out according to a stereotyped pattern or an unrealistic plan worked out too far ahead of time as we used to do. We are no longer obliged to try to maintain what was euphemistically called "continuous air cover," which in practice was about as much of an obstacle to the enemy air force as a net is to rain. In addition to these overall advantages, we are firmly convinced that the presence of the forward air CPs has also markedly raised the level of discipline and the self-confidence of our pilots.

We have adopted the practice of having not only air division, brigade, regiment, and squadron commanders at the forward CPs, but individual pilots as well. In this way, each flier understands and accepts the fact that many eyes are following him while he is in action in the air, and that they see all that goes on. As a result, he has an increased sense of responsibility and of being a self-

The Struggle for Mastery of the Air on the Northwestern Front 115

confident member of a closely knit team, and he performs better under the heavy stress of air combat.

In addition, every pilot who returns to his air regiment after having been at the forward air CP becomes a first-rate propagandist among the other pilots for telling them what air support really means to the ground troops.

All of these measures enormously increased the value of the air power available to us.

We began the air offensive on the eve of the ground offensive. The air offensive was launched with a series of strikes against enemy airfields. After careful reconnaissance Major Vasilev's Shturmoviks struck hard at the enemy fighters on the ground. Taking off while it was still dark, just at dawn the Shturmoviks caught a group of Messerschmitts lined up for refueling and destroyed no less than 12 of them. Later, in the early evening, the Shturmoviks came on another group of German fighters in the process of dispersing on an airfield for the night and shot up a number of them.

Strikes like these at enemy aircraft on the ground weakened the Germans somewhat and brought about something like an equality in numbers between us. But however successful our strikes against enemy airfields may be, they cannot decide the question of mastery of the air by themselves; they are useful only in setting up favorable conditions for the subsequent air battles in which the question will be decided.

The air battles for supremacy began by our sending out our best pair to fight the pairs of Messerschmitts that were patrolling various aerial sectors near the battlefield.

When the first German pair met ours, it did not think it necessary to call for reinforcements; it engaged our pair and immediately fell into the trap we had set for it, for the German pair had not noticed another pair of our aircraft that had been flying somewhat higher. This second pair of ours dove on the Germans. Major Maidenov guided his No. 2 pilot as they both dove on the Germans so skillfully by radio that they together threw the German pilots into total confusion and panic, and the two Messerschmitts collided in midair. A second German pair that came to the help of the hapless first pair arrived too late, and seeing what happened to the first pair, it flew off without giving battle.

This victory had a decisive psychological effect; it can be said to have brought about the turning point in the situation in the air on our sector of the front. Thereafter, our fighters whenever they saw any German aircraft aloft immediately engaged them without hesitation.

Senior Lieutenant Puchkov, with a young, relatively inexperienced pilot as his No. 2 man—Lieutenant Marchenko—engaged a pair of German aces, and after a short dogfight, both Germans were shot down. One of them was taken prisoner: Lieutenant Werner Fess, who had been an instructor in advanced flying.

Another young flyer, Sergeant Chulaev, took on three Messerschmitts single-handedly. He shot down two, and the third he drove away. These initial successes of ours sobered and frightened the conceited German aces. Losing their self-confidence, the Germans took to flying not in pairs but in large groups. After losing a number of their pilots, the German command began to send out their planes in groups of six or eight and ordered their pilots not to engage our planes except where they had a clear numerical superiority.

Once the Germans sent up a group of eleven aircraft against four of our fighters led by Major Maidenov. Our planes attacked boldly. The fight was decided in our favor when we sent up a second group of four. The Germans quickly sent in eight more planes; eight Yak-1s were involved against 19 Me-109s and Me-109Fs. Senior Lieutenant Motus attacked four of the enemy, and heavily wounded, he still was able to down two of his opponents and drive off the other two. In the whole engagement, the enemy lost six Messerschmitts that day and showed that they were soundly beaten by not returning. On the following days, our fliers destroyed additional enemy aircraft. The overall result was that the sky was swept clean of German fighters, and the German bombers no longer dared venture without fighter cover to help their hard-pressed ground troops. Their reconnaissance and artillery fire control were also knocked down in numbers, while our dive bombers and reconnaissance aircraft were able to fly at will over the front with no special difficulty.

Thus in a relatively short time we were able to achieve air superiority with forces about equal in numbers to the enemy's. The same Soviet pilots who just a short while before were lacking in self-confidence and customarily bunched up in large formations whenever a German ace appeared were now well organized, and they shot down and chased off the German aces. They now were the masters, the initiative was theirs, and they had caused the enemy to be hesitant and overcautious in combat.

Lieutenant Werner Fess, the German ace who was taken prisoner after he was shot down, stated that he thought he had been engaged by English pilots. Evidently the German aces, having taken a beating, could only explain it to themselves by imagining that English fighters had shown up on the Soviet-German front. The saying of Suvorov paid off handsomely: "In war, do what the enemy does not expect of you." Our fliers were amused at the speculations of Lieutenant Fess; they said they hoped that the Germans might be equally surprised at the appearance of Russian tactics on the English-German front.[1]

Of course the enemy will not take this loss of air superiority passively, and we must anticipate countermeasures on his part. We must further improve our organization for combat and our alertness. For we have shown that by bold and decisive actions we are able to seize the initiative in the air and attain air superiority. Now we must mobilize all the strength and resources we possess, so that we shall surely be able to repeat this experience on the broadest possible scale.

We have many fine planes and outstanding fliers. We must emphasize organizing ability, skill on the part of air commanders, firmness, and precision in the direction of air actions. If we can accomplish these things the combat work of our pilots will show up to best advantage.

Note

1. No Lieutenant Werner Fess is listed in any German aces directory—Ed.

The Battle of Moscow did not involve fighting in major urban areas, and in fact, the Germans managed by flanking maneuvers to cut off cities such as Minsk and capture them with relatively little fighting in the urban area. What is described here is combat in Stalingrad that was taking place while this report was being prepared. The Soviet tactics here are the classical "no-step-backward" type of defense where every building is turned into a fortress. As it turned out, these tactics were fully deployed only by the Soviets in Stalingrad and later by the Germans in 1944-45. Strangely enough, the report does not mention the use of snipers, which were used with great effectiveness by the Russians in Stalingrad—Ed.

10
The Defense of a Large Populated Place

ALL cities and large populated places, no matter how far they may be from the front line, should be made ready for defense.

The Organization of the Defense of a Populated Place

The principle of a stubborn all-round defense should be the basis of the organization of the defense system of a populated place. Every house, every street, and every part of a town must be converted into a fortress, capable of holding up the enemy for a long time and capable also of conducting a prolonged defense even in total encirclement. The overall defense system should be arranged in such a manner that the enemy will not be able to break through the field fortifications flanking the town and then cut off the town from the bases in the rear and deprive our forces of freedom of maneuver, supplies, and evacuation routes. The struggle for lateral and rear roads and railroads is an integral part of the battle for a town or populated place.

The defensive positions around a populated place as well as the defense of the place itself must be laid out along naturally favorable lines. For the defense, the most must be made of bluffs, draws, railroad cuts, individual heights, and crests.

The close-in defense of large populated places should be built on the same principles that govern the organization of fortified areas: i.e., a series of defensive lines prepared beforehand, each consisting of a series of strong points and centers of resistance, with the whole system closely integrated and arranged for mutual fire support.

The more skillfully the defensive position is chosen from the point of view of antitank, antipersonnel, antiartillery, and antiaircraft defense, the better it can be defended, the smaller the forces that will be required for its defense, and the greater the losses the enemy will have in attacking it.

The commander of a defended populated place must have at his disposal a strong mobile reserve that can be employed piecemeal in various directions or as a single command in a single direction.

The defense plan of a large populated place is part of the overall operational plan of the army or army-group commander, and it is closely tied in with the overall defensive system and defensive lines developed by the army or army group.

The defensive plan for a populated place includes the following:
- The organization of direction and control of the troops defending the given populated place and the organization of closest cooperation between them and detachments formed on a provisional basis from local inhabitants;
- Cooperation between the forces defending the populated place and the field forces operating outside of it;
- Echelon defense throughout the full depth of the populated place and preparation to defend stubbornly each part, each block, and each individual building;
- The organization of defensive measures within the town and its environs, and the setting of deadlines for the completion of these defensive measures;
- The organization of antitank defense;
- The organization of antiaircraft defense, chemical defense and a firefighting organization;
- Arrangement for the use of antiaircraft artillery both for antiaircraft missions and direct fire ground missions;
- The establishment of a strong mobile reserve at the disposal of the commandant of the fortified town;
- Organization of supply and evacuation services;
- The accumulation of emergency reserves of ammunition, rations, fuel, and materiel; and
- Application of all industrial resources within the town to the task of aiding the defense of the place.

The defense of a populated place consists of the development of a system of strong points within the town, and one or more defensive lines and switch positions of the field fortification type outside the town and tied in with the defenses within the town, the whole to take full advantage of the natural defensive characteristics of the terrain.

For convenience in control, the suburbs and approaches to the town are divided into sectors. The number of sectors depends on the number of major approaches to the town.

The internal defense of the town is also divided into sectors, each consisting of a number of strong points and centers of resistance. The number of sectors depends on the number and importance of the principal buildings or blocks within the town that can be converted into strong fortresses.

The strong points and centers of resistance should be closely tied in with each other.

Each strong point or center of resistance should be a fully self-sufficient element, capable of waging a stubborn and prolonged all-round defense. For the efficient direction of the defense of the town, an interior defense staff is set up, headed by a commandant. The internal defense commandant had under him a number of sector commandants. Each sector commandant is the commander of the formations and units that are deployed within his sector. The commandants of combat subsectors and their staffs are organized according to the same principles.

Among the elements making up the garrison of a sector and of a strong point are army units, NKVD units, city police (militia), units of armed workers, antiaircraft units, and fire department elements. These elements are quartered in the sectors they are to defend.

The local population must be made ready for active participation in the defense of the town. Armed detachments are formed beforehand in the various parts of the town, each prepared to defend objectives in the part of the town where they regularly work. Politically hostile and unreliable elements should either be isolated or be evacuated from the town.

In populated places prepared for defense, each locality from which effective fire can be delivered must be converted into a strong point. Each house, each factory, each warehouse—all of these must be made into fortresses, and each one must be defended by a garrison consisting basically of the men who live or work in it, somewhat on the guild principle. This can be demonstrated by the example of the defense of City N in which Factory B is a combat subsector. The garrison of this particular strong point (or subsector) is made up of the armed guards of the factory and of the volunteer workers detachment recruited from among the workers of the factory and of various smaller detachments recruited on the guild principle from among workers in neighboring smaller establishments. The commandant of this strong point is the chief of the factory security detachment. The logistical element of the defense force of factory "B" is made up of the administrative elements of the factory itself.

In City K some warehouses have been effectively converted into strong

The Defense of a Large Populated Place

points. All the ground covered by one complex of warehouses constitutes a combat subsector, divided into a number of strong points, each one of which is an individual warehouse. The garrison of this particular combat subsector consists of the regular guard detachment of the warehouse complex, of its firefighting detachment, of groups of workers and other employees, and of the administrative and housekeeping force of the warehouses—these latter constituting the rear service element of the garrison. The commandant of the combat subsector is the chief of the warehouse complex.

The headquarters for the defense of a populated place of large size should if possible be located some 20 to 30 kilometers outside the town itself. The defensive system of the outskirts of a town is set up along the same lines as a field-fortifications system and consists of battalion strong points having a depth of 6 to 8 kilometers. Such strong points may be 10 to 12 kilometers apart, with intermediate smaller strong points to tie the main ones together.

City K had on its outskirts three or four lines of field fortifications. The enemy repeatedly attacked them with superior forces, but he had little or no success and took heavy losses. Then, concentrating overwhelming forces, and at great expense, he was able to break through one defensive line on one sector, and through two on another. But as a result of these attacks, the enemy wore himself down to such an extent that he was unable to assault the city itself and had to break off action for a long time. The garrison of the town maintained its defense on its forward lines and counterattacked the exhausted enemy, causing him considerable additional losses.

The headquarters of the town defense proper may be located outside and in front of the town or on the actual edge of the built-up part of the town, depending on the terrain and on the defense plan. When the headquarters of the town defense runs directly along the edge of the town itself, it is necessary to set up more than normally dense combat security outposts out in front.

In all cases, heights adjoining towns must be integrated into the overall defense system of the town.

The defense system within the town or populated place itself should include:

1. A series of strong points, mutually tied in by flanking cross fires and covered by antitank and antipersonnel obstacles, the whole complex covered and supported by machine gun, mortar, and artillery fire. All cellars and cellar windows from which flanking fire can be conducted should be reinforced and prepared as firing points. All buildings and all entrances of buildings, either into the street or into yards, should be covered by flanking fire.

All stone structures should be linked together into centers of resistance by cutting through abutting walls so as to provide covered communications routes between them. Walls should be reinforced with beams and earth, and firing apertures should be punched through the walls. Special attention should be paid to making underground structures ready for defense, and some

Battle for Moscow

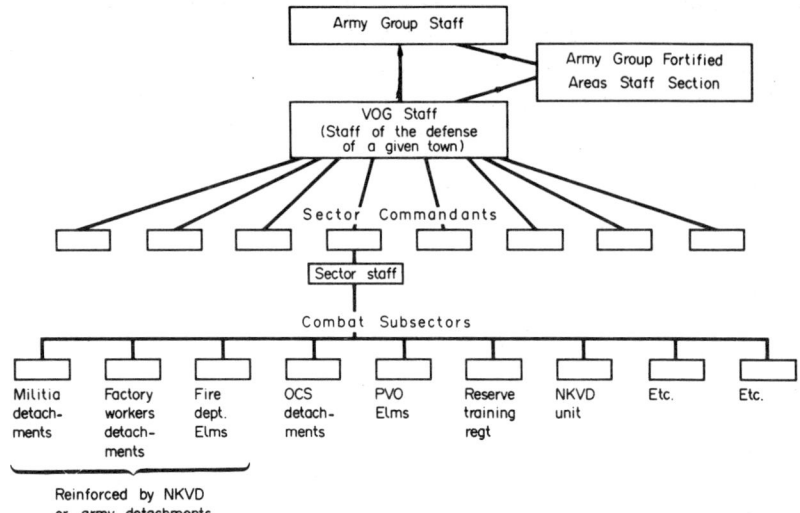

FIG. 1 Chart for Organizing the Defense of Populated Areas

underground installations should be prepared for use as shelters and first-aid stations. Wells and the ditches, covered ditches, and underground water mains or sewers can be used as covered communications routes.

To thicken and strengthen the firing system of the strong point, one can use reinforced concrete turrets, knocked-out tanks, tank turrets, cast-iron cupolas, dug-in tanks, etc.

2. A mobile reserve, whose task is to counterattack and destroy any enemy forces that succeed in breaking into the defended town. The mobile reserve includes groups and detachments that cover the intervals between strong points, covers sectors not otherwise covered by fire, and sectors or points where a full-time or constant garrison is not needed.

A populated place, depending on its size, may include anywhere from a single company strong point up to several battalion strong points, but under any conditions, it must have a fully developed all-round defense.

The central part of the town should be the location of a special strong point that includes not only its regular garrison but and additional mobile reserves at the disposal of the commandant of the town.

The strong points should be laid out in such a way as to cover adequately the most important directions and approaches. Intervals should not be left between them, and the boundaries between them should run along small streets or alleys in such a way as not to be noticeable. Large, wide streets, particularly those that lead out on to the main highway, should be assigned as the backbone of a single defensive sector to be held by a detachment of not smaller than company size.

Parks and public gardens in towns must also be prepared for all-round defense; buildings in them, and fences, barriers, and other installations are adapted for the defense, and additional works are built.

At the decision of the town commandant, separate buildings or groups of buildings in front of the town but not part of its overall defense system may be taken down if they appear likely to serve as cover for the enemy or if they interfere with the fields of fire and observation of the defenders.

3. The fire system of a strong point is organized mainly by adapting existing buildings and structures for the delivery of surprise fire and flanking fire from them. In addition, special firing positions may also be built in the place in order to take streets and public squares under fire.

Machine guns and individual cannon are sited in the lower stories of buildings to be able to deliver grazing fire and to reduce the amount of dead space wherever possible.

Some mortars and machine guns are sited in the upper stories and on the roofs of buildings. Embrasures are prepared in the walls of building, and windows are narrowed down to provide good firing positions for individual riflemen.

Wide use must be made of submachine gunners who ambush and attack from the rear any enemy groups that may have broken into the position. The submachine gunners also have the task of separating enemy infantry from their tasks.

Antitank rifles and guns are echeloned in depth and grouped mainly in the directions most accessible to enemy tanks. They are sited behind barricades, antitank obstacles, dragon's teeth, mine fields, roadblocks, traps, and specially built timber-earthen works and permanent-type works.

Antiaircraft artillery also has the secondary task of conducting antitank fire. Therefore antiaircraft artillery is generally sited along likely tank approaches. Tank-hunter groups, armed with grenades and Molotov cocktails, are placed in buildings next to barriers in streets.

In the defense of one of our towns, the fire system was organized in the following manner. The barricades at street corners were built in such a way that each street corner would be under enfilade fire from several directions. These barricades, however, did not interfere with the movement of our own transport traffic along the streets. Barricades set up as antitank obstacles were prepared for the defense; they had embrasures for rifle fire. The windows of buildings were mostly bricked up, but embrasures for machine guns and elbow rests for riflemen were prepared. All the outside doors of the buildings were bricked up, and the bricking was reinforced with sandbags or beams.

If the headquarters is out in front of the town, the fire system is organized along normal lines for field fortifications, but particular attention must be given to covering roads leading to the town.

4. All roads not needed by the troops holding the field fortifications in front of the town should be destroyed in order to limit the enemy's freedom of maneuver. The remaining roads should be made ready beforehand for destruction if needed.

On the approaches to one of our big cities, one road only was left open for every 50 kilometers of front; the rest were made unusable before the enemy reached them. Three main highways lead to City X from the enemy side. All of them widen out into main streets within the city. In order to prevent the enemy tanks from moving straight up these highways into the city, each of them was blocked with antitank ditches. Temporary approaches to the city were arranged, using detours and secondary roads, and these also were equipped with ready-made antitank obstacles that could be moved into place on a short notice.

The division of City X into sectors (and the division of the sectors into subsectors) was done in such a way that every major street leading or linking up with the highways outside the city ran through the middle of a sector and subsector. All streets in the area of the first subsector were covered with cross fire from antitank weapons including guns.

In view of the difficulty and complexity of directing combat actions within a town and the difficulty of observing the course of combat within it, a comprehensive net of observation points should be set up, located in attics and on rooftops. These points should have telephone communication, and they should also be able to communicate with one another by visual signals, including light signals at night.

In City P, the observation points system was set up in a way that tied it into all the observation points of the antitank defense system. All church-like buildings were adapted for observation. The chimneys of factories temporarily not in production were particularly useful. Platforms were built inside the chimneys, and embrasures were knocked through the chimney wall to give good vision.

In addition to observation points, local message centers and signal posts must be set up.

Employment of Artillery

In the defense of a town, artillery is deeply echeloned; it has a thoroughly developed net of observation points and a communications network including runners, motorcycle riders, etc., as well as telephones.

Mobile antitank artillery reserves should be established, and a plan worked out ahead of time for their employment and movement under various contingencies.

The artillery fire system should be organized in such a way that all approaches to the town can be brought under flanking fire or frontal fire from batteries or from individual pieces sited in buildings or in blockhouses.

Until the battle moves into the town itself, the artillery is directed by the senior artillery commander. Deployed in firing positions in garden squares and other open places within the town, and partly outside the town, the artillery's task is to disrupt the enemy's combat formations as he is moving toward the town, causing him losses as he is concentrating his forces for the assault. During this phase, the artillery carries out its mission in a perfectly ordinary manner, as if it were in the defense in the field.

But during combat within the town, artillery direction is decentralized; individual pieces are subordinated to platoons and batteries to companies, in order to get better and closer coordination.

Antitank guns, regimental guns, and a part of the 76-millimeter guns of divisional artillery are sited as individual pieces in streets and at crossings along the most likely avenues of approach for enemy tanks. These pieces are set up in firing positions with stone barriers and obstacles to protect them, and they are organized to provide mutually flanking fire.

Antiaircraft guns, whenever enemy tanks show up in their vicinity, take the tanks under direct fire.

Employment of Tanks

In the defense of a large town, tanks are used for the following:
- As a mobile maneuver group to strike counterblows against enemy tanks and motorized infantry on the immediate approaches to the town and in its outskirts;
- For combat with enemy tanks and submachine gunners who may have broken through to squares and wide streets within the town; and
- For ambush actions, being used as mobile or stationary firing points either dug in, or hidden behind buildings, and so on.

During the period of combat for the town, our tanks as a mobile counterattack shock group must be kept in the directions where the enemy tank and motorized infantry are most likely to attack.

Generally in attacking a town, the enemy begins with groups of five to fifteen or more tanks accompanied by submachine gunners in two or three directions, later committing tanks and motorized infantry reserves at the point where he has made the most gains. Sometimes the enemy tries to infiltrate individual tanks and small groups of submachine gunners through our outer lines at whatever costs, so that they can later link up on the immediate outskirts of the town. Therefore, our senior tank commander must draw the enemy tanks into combat on the outer defensive positions under conditions that will be least favorable to the enemy tanks; he must seek to disrupt the enemy's combat formations and lead the enemy tanks into the fields of fire of our artillery and draw them into tank traps. Individual enemy tanks that succeed in breaking through to the immediate outskirts of the town are destroyed by our tank reserves.

Combat for a town is divided into two phases. In the first phase, which involves actions on the approaches to the town, the maneuverability of tanks is not impeded, and the tanks should be used en masse. The combat formations of our tanks should be compact, and there must be a mobile reserve. If the enemy succeeds in breaking through the first tank echelon, then he must be met and defeated by the mobile tank reserve on the approaches to the outskirts. Artillery infantry and submachine gunners must work in close cooperation with tanks.

During the second phase, tanks are involved in street fighting. In this phase, tanks can be used in small groups and as individual machines for the destruction of enemy tanks, armored cars, or motorcyclists who have broken into the town and also for the suppression of enemy soldiers who have taken cover in buildings.

In street fighting it is also sometimes possible to use tanks in groups of five or ten vehicles, moving at high speed and shooting rapidly at point blank in order to demoralize the enemy and create panic in his ranks.

In organizing tank ambushes, tanks should be used in groups, for in this way one can achieve massed fire, and it is possible to go over to the counterattack quickly with a number of tanks.

Employment of Reserves

Experience in the defense of large towns demonstrates the necessity of reserves at the disposal of the town commanders. The size of the reserves depends on the size of the garrison itself, and on the number of sectors and subsectors in the town.

In a battle for a sizable defended town, the enemy will seek to break into the town not only by trying to establish an overwhelming superiority of force in whatever direction or directions seem most promising, but also by seeking to infiltrate small groups through weakly defended sectors.

In order to make the reserve as mobile as possible, it is necessary to mobilize all the motor vehicles available locally and to give to the reserve all the vehicles belonging to units defending the town that can be spared. As part of the reserve, there should be antitank guns that can be carried on trucks. The detachments that make up the reserve should have stores of grenades and inflammable bottles; and they must be able to conduct combat at close quarters with the bayonet and also be able to deal with enemy tanks with grenades and Molotov cocktails.

The general reserve is at the disposal of the city commandant. This reserve must not be committed except under the most pressing urgency, but on the other hand, it must be committed in good time and not held out so long that it cannot affect the course of the battle.

There may be occasions when the reserve is committed piecemeal in various parts of the defense. The defense command, in assigning tasks to these reserve elements, must also see to it that coordination is established among the units already in action on the various sectors and the reserve units that are committed to help and support them.

The skillful use of his reserve by the commandant always makes it possible to fend off the danger of an enemy breakthrough. If there is smooth cooperation among all elements, the defending forces of a town are able to exhaust the attacking enemy and then throw him out of the town.

Engineering Measures

In preparing a town or populated place for defense, it must be kept in mind that it will be defended by a limited number of troops.

The degree of completeness and strength of the defensive engineer works depends mainly on the time available to prepare them. All available local resources should be exploited in preparing the town for defense. If there is time, the engineer works in a defended town should be continually strengthened and improved.

In City N most of the factories and shops, in addition to their basic production, were turning out armored cupolas and firing points. For this, they used existing stocks of sheet iron, as well as the turrets of captured tanks. Construction organizations (civilian) that had concrete mixers and concrete factories prepared prefabricated parts for reinforced concrete defensive works. This, together with the improvised armored cupolas turned out by metal working shops, hastened greatly the preparation of the city for defense.

In City K, one of the warehouse complexes was excellently prepared for defense. Embrasures were cut in the warehouse walls for light weapons. The premises of this warehouse group were very large, so brick strong points were built up in them, abutting the walls from the inside. These were protected on the outside by double rows of rails driven into the ground and by I-beams as well. Entrances to buildings were bricked up, and buildings that were not part of the defensive complex were either bricked up or torn down. All passages between buildings were also blocked.

In preparing a town for defense, first barricades must be set up around the outskirts, and these must be covered by firing points. Obstacles and barriers must be set up consisting of rail or trolley-track rail. Separate houses interfering with fields of fire must be torn down; buildings and streets must be mined so that all approaches to the defended place will be covered.

Barricades at street crossings must in all cases be covered by flanking machine gun and artillery fire. Houses abutting barricades must be made ready for all-round defense. Large stone or brick buildings located at important points must be prepared as separate strong points. The lower stories are prepared so that machine gun and direct-fire guns can be sited in them. The second and third stories are arranged to accommodate individual riflemen and submachine gunners. The basement is reinforced and shored up to serve as a shelter. In each strong point, there must be gathered beforehand reserves of ammunition, food, medical supplies, and drinking water.

In order to give the garrison freedom of movement within the town, passages are cut through the walls of buildings leading from one quarter of the town to the next. All unnecessary doors, windows, and gates are sealed up, so that the enemy will not be able to break unexpectedly into a building. The garrison of a strong point may not leave it unless at the written order of the next higher commander.

In case the town or city has to be evacuated by our forces, a plan is drawn up prescribing what demolitions are to take place, the order in which various factories and installations will be evacuated, and when demolitions will be carried out. The plan also assigns the responsibility for all the prescribed actions individually and states who bears general responsibility for the accomplishment of the plan in each quarter or ward of the town.

Things having military significance must be destroyed as a matter of priority—bridges and culverts before the town and on the main routes that the enemy will use, military factories and installations, power stations and substations, all signal equipment and installations, warehouses, stations, aqueducts, trolley and bus parks, and workshops. Booby traps are liberally planted.

Such measures are taken upon the abandonment of a town only on the specific orders of the army or army-group commander.

Camouflage

A large town or city as a rule will be an objective of enemy air attacks. These attacks will have as their aim the destruction or neutralization of power stations, telegraph, telephone, and radio stations, highways and railroads, aqueducts, ammunitions factories, warehouses, and other rear area installations. The enemy will have maps and town plans showing the ward and the street where important objectives are located, and he will have good orientation directions to point out accurately the location of these objectives to his air force and how to approach them.

The task of camouflage is to deceive the enemy and confuse him by erecting false buildings and installations, changing the shape and form of existing ones by painting and false roofs, etc. It is essential to remember that it is useless to camouflage just one single important objective, for the enemy pilots will be able to orient themselves to it easily by referring to other known orientation points. Therefore the camouflage of a city should provide for the change in the configuration of its principal existing buildings, the building of false squares and streets across existing buildings with camouflage materials, the setting up of new sections of the city through the use of fabric on light frames, etc., the erection of new small bridges out of camouflage materials, and the creation of the illusion that existing bridges are knocked out.

The camouflage of rail lines is especially difficult. It is necessary to camouflage existing railroad stations and then set up imitation ones nearby and also to imitate the night lighting of the right of way, switches, and signals, etc.

On lakes and ponds, floats can be set up to simulate buildings, and if they are spaced right, the illusion of streets can be created.

The Organization of Communications

In organizing the defense of a town, the greatest possible use must be made of already existing local signal communications facilities. When a town is put under an emergency regime on the approach of the enemy ground forces, the chief signal officers of the units defending the town undertake the mobilization of all signal equipment and personnel in the town and integrate them into the military signal organization of the command.

The signal organization plan provides first of all for direct and indirect wire communications among the various sectors and subsectors and among all military installations.

A double wire communication net, with the wire protected by being laid underground, constitutes the basic and most dependable form of communication in the defense of a town. The basic form of signal communication between the town and military installations or units outside the town is radio.

In order to protect the basic signal installations in the town against enemy air or ground attack and against sabotage and espionage, a special security force is set up.

A chief is designated who is responsible for each important signal installation. Less important signal installations do not have chiefs, but someone in the building or place where they are located is specifically made responsible for them. This responsibility includes organizing a system of checking and control and permitting access to the signal facilities only to persons carrying valid passes.

In order to avoid the enemy listening to our phone conversations, the appropriate signal chiefs must constantly check to see that the wires and cables running through areas occupied by the enemy are not tampered with. Important phone conversations or radio messages, having to do with operational matters, are transmitted in prearranged code.

The plan of signal organization must provide the men and the resources to prevent our lines from being damaged, and they must also provide for reserves of signal equipment.

In addition, the signal organization plan includes:
- The reinforcement of signal resources of important military installation;
- The removal of important signal centers and pieces of apparatus to more defensible and secure locations, usually to underground shelters;
- Laying of new signal lines through existing underground water and sewer pipes;
- The use of public address systems for broadcasting general alarm signals and general commands to the population;
- Mobilization of all available equipment for visual and sound signaling, such as electric pocket flashlights, factory and train whistles, etc.

Chemical Warfare Defense

In case of chemical warfare attack, it is essential to have the garrison and population of the town prepared for chemical warfare defense. For this purpose, a number of shelters should have been prepared beforehand, consisting mostly of the basements of apartment houses and other dwellings.

These shelters should be able to take a 100-kilogram bomb without suffering damage. In order to strengthen them, additional reinforcing beams are installed to shore up the first floor, and slabs of concrete or layers of sandbags are laid over the floor of the first story. Shelters should not be located next to fuel dumps nor next to highly inflammable buildings. There should be separate shelters for military personnel and civilians.

Both the military and the civilian population should be given the chemical-warfare-alert signal and should be given explicit instructions as to where their assigned shelters are to be located. The shelters should be equipped with air filters. If there are no readily available factory air filter systems that can be used, then a simple field-expedient sort of charcoal filter system can be improvised.

Fire-fighting Service

For fire fighting and the smothering of incendiary bombs special fire-fighting teams are set up in each ward, each block, and each house, consisting of the local inhabitants. Special attention must be given to the training of these teams or commands. A really serious fire in the city could make it necessary for the garrison to abandon the houses, blocks, and even whole sections of the city that had been prepared for defense. In this case, the defensive capabilities of the garrison would be greatly diminished.

The defense of a populated place depends to a large extent on the stubbornness, self-discipline, and capacity for self-sacrifice on the part of the troops defending it, both within the town and on its approaches.

The series of battles for Stalingrad proves that units that make the best use of their resources of men and materiel, coordinate skillfully with the guns and tanks attached to them, and keep the initiative by constantly maneuvering and counterattacking can keep the Germans from advancing even a single yard.

Following is a discussion of the antiaircraft tactics in the first year and a half of the war when the Germans were engaged in some strategic bombings against the Soviet Union that were soon to cease except for a few harassment raids and the famous 1944 raid on U.S. Air Force shuttle bombers in Poltava. On the eve of the war, Stalin purged Colonel General G.M. Shtern, commander of antiair defense troops (the PVO), indicating perhaps a lack of satisfaction with the performance in this area, and appointed Colonel General N.N. Voronov, the future commander of Soviet artillery, in his place. The Soviet antiaircraft forces performed no worse than the other units when faced by the German onslaught, and they certainly did little to defend the exposed front-line airfields that were the primary target of the Luftwaffe. This was partially due to surprise and lack of radar, an area in which the Soviets were to remain deficient throughout the war—Ed.

11

Antiaircraft Defense of a Major Center
(Based on a Year's War Experience)

A major city, with its important concentrations of major installations of an administrative-political, economic, and transportation type, presents an especially attractive target for air attack.

The tasks of the antiair defense troops (PVO) in the organization of the defense of a major center include:

1. Active operations by fighter aviation of the PVO with the object of destroying enemy aircraft and ground forces over enemy-held territory (as in the operations of the fighter aircraft of the PVO in the defense of Moscow, Leningrad, Kiev, and Stalingrad);

2. Timely warning of PVO units and of likely objectives of enemy air attack of an impending air attack;

3. Active antiaircraft fire against enemy air strikes, on the approaches to the objective as well as over the objective itself;

4. A thoroughly developed system of camouflage of the objective as a whole, as well as of its most important buildings and installations;

5. Rapid neutralization of the effects of an enemy air raid.

The basic elements of the antiair defense of a major city include the following:

- Active air defense;
- Air warning service; and
- Local air defense.

The resources of active air defense include fighter aircraft, antiaircraft (AA), artillery and machine guns of all calibers, barrage balloons, searchlights, and sound detectors. They are all concentrated on the task of holding off and turning back enemy air raids.

The antiaircraft service is organized within the city and includes all measures for the camouflage of individual objectives as well as of the city as a whole; for the erection of false structures; and for the chemical, firefighting, medical aid, and emergency restoration work within the city.

The warning system is intended to ensure that all AA defensive resources will be brought into action in good time.

Enemy Tactics in Air Raids

The enemy uses a wide variety of tactical procedures in conducting air raids against targets in our country.

One of the characteristic tactical procedures used by the Germans in attacking especially important targets from the air is to launch a number of large groups of aircraft against the target in the following manner:

- In the beginning, a rather small group flies over the target to try to discover the pattern of AA defense of the target;
- Following the first group comes the neutralization group whose mission is knock out or neutralize our fighter airfields and AA installations. This group, consisting of bombers and fighters, comes in at low level, bombing and strafing; and
- Following the neutralization group or echelon comes the main body of bombers. They bomb the target in horizontal flight and with dive bombing.

The main body of bombers in operations against objectives and points in our immediate rear are accompanied by fighter cover; the fighters fly somewhat ahead of the bombers and 500 to 1,000 meters higher. After the bombing has begun, some of the fighters continue on with the bombers that have dropped their bombs to cover them on their return, while the rest remain over the target until the bombing has been completed.

For orientation of his bombers in flight, the enemy employs radio beams and light signals made by his agents from the ground near the target. The Germans make wide use of pathfinders for guiding their bombers. The planes and their pilots have made a previous reconnaissance over the target area and have oriented themselves on the exact location of the target and of our antiaircraft artillery (AAA) installations. Then, in the raid itself, they each lead in a sizable group of bombers and point out the targets to them.

The altitude at which the German bombers fly during the raid is between 3,000 and 8,000 meters. The altitude depends on the nature of the target, the weather, and most of all on the number and effectiveness of AA weapons.

The enemy chooses the particular tactical form for each air raid after a careful study and reconnaissance of the AA resources at the point he intends to bomb. Thus, we cannot say, based on the experience of the first year of war, that the enemy follows any set pattern in his air raids.

Of all the enemy flights deep over our territory, nearly 70 percent have consisted of reconnaissance-bomber flights by single bombers. But this gives a clear idea of the great importance the enemy attaches to the reconnaissance of our rear and particularly to the reconnaissance of the grouping and dispositions of our AA defenses.

Night raids against large places take place either in the form of flights by single bombers or by groups of varying sizes; in both cases the enemy aircraft come in deeply echeloned and often simultaneously from several directions.

In order to locate targets in night bombing, the first group of enemy aircraft illuminate the area with flare bombs and drop clusters of incendiary bombs on the target. The following waves orient themselves by the light of the fires caused by the incendiaries and carry out their mission by dropping high-explosive (HE) bombs.

In the German air force much attention is given to methods of achieving surprise in attacking towns and important points, and the Germans are skillful at it. They approach the target from out of the sun; they dart out of the clouds with throttled motors; and they follow erratic courses. All these measures are designed to nullify the effectiveness of our AA guns.

In air raids on especially important points and installations, the Germans sometimes use the tactic of a prolonged attack, the whole action taking as much as five or six hours, with intervals between waves or between flights by individual planes of 30 or even 40 minutes. In several cases the following order of flight has been observed in such raids: at the approach to the target, enemy bomber groups break up into smaller groups or even disperse as individual planes. Then they come in over the target from various directions, and after having dropped their bombs, many of them fly back over the target one or more times so as to confuse our AA defenses and keep the people in the town under strain and terror.

Bombing small targets or individual objects (railroad bridges, individual factories, etc.) is carried out from altitudes of 600 to 2,000 meters. The enemy bombers fly in close formation, with dive bombers making their passes at the target one after the other. In the latter case, the dives follow closely one after the other; the first plane will not have come out of its dive before the second is bearing down on the target. Sometimes this type of operation will be carried out with enemy planes flying in column formation, either straight or in echelon at an acute angle from the line of flight. In raids on rail junctions and roads, the enemy does his bombing along the axis of the roadbed or road or comes in at an angle of 30 to 45 degrees.

In order to achieve surprise, sometimes the enemy bombers come at one target, but just before reaching it, they veer off and approach the real target from an unexpected direction.

When in the zone of our AA fire, enemy aircraft execute evasive measures by rapidly losing altitude, or by losing altitude and at the same time changing course.

When they come under our AA fire, enemy bombers often jettison their bombs outside the target area.

In some cases, the Germans carry out simultaneous strikes against the target and against the AA defense at and near the target. In this case, the enemy bomber force is usually divided into parts. The first carries out its strike against the target and draws the fire of our AA weapons, while the second group comes in a trifle later and strikes at our already-engaged AA weapons.

Sometimes the enemy bombers do not come at once within the zone of our AA fire; they skirt along its edge, probing for thin spots, and then on finding one, they break through to the target.

In night raids, individual enemy aircraft attach themselves to the combat formations of our aircraft that have come up to oppose them. Then the enemy plane accompanies our planes back to their airfield, and as our planes are landing, the enemy planes suddenly drops its bombs.

The enemy is particularly sensitive to having his planes caught in the beam of our AA searchlights. If an enemy plane is caught by one of our searchlights, it at once begins wild and erratic maneuvers to escape the beam at all costs, and while it is in the beam, it fires long machine gun bursts astern and to both sides obviously fearing that it will be attacked by our fighters.

Until May 1942, the enemy would come into the zone of action of our searchlights at Leningrad only at altitudes greater than 5,000 to 7,000 meters.

In daylight raids against our airfields, the enemy tries to achieve surprise by flying out of the clouds suddenly or by coming in from the sun with throttled-down motors. Sometimes he first drops smoke bombs in order to blind our AA guns and aircraft.

The main mass of the enemy air force is employed, whatever the depth of penetration over our rear, in the direction of his main ground force effort. Bomber operations in our rear reach a depth of 600 kilometers, while enemy reconnaissance aircraft have penetrated as far as 1,200 kilometers.

Combat Employment of AA Defense Resources

The grouping of AA artillery in the defense of a major center depends on the size and configuration of the area to be defended, the significance of the

Antiaircraft Defense of a Major Center

individual objectives within the general area, and the quantity and calibers of AA guns that are available.

In its raids against our cities and important points the enemy air force uses varying tactical methods and carries out its raids at all altitudes, beginning with the very lowest and ending at altitudes that represent the practical effective ceiling from which bombs may be dropped with any hope of striking at or near the target.

Fire from medium-caliber AA guns forces the enemy to keep his aircraft at a considerable altitude. But since bombs dropped from high altitudes are notoriously inaccurate, the enemy seeks accuracy by divebombing, and he accepts the fact that in so doing his losses from AA fire are bound to be greater.

To reduce his losses, the enemy first strikes at our AA firing points, with his aircraft spread out in the zone of our AA fire both in depth and at varying altitudes, to complicate our efforts to deliver massed AA fires.

This enemy air tactic emphasizes the necessity of having AA weapons of all calibers grouped together in an air defense complex. The presence of small-caliber AA weapons makes it much easier to fight enemy dive bombers.

Thus, only by integrating the fire of all calibers of AA weapons, including .50-caliber machine guns, can one achieve the best means of combatting the enemy aviation.

As the experience of the war has shown, the combat deployment of AA artillery should be on an all-round defense basis. This will permit our AA weapons to oppose enemy air attacks from any direction, and with such a deployment, our AA weapons will be able to deliver massed fire for the simultaneous repulsion of a number of waves of enemy aircraft attacking from different directions.

When a large quantity of AA artillery has been massed for the defense of a place, the zone of its fire can be moved out to cover the approaches to the defended place. The depth of the zone of fire is determined by the number of AA guns available and by the relative degree of importance of the various approaches to the defended place.

The artillery chief who controls the AA artillery should have a highly mobile AA reserve group. Depending on the circumstances, he can rapidly shift this group to reinforce the AA defense on one or more of the approaches or to defend particularly important objectives within the place itself.

In organizing AA defense, consideration should be given to high-priority objectives within the town and special AA groups should be organized and sited to defend these objectives, even at the expense of the overall density and effectiveness of the AA defense.

When there are several AA regiments in the defense of a large place, the town should be divided into sectors, each of which as a rule is defended by one AA regiment. The sector, in turn, is subdivided into AA battalion areas. The commander is located in the center of the sector, but somewhat toward outer battery positions.

It is important to avoid any sort of stereotyped layout in the combat deployment of AA units or defensive complexes. The enemy will soon catch on to any set-piece layout. It is essential also to keep in mind that the enemy in his air raids will try to neutralize the fire of our AA defense system. Therefore, it is necessary to be able to shift quickly and modify the combat layout of our AA positions. However, changes in the combat dispositions of AA units should not make it necessary to change the locations of any of the other elements of the units (fire control, command posts, etc.). It is usually sufficient to work out beforehand a number of variants of the basic position to be taken and then to make arrangements for shifting from one variant to another as quickly and smoothly as possible. These arrangements include preparing alternate firing positions, being able to rearrange signal communications quickly, and making arrangements for new or alternate supply routes, etc.

In determining how much AA artillery will be needed for the defense of a place, it is necessary to consider the quality of the enemy air force, the kinds of AA pieces available (rate of fire, caliber, etc.), and the average number of rounds necessary to shoot down each enemy aircraft.

The matter of rate of fire and also of muzzle velocity has taken on increased importance in view of the increasing speed of enemy aircraft.

In organizing an AA defense system, it is necessary to try to concentrate a large number of batteries capable of putting up a heavy volume of fire against as many different air targets as possible.

Experience shows that an adequate AA defense system of a major center requires a series of antiaircraft artillery rings around it. The most favorable distance between the individual batteries and between the rings, in order to be able to cover as large an area as possible yet achieve sufficient density of fire, is on the order of 3 kilometers.

On the average, a large city will require from 500 to 2,000 AA artillery pieces for its antiair defense.

The observation system of the AA defense complex of a large city is organized on a centralized basis, with the senior artillery chief prescribing exactly how it will be set up. The outer ring of observation points should not be less than 15 kilometers in front of the firing positions of the outer batteries, in view of the high speed of modern aircraft.

AA battalions in the second, third, and successive inner rings of the defense set up forward and lateral observation points. These should be sited to provide a good overlap in observation, with some of the observation points of one battalion actually being located in the area occupied and defended by its immediate neighbors.

Changes in the Combat Formation of AA Artillery during the Course of the War

In the beginning of the war, the battalion command posts were located in the middle of the area occupied by their batteries. Experience has shown that the

Antiaircraft Defense of a Major Center 137

command post should be located directly adjacent to one of the battery positions. In this manner, it is possible to avoid having the enemy dive bomb the command post in relative safety. Furthermore, it simplifies fire control and economizes in wire and ground security personnel as well as in the use of motor transport and fuel for the bringing up of supplies.

The command post of separate battalions and regiments that had been located in towns or points being defended have had to be moved out into the field. This has strengthened the measure of control the commander can exercise over his batteries and also has reduced the likelihood of unnecessary losses in headquarter personnel. But with this arrangement, special attention must be given to ensuring that wire communications are absolutely dependable.

In the beginning of the war, battery operational control points were set up 12 kilometers or less from the batteries themselves. Such a distance, however, in view of the high speed of modern aircraft, failed to give the batteries timely warning to open fire on the enemy. Experience has shown that such points must be at least 15 kilometers from the battery firing position.

Machine gun positions were set up as far as 500 meters from the battery firing positions in the most likely directions of enemy air attack. To heighten the effectiveness of antiaircraft machine gun fire against enemy ground-attack planes and dive bombers striking at the battery position, it has been found better to disperse the machine guns at no greater a distance than 100 to 200 meters from the battery positions themselves.

Losses from enemy bombs dropped on battery positions have led to the conclusion that it was desirable to increase the distance between individual pieces and between the pieces and the battery fire control device from 25 meters to 50 to 100 meters. Such an open-order disposition of batteries has reduced damage from enemy bombs.

In order to deceive the enemy as to the layout of our AA defense system under night conditions, it is desirable to set up false AA defense areas near real ones and to simulate AA artillery and searchlight activity in the false areas. In one of his night raids against Moscow, the enemy dropped over 200 high explosive bombs on false positions.

Direction. The conditions under which antiaircraft defense combats are carried out demand clear-cut and accurate direction and control to work out the data concerning the approaching enemy. The AA commander, moreover, must make fast decisions on the basis of data given to him and must transmit it with all possible speed to his subordinates. In this connection, it must be kept in mind that the enemy is approaching his target at a speed of 5 or 6 kilometers per minute. It might seem under these conditions that a greater centralization of control is necessary. But in actual fact, to control the AA activities over an area of several tens of thousands of square kilometers on a centralized basis is an extremely difficult task. On the other hand, the experience of the war has shown that too great a decentralization is equally unwieldy.

The AA command of a city will not always be able to foresee the precise nature of an enemy air raid. The situation will not become even approximately clear until the enemy raiding force has come within range of our warning service. But this will not give enough time to coordinate fully the actions of the AA artillery with the other elements of the AA defense. Yet on the other hand, everything possible must be done to coordinate as quickly as possible the actions of the various AA elements of the particular area defense.

The direction of AA artillery defending a place against an air raid should as a rule be centralized. The actions of the AA artillery should be directed by the senior artillery chief present, who plans the combat activity of all AA units throughout the battle and assigns additional tasks as necessary during the course of the battle. Centralized direction facilitates the rapid shifting of fire and makes it possible to mass fire in the decisive directions, in terms of the overall defense of the place.

The experience of the war confirms the basic validity of these general principles concerning the direction of AA artillery. But the difficulty of centralized control increases as the enemy approaches the defended place, so that there must be a balanced integration of centralization and decentralization in the control of AA artillery during actual combat. The relative stability of the AA defense of a city makes it possible to work out this balance and to improve the organs of control and direction.

Reconnaissance. The experience of the war shows that the timely entrance of AA artillery into the battle against enemy air raids is in direct proportion to the quality of AA artillery observation. Numerous examples prove this. If AA observation points are located too close to the firing positions, if the observers cannot quickly recognize enemy aircraft by their silhouettes and by the sound of their motors, if the personnel at observation posts and at battery command posts are not constantly on the alert, and if the results of observation are transmitted late and incorrectly if these things occur, then the enemy aircraft have a good chance of "appearing suddenly" over the target, dropping their bombs, and getting away without harm. On the other hand, in cases where AA observation and reconnaissance is alert and active and carried out in accordance with the regulations and the experience we have had thus far, it is a sure bet that the AA artillery will open fire in good time against the enemy aircraft and achieve worthwhile results.

Methods and Types of Fire. Up to now during the war antiaircraft artillery has used salvo fire and continuous fire. Fire has been conducted with normal direction methods and with alternate or supplementary fire-direction methods.

Antiaircraft artillery has fired barrage fire, fire against ground-attack

Antiaircraft Defense of a Major Center 139

aircraft, against descending parachutists, and against ground targets including tanks, armored cars, and infantry, without AA fire control mechanisms.

Against individual aircraft or groups of aircraft, under conditions of normal visibility, fire with normal fire-direction methods is the most effective. In this connection, the initial shots should be very carefully calculated and fired slowly enough that they can be accurately observed.

At one time during the war against rapidly maneuvering air targets, we conducted fire with deliberately scattered bursts, but experience has proven that such fire is not effective. At present it is considered that fire controlled by AA fire-directors against aircraft using evasive tactics is not worthwhile. An immobile AA barrage is more effective.

At night and during the day when visibility is limited, as a rule barrage fire is used.

AA fire at night is conducted with AA fire control directors only against targets illuminated by searchlight beams. Once we have good radar fire control, we shall be able to use directed fire against enemy aircraft both at night and in bad daytime visibility; this will not only be possible, but it will be essential if we are to achieve the greatest effectiveness in our AA fire.

AA artillery is often obliged to use alternative methods of fire control in cases where elements of the regular fire control instruments fail to function properly. In some instances, it is necessary to have recourse to direct fire, with visually estimated leads on the enemy aircraft under fire.

The employment by the enemy of high-speed aircraft (fighters and ground-attack planes) for the neutralization of our AA batteries has obliged the latter to use something better than the old-fashioned firing methods in such cases. The old methods, worked out at a time when aircraft speeds were less than they are today, quickly proved to be unsatisfactory. We shortly worked out new methods of fire against ground-attack planes that are now used by all our AA artillery. Experience shows that if the new method is correctly used and if the data are correct, the enemy aircraft are shot down by the first AA bursts. Thus, for example, in an air raid over Leningrad, the 351st AA Regiment shot down some fourteen enemy aircraft, of which twelve were hit while they were dive bombing or strafing our AA positions.

Ground-attack planes generally attack AA firing positions from the rear when the AA battery is firing against high-altitude targets. In such a case, one or two guns — depending on the circumstances — must transfer their fire to the enemy ground-attack planes.

Experience has shown that in taking data from the man who is handling the stereoscopic fire control instrument, anywhere from 100 to 200 meters additional lead must be calculated, depending on how well-trained—and therefore on how fast—the operator is in transmitting his data.

In the first phase of the war, AA barrage fire was conducted in accordance with the *1939 Regulations for AA Fire*. In the first enemy air raids, the methods prescribed in this manual were proven to be relatively ineffective and cumbersome as far as control was concerned. During the course of the war, new barrage fire procedures have been worked out; they are far more flexible and make it possible to conduct moving AA barrage fire in various directions up to the limit of the range of the AA pieces involved.

The new method of conducting AA barrage fire uses up a great amount of ammunition, but its effectiveness is far greater than that of the older method.

Effectiveness of AA Artillery in Combat Against the Enemy Air Force

During the war so far, AA artillery has shown that it is a powerful weapon in combatting enemy air raids. Thus, during the first year of the war, 34 percent of all the enemy aircraft shot down over our territory have been accounted for by AA artillery.

The amount of rounds of medium-caliber AA ammunition necessary to shoot down an enemy airplane, using tracking fire, is on the order of 530 rounds per plane, while some 1,500 rounds of small-caliber AA ammunition are needed to account for one enemy aircraft. These data are an overall average; in individual cases there are very great variations. For example, in one action, the AA artillery pieces in Kiev expended 85 rounds and knocked down two enemy aircraft. In that case 43 rounds were used and five enemy aircraft were shot down, for an average of 133 rounds per plane. But in this case, more than the normal amount of rounds was spent in barrage fire.

The increasing power of our AA artillery has obliged the enemy to give serious consideration to planning his air raids. There are many examples to show that when AA artillery was not present, the enemy air force strafed and bombed the target from any altitude he desired and from any direction.

On the other hand, when the target was defended by AA artillery, the altitude at which the enemy planes flew over was a good bit higher, there were fewer passes over the target, and the enemy quite often failed right up to the end to accomplish his mission.

ᛋMany of our AA batteries are excellently trained and highly effective, but there are still a number that show various shortcomings that reduce their combat effectiveness. The most important of these shortcomings include:

- Poor procedure in discovering and identifying targets, and faulty aiming procedure, which leads to delays in opening effective fire;
- Careless preparation of artillery pieces and aiming devices for action and lack of preparation before opening fire;
- Too careless or hasty preparation of firing data, simple target designation by offhand visual estimates, or incorrect setting of fire control mechanisms; and
- Inadequate knowledge of the rules of fire and of the provisions of the manual and regulations on the part of command personnel.

It is an established fact that the enemy air force goes into action against AA artillery when the latter seriously interferes with the accomplishment of the

Antiaircraft Defense of a Major Center 141

enemy air mission against a defended place. Efforts to neutralize AA weapons may take place at the same time as the raid on the city the weapons are defending, or there may be special air attacks just against the AA defenses.

Divebombing is carried out mostly by Ju-88, Ju-87, and Me-110 aircraft, which fire on our AA batteries with their cannon and machine guns. There have been individual cases when the enemy has bombed out AA positions from horizontal flight at altitudes of 1,000 to 2,000 meters. In neutralizing AA batteries, the Me-109 is sometimes used; it hedgehops and comes in to strafe our positions.

In most cases, the enemy achieves little in his attacks against our AA positions, as can be confirmed by many examples.

On 29 August 1942 a railroad AA battery near Leningrad was hit three times during that one day by enemy air groups of bombers and ground-attack planes. There were thirty to forty planes in each group. The bombers came in at 2,000 meters in level flight and dropped their bombs and then strafed our positions. But the battery stubbornly kept up its fire throughout the attacks, and as a result, three Ju-88s were shot down while our losses amounted only to four men wounded.

On 2 September 1942 the 12th Battery of the 351st AA Regiment, which was defending a bridge over the Neva River, was struck by some sixty Ju-87s and Me-109s. The enemy divebombed the battery and strafed it, making three passes. Yet the battery sustained no losses.

On 21 September 1941, thirty-two Ju-88s and some twenty-five Me-110s attempted to bomb a power station. The enemy discovered our AA battery defending the station when the battery opened fire. He sent some Me-109s and Me-110s to attack the battery and strafe it with cannon and machine gun fire. The battery continued to fire, using two guns to shoot at the bombers and two to shoot at the ground-attack planes that were attacking it. Four enemy aircraft were destroyed, while the battery itself sustained no losses.

The 2d Battery of the 256th Antiaircraft Battalion defending Zhitomir was attacked by twelve Me-111s coming in four converging groups. The battery maintained its fire and obliged the enemy to jettison his bombs and break off the attack.

The 6th Battery of the 183d AA Regiment got a direct hit on an Me-109 in its first salvo.

During a single day, one battalion of the 351st AA Regiment shot down fourteen enemy aircraft.

Near Odessa the 5th Battery of the 638th AA Regiment shot down five enemy aircraft in a single day.

The AA artillery defending a bridge across the Dneiper successfully repulsed no less than 150 enemy attacks against the bridge and preserved the bridge intact until our forces had taken up new positions on the east bank.

Combat experience has shown that well-developed engineer works on an artillery battery position provide adequate protection against bomb splinters, even when the bombs hit very close to the battery position. A battery of the 745th AA Regiment defending the Dnieper River crossing near Rogachev that was well protected with field works was attacked nineteen times by enemy bombers that dropped over 100 bombs. Yet the battery never ceased functioning; it lost only six men dead and wounded and had two of its guns and a rangefinder only temporarily put out of action.

On the other hand, batteries that neglected to dig in properly took serious losses. Thus, a battery of the 64th Independent AA Battalion, which was defending near Borisenki (western front) in April 1942, was attacked by enemy aircraft. The battery was totally without engineer works or other comparable protection. As a result, it suffered heavy personnel losses, and all of its materiel was put out of action.

An equally important requirement in maintaining the effectiveness of AA batteries is changing firing positions, especially after enemy air reconnaissance has spotted them or after an air raid. Failure to observe this rule can lead to unnecessary losses.

The 41st Independent Armored AA train, which was defending a railroad bridge across the Ugra, occupied the same firing position for ten days, even after several enemy air raids against the bridge it was defending. Then, on 22 May 1942, six enemy dive bombers dropped several dozen bombs on the train or near it and shot it up and strafed it. Two guns, a fire-director, several AA machine guns, and a number of personnel were put out of action.

AA Artillery in Combat with Enemy Ground Forces

In addition to its basic mission of destroying enemy aircraft, AA artillery conducts active combat against enemy ground troops, including tanks, armored carriers, motorized infantry, infantry parachutists, etc.

Very often, AA artillery actions against enemy ground troops were not purely defensive in nature. In many cases AA guns have constituted the backbone of the antitank defense system. The AA artillery of Moscow, Leningrad, Tula, Voronezh, Stalingrad, and other cities has played an important role in combat against enemy ground troops. AA batteries close to the actual front line have successfully cooperated with our ground troops in throwing back the enemy with heavy losses to him in personnel and materiel.

Fire against ground targets has become an everyday matter for our AA gunners. The high muzzle velocity and high rate of fire of AA pieces and their extreme accuracy has made it possible for individual AA batteries in a single day to knock out as many as eight to twelve enemy tanks. No enemy tank is armored well-enough to be able to stand up against the armor-piercing round of our medium-caliber AA gun.

Success in antitank fire depends on careful adjustment of the sights, skillful fire direction, well-trained pointers, and brave and steady gun crews.

AA batteries with their fire have beaten off numerous German infantry attacks, and quite often they alone have been able to hold off greatly superior forces. Artillery fire against infantry achieves its effect not only through the deadly action of its rounds but also through the shattering effect it produces on enemy morale. Use of AA guns for firing against enemy tanks and infantry has proven to be highly effective. Following are some illustrative examples.

On 17 August 1941, the 21st September AA battalion was obliged to devote all its energy to combat with the enemy ground forces, since our infantry had been forced by enemy motorized units to withdraw. On this one day, the battalion destroyed 8 enemy tanks with its fire, as well as 3 guns, 4 mortars, and nearly 150 enemy motorized infantrymen. The enemy infantry was obliged to go over to the defense.

On 20 and 21 August 1941 batteries of the 34th and 141st Independent AA Battalions conducted fire against enemy ground troops at ranges of up to 9 kilometers. According to eyewitness reports of our front-line troops, the enemy took heavy personnel losses as a result of this fire.

The 114th Independent AA Battalion, which was defending the bridge across the River Oster, held off with its fire a group of German tanks which had broken through farther to the west and had come up to the river; the AA pieces knocked out seven enemy tanks and held the remainder off until our forces could come up and relieve it by taking up a new defensive position along the river.

On 11 December 1941 batteries of the 13th Independent AA Battalion shot up a force of enemy motorized infantry. The batteries expended 283 rounds, knocking out some 30 motor vehicles loaded with infantry and supplies.

In the Medevezhegorsk direction (Karelian front) a single AA gun of the 298th Independent AA Battalion held off an enemy tank attack for several hours, covering the withdrawal of our infantry, until finally it was knocked out by a direct hit from an enemy heavy tank.

AA artillery very often suffered losses in combatting enemy ground troops through having no armored shields on its guns or by failing to use appropriate camouflage and cover measures and to comply with the regulations governing ground-antitank action.

It has been clearly demonstrated that it is highly undesirable to use AA artillery without prime movers. When AA artillery is deprived of its mobility (especially in winter and in bad weather), it becomes decidedly more vulnerable.

It often happens that when the enemy ground troops approach close to a point being defended against enemy air attack by AA artillery the latter is entirely and totally reoriented to the task of defending against enemy ground attack. This is wrong, for then the enemy air force will be able without interference to attack the AA artillery, which is absorbed completely in its ground missions. Consequently in a situation like this, it is always necessary to decide how much of the AA artillery energy must be taken up by ground missions and how much must be left for the basic antiaircraft mission. The decision must be made in each case on the basis of the concrete situation. And the decision must be made by the commander and his staff who are well oriented on both the ground and the air situations.

It is necessary to call attention to the fact that the commanders of antiaircraft units and formations that are assigned ground tasks do not generally coordinate their actions closely enough with those of the ground troops. Generally they and their staffs are not well informed concerning the ground situation, and usually they do not organize efficient reconnaissance of the enemy nor do they establish sufficiently close liaison with their own neighboring ground elements. This shortcoming must be observed.

For effective and correct antitank defense, the following are necessary:

- Careful choice of firing positions with the greatest possible exploitation of natural cover and natural obstacles. If these are not present, then the firing positions should be well prepared with engineer work;
- Accurate preparation of firing data (registration on given lines or points, making sure that the gunners know the orientation points and registration points) for ground firing;
- Dependable signal communication among batteries and arrangements for mutual fire support;
- Preparation of alternate firing positions and earmarking of prime movers to move the pieces rapidly from one firing position to another;
- Organization of small groups to liquidate enemy submachine gunners and mortars that may threaten our gun positions; and
- Establishment of signal communications and arrangements for cooperation with the combined-arms commander for careful and continuous reconnaissance of the enemy's ground troops and of the enemy air force.

Employment of Antiaircraft Machine Guns

The basic mission of AA machine guns is to combat enemy aircraft operating at altitudes up to 1,000 meters (in the case of the 7.62-millimeter MG) or 1,800 meters (in the case of the 12.7-millimeter MG).

AA machine guns in the AA defense system of a city or major point are used for the following tasks: to strengthen the defense of particularly important installations or objectives within the city against low-flying enemy aircraft and against enemy dive-bombers; and to cover and protect antiaircraft artillery searchlights, barrage balloons, and other antiaircraft installations either in position or in bivouac.

The combat development of MGs should enable them to conduct fire over the objectives they are protecting from camouflaged or covered positions.

Sufficient density of fire against a single enemy air target can be achieved by a single quadruple 7.62-millimeter MG mount or by two 12.7-millimeter MGs.

The direction of machine gun fire, when machine guns are an element of the defense of a city or important place, is centralized as a rule. But fire is opened at the initiative of the commander of the machine gun squad or platoon.

On the Leningrad Front there was a case of one enemy aircraft shot down in which were found hits by 2,281 machine gun rounds.

Coordination Between Antiaircraft Elements

The forms and methods of coordination in the defense of a major center or city include the following:
- Coordination of zones of responsibility, delineated by area altitude, and direction;
- Coordination of all active defense resources in each zone; and
- Interlocking the various types of coordination.

Whatever form of coordination is used, it should be designed to ensure the maximum effectiveness of all forms of defense resources (artillery and fighter aviation), and it should also be designed to reinforce the effect of each form of antiaircraft weapon. It should also be aimed at bringing the battle to the enemy air force on the approaches to the city as much as possible, rather than allowing him to penetrate the air space over it.

The experience we have gained in combat confirms generally that the forms and methods of coordination of antiaircraft defense that had been worked out in peacetime are generally sound. But from our combat experience, we have been able to develop these methods further and supplement them in some respects.

Above all, experience has shown that the most favorable setup is one that includes all calibers of artillery and with the tasks assigned to each weapon being those that are best fitted to its tactical-technical characteristics.

The organizational framework for successful defense coordination is the body of planning and operational documents that are worked out beforehand and on the basis of which the battle is conducted.

Basically the plan of coordination of combat is drawn up to provide several variants of an action, showing for each variant what the missions of the various elements will be and the order in which each of these missions will be fulfilled as a part of the overall action. The variants should be simple and readily understandable. But in any case, the rapidly shifting situation will make it essential for the commandant and his staff to exercise personal direction over the complex situation as it develops and make necessary changes in the procedure set forth in the coordination tables.

The success of a defensive action depends on the precision and clarity with which the command directs the course of the combat action. Rapidly changing situations in the air and the speed with which the battle itself takes place and progresses both make it essential for all echelons to exercise the greatest economy in time and in effort to react quickly and flexibly. For this reason it is essential for the senior ground command and the senior fighter air defense commander to be located at the same command post.

The employment of fighter aviation on the outer approaches to the defended city or place, and the use of fighters in the zone accessible to antiaircraft artillery, with the fighters in the latter case being able to choose their own targets of opportunity as the situation presents them, have both been proven during this first year of war to be correct and useful procedures.

The organization of combat involving fighter aircraft and antiaircraft artillery in action in the same zone is an extremely complex matter. The basic principle governing this situation is that the fighters have priority at enemy targets while they are in the zone. The artillery breaks off fire until the fighters have broken contact with the enemy, after which the artillery resumes its fire on the enemy aircraft. When there are several targets in a given zone, the fighters choose theirs first. The artillery fires on those not engaged by the fighters. In such joint actions, coordination depends on the most highly developed teamwork between the fighter aircraft in the air and the battery commanders on the ground. In an action against a single target, the artillery takes the target under fire until the fighters can engage it; then the artillery breaks off fire immediately. At night, if fighters approach an enemy aircraft that is caught in the beam of our searchlights, the fighters fire on the target with tracer rounds as a signal that they are engaging the target. At this signal, the artillery stops firing.

It must be pointed out that patrolling in nighttime by our fighters of a zone within the range and area of responsibility of artillery—even when the fighters patrol at great heights—is an interference with the work of our ground sound-detectors; it confuses them and diminishes their effectiveness, and it can sometimes lead to faulty identifications with our artillery opening fire against our own patrolling fighters.

When the front line on the ground moved very close to Leningrad, it was necessary to modify air-ground coordination procedures.

Our searchlights could not get sufficient warning to seek out specific targets. What it amounted to was that the artillery and the fighters as a general rule had to operate in the same zone. So special coordination procedures were worked out to fit daytime, nighttime, and bad-weather conditions. At night, under any conditions, the fields of action of artillery and of fighters were prescribed, with the artillery not firing over a certain altitude nor the fighters operating below this altitude. Coordination in general was again based on the principle that fighters have priority in the choice of targets.

In the beginning, there were quite a few cases of our artillery firing at our own fighters. But as time went on, and our ground personnel became accustomed without fail to distinguish the sound of friendly and enemy aircraft motors, these incidents stopped. The most essential thing in fighter-artillery coordination, as the experience of the defense of Leningrad clearly showed, is that the pilots and gunners be thoroughly grounded in the principles and procedures of coordination.

Coordination of fighters and artillery in a single zone for night actions has taken place very little in the troops of the PVO (antiaircraft forces), and this is a matter that will have to be worked out in the future.

The enemy air force often makes use of clouds when it attacks a target. This brings up the matter of fighter artillery coordination under such conditions. It is possible for one or both to go into action against the enemy when he is in the clouds; but when both fighters and artillery are dealing with the enemy under these conditions, there must be the strictest delineation of their zones of responsibility, measured in terms of altitude.

When fighters go into action in the zones of searchlights, they must exercise the greatest discipline in their flight so as not to interfere with the effective work of the searchlights. If they approach from the enemy side, the noise of their motors will make it difficult for the searchlight crews to detect the sound of the enemy's motors, with the result that the searchlights may fail to pick up the enemy in time and may not be able to track him. Our pilots must know the searchlights and must respect them.

Our fighters, when they are waiting to meet the enemy aircraft in a zone covered by searchlights, should themselves fly or circle about in the middle of the zone. In this way, they will be able to engage the enemy near the outer edge of the zone and hope to be able to prevent him from quickly turning back and avoiding the searchlights. If the enemy is obliged, or by choice continues, to fly through the searchlight zone, he runs a good chance of being caught in a searchlight beam, and our fighters will have the opportunity to make several passes at him before he can get free of the searchlights.

One shortcoming that has been noticed in the joint employment of artillery barrage balloons is that the balloons have taken quite heavy losses as a result of barrage fire. Such losses can be greatly reduced if the artillery strictly observes the rule not to fire at altitudes lower than 1,000 meters above the level of the barrage balloons; such an interval in altitudes leaves the balloons in relative safety.

Guiding Our Fighter Aircraft to Contact with Enemy Aviation

The basic means for guiding pilots to contact with the enemy air force have been white cloth signal markers (for daytime use) and auto headlights and other light signals (for night use) employed by target direction centers.

But air combat experience from the very first days of the war made it clear that such methods were not adequate for guiding our fighters quickly enough to contact with the enemy. They took too long, considering the speed of present-day aircraft, and they tended to distract the pilot's attention. He had to spend too much time and energy watching for ground signals and sometimes found himself at a disadvantage in air combat as a result. Nor did the system of wire communication between the air and ground target direction centers work much better.

It became necessary to work out a system that would make it possible quickly and surely to guide our fighters to contact with the enemy.

After analyzing the problem and considering what technical resources were available, it seemed possible to solve the matter by using special spotting devices and radio instruments, together with the already existing target direction centers.

Further experience showed that the basic and best means was to use radio to convey information acquired by means of radar. All the other means, such as target direction centers using white cloth markers, light signals, artillery bursts, etc., must be considered secondary means.

Under night conditions, radio and radar are particularly useful not only in guiding our fighters onto the enemy but also in aiding them back to their airfields and helping them to land.

The target direction centers, which are operationally subordinate to the senior commander, are useful auxiliary resources for guiding our fighters to contact with the enemy. In daytime, these centers may use cloth markers or arrows in addition to their radio, and at nightime they use the most varied types of light signals.

Experience has shown that motor-vehicle headlights are the simplest and most effective form of light signal. Codes can be worked out by which it is possible to give our pilots quite precise and full data quickly. This is an inexpensive and quickly established system.

To solve the problem of guiding our fighters to contact with the enemy, it is necessary to

- Define the sector of action of each air unit constituting a part of a given air defense system;
- Allot sufficient radar apparatus, radio equipment, and target direction centers to each sector;
- Define the fighters' sequence of actions in their own combat zones, in the zones of fire of the artillery, and at night in the zones covered by searchlight batteries;
- Set up and equip target direction centers covering the outer boundaries of each of the zones of action of the fighter elements;
- Provide the target direction system with adequate signal equipment;
- Reinforce ground control points and radar stations with suitable local personnel;
- Specifically appoint responsible persons who will have the duty to see that the data concerning enemy flights are transmitted in a timely manner to our fighters and define precisely their responsibility;
- Set up a voice code to be used between ground posts and aircraft including call signs;
- Ensure that all ground controls involved in directing our fighters have the means with which to receive timely and accurate data; and
- Constantly train all elements of the direction system and ensure that there will be full synchronization in the work of all these elements.

Only by doing all these things can the PVO and air commanders be sure that they can successfully bring their planes in contact with the enemy in good time.

Naturally, if no radar equipment is available, then the direction system must make wide use of radio and of ground direction centers.

The following incident serves as an example of effective use of radio to direct one's fighters onto the enemy who is trying to carry out an air raid or to conduct air reconnaissance for one. On 11 July 1942, two pilots of the 731st Fighter Flying Kittyhawks [U.S.-made P-40 fighters] were directed by radio into an enemy Ju-88 that was on a reconnaissance mission. The fliers intercepted the enemy aircraft at an altitude of 7,000 meters, but they were not able to shoot him down as he quickly dived and was able to shake them. But the control point of the 731st Fighter Regiment still was able to track him through radio reports, and it sent another pair of fighters after him. These two Kittyhawks, getting the bearings of the enemy by radio, intercepted him at an altitude of 4,000 meters. The Ju-88 dived again, this time to hedgehopping height, but the pair of Kittyhawks kept him in sight and dived to his altitude, destroying him shortly.

VNOS (Air Observation, Warning, and Liaison Service)

The VNOS system as it was organized before the war, with a breakdown into a number of VNOS area subdivisions with those covering areas over which fighter aviation would be operating being more densely covered, has in general worked out very well. The organization of VNOS points (company, battalion, and regimental posts) and the procedure followed in the posts have changed but little during this first year of war. There have been a few improvements, designed to streamline and smooth out their work.

The location of VNOS posts in populated places, which was common early in the war, was disadvantageous, for their all-round field of vision was usually limited. Now they are regularly located out in the open and away from roads and railroads. Their field of vision is thereby much improved, and furthermore, they are free to detect enemy aircraft by sound-detection methods without the interference that is normal from city or railroad noises at night.

In the organization of VNOS, the principal weakness is in tying in one VNOS area with the next and particularly in coordinating the VNOS service of PVO Strany with PVO Voisk (Strategic Antiaircraft Defense and Practical Antiaircraft Defense). In this latter case, it often happens that there are holes between the one and the other through which the enemy air force can penetrate without readily being detected.

Experience has shown that it is advantageous to locate company battalion and regimental VNOS posts at or very near to the command posts of the antiaircraft artillery commander responsible for the defense of the area. In this way, the latter can obtain the most timely information quickest concerning the air situation. If the company, battalion, and regimental VNOS posts are located at some distance from the command posts, then there is an inevitable time lag in reporting to the latter, with the results that the whole defense process is slowed down and often fails to function properly.

The practice of having several air reconnaissance centers in a single place is not good practice. Time is lost in forwarding information concerning the air situation, channels are overcomplicated, the desirable degree of centralization does not exist. It is preferable to have a single responsible VNOS center in each defended place, with all reports flowing through it to the antiaircraft defense commander.

Reporting on the air situation from areas where AA artillery and searchlights are located is the responsibility of these units. They conduct their own VNOS activity. The antiaircraft commanders must always see to it that the reports sent in by these elements are quickly put into the right channels so that all interested parties receive them as soon as possible.

Detection of Enemy Aircraft

The practical experience of the first year of the war shows that the principal means by which VNOS posts detach enemy aircraft is through identifying the sound of their motors. After that comes visual identification. From 20 May through 4 June 1942 at the main VNOS post of a divisional PVO area, some 4,162 reports of identification of enemy aircraft flights were made. Of these 2,478—or about 60 percent—were based on auditory detection, and 1,684—or about 40 percent—were made on the basis of visual identification. In the far north, where the atmosphere is exceptionally clear in good weather, most enemy aircraft (particularly large groups of them) were first identified by sight at a distance of 15 to 20 kilometers and then confirmed by the sound of their motors. [The figures in the chart listed in the report do not correspond to these figures—Ed.]

Experience in VNOS post activity provides the basis for the following general conclusions concerning auditory detection:

- If the enemy is flying at an altitude of from 500 to 5,000 meters, he will be detected in quiet, windless weather at a distance of 8 to 10 kilometers. If the wind is blowing from the enemy direction, he will be detected at a distance of 8 to 15 kilometers; and if the wind is blowing in his direction then he will be detected at a distance of 4 to 8 kilometers;
- If the enemy is flying lower than 500 or higher than 5,000 meters, then the distance at which he will be detected is markedly shorter.

Aircraft flying at from 500 to 5,000 meters' altitude can be picked up by visual observation in cloudless or nearly cloudless weather at a distance of 5 to 6 kilometers. If the planes are flying higher or lower, the distance is diminished to between 2 and 3 kilometers.

In the following table is shown the method by which aircraft were recognized

Antiaircraft Defense of a Major Center

No. of aircraft reported by the principal VNOS posts in the PVO area from 25 May through 4 June 1942	Auditory identifications		Visual indentifications		Not identified through reports	
	No.	Percent	No.	Percent	No.	Percent
4,162	1,721	41.4	2,126	51	315	7.6

Note: Of those listed as not identified, sixty were friendly aircraft incorrectly identified as enemy aircraft. This amounts to 1.4 percent of the overall total.

by VNOS posts in one of the PVO areas just behind the front.

Aircraft that appeared in the area of responsibility of VNOS posts that were flying at great altitudes (over 5,000 meters), in clouds or behind them, or in foggy weather or at night were for the most part identified by the sound of their motors. Visual identifications were dependable only at low or medium heights and under favorable conditions of visibility at distances of not over 5 to 6 kilometers.

Many aircraft—both ours and the enemy's—that have to be identified by some single feature proved difficult to identify with certainty at altitudes of over 3,000 meters or distances of over $3\frac{1}{2}$ kilometers.

And if one takes into account that the enemy for the most part flies either at night or at great heights during the day or in weather that makes identification hard, then he must recognize that visual identification has serious shortcomings as a regular measure to depend on. This makes auditory identification all the more important and emphasizes the necessity of carefully and continually training VNOS post personnel in this skill.

It is necessary also to bend all efforts to correcting the mistakes that are still quite common, where VNOS posts let enemy aircraft slip through undetected, detect them too late, estimate the air course incorrectly, or fail to give timely warning of the aircraft they have identified.

With this in mind, it is essential to pay particular attention to the following shortcomings.

Some posts are incorrectly deployed, with far too great intervals between them, so that there are sizable gaps not under observation in the area of responsibility of the VNOS element to which these posts belong. One still finds a fair number of VNOS posts set up in town or villages, along roads or railroads, or near tall trees. This makes it more likely that enemy aircraft will be able to get through their observation undetected, and it interferes with efficient detection, both visual and auditory.

In many VNOS posts, the listening posts are incorrectly laid out, or in fact, none worthy of the name are built, with the listeners simply standing out in the wind. Course-of-flight indicators are frequently incorrectly oriented. These failings markedly reduce the accuracy and effectiveness of auditory identification.

Often the telephone machines at the VNOS posts by which they convey their reports to the company or battalion command posts are located not directly at the post but in a building nearby. This is bad, for it obliges the

VNOS observers to leave their post and waste time getting to the phone to make their reports.

VNOS Signal Net

This net is based for the most part on the facilities of the Peoples Commissariat of Communications. Sometimes it uses the existing signal facilities of other government departments. These together generally proved equal to the task, and it was necessary only rarely to use the telegraph facilities that are organic to the VNOS system.

Time lag in sending in VNOS reports of aircraft sightings was generally not because of any technical difficulties with equipment, but because of poorly organized procedure or slovenly work at the VNOS posts themselves or at the telephone switchboards of the Peoples Commissariat of Communications.

The signal net worked efficiently when the personnel of the Peoples Commissariat of Communications and of other departments involved were given explicit and clear instructions to follow and then their work was systematically checked by VNOS command personnel.

In large telephone centrals through which many messages were sent by VNOS, it was found desirable to station permanently a responsible VNOS officer who had the task of ensuring that the VNOS messages were given the highest priority and were put through in the shortest possible time. This procedure paid off handsomely.

Reporting on the Air Situation

If local PVO elements and the troops themselves can convey timely warning of what appears to be an impending enemy air raid, the PVO system and other military and economic elements can make ready to repel the attack and also can take appropriate passive air defense measures. The priority in which agencies are warned is fighter aircraft, antiaircraft artillery, industrial air targets, and the population and the troops. In order to gain time, warnings should be sent out simultaneously—or as nearly so as possible—over all lines. Appropriate measures should be taken to organize both equipment and personnel to this task.

In air warning procedure, experience has shown that the following must be done:
- When warning messages are sent by radio, the recipient must acknowledge the message by responding to the sender. In this way, false air warnings transmitted by enemy radio stations can be shown up;
- Have radio facilities alerted to replace wire facilities in case of failure of the latter;
- With unmistakable clarity and as a matter of first priority, warn fighter air defense CPs and airfields, and also Red Army fighter reserve units that may be in the general area;

Antiaircraft Defense of a Major Center 153

- Warn local NKVD staffs and the authorities of civil government in the threatened area; and
- Special attention must be paid to warning neighboring units.

In warning the local NKVD authorities, the headquarters of local factories, and the civil population (including the population in rural areas), it is essential to make the widest possible use of non-military as well as military communication facilities.

Counteracting False Reporting

In the beginning of the war, the enemy's spies in this country began to transmit a great number of false air raid warnings on the wavelengths reserved for such reporting. These enemy agents were sometimes successful in misleading our PVO commanders, particularly because of our poor signal discipline and because we did not make a practice of checking back on our messages to the sender or supposed sender.

The following measures are used in counteracting false air warning reports:
- Strictest discipline in telephone conversation;
- Checking any doubtful messages by calling back the sender and verifying the message;
- Training, practice, and synchronization of the work of telephone personnel, VNOS posts, and civilian telephone offices to the point where all are completely familiar with each other's procedures and even know each other by first and last name and can identify each others' voices;
- Instructing civilian switchboard personnel at telephone centrals not to let anyone except VNOS people use "air raid priority"; and
- Not permitting any civilian phone subscriber whose phone can be reached by unauthorized persons to use the "air raid priority" call.

The Interval between VNOS of PVO Strany and VNOS of PVO Voisk

Operations of VNOS of PVO Voisk as a rule cover an area that runs directly along the front. The dispositions of PVO Strany VNOS posts and army or army-group PVO VNOS posts should be coordinated with the senior artillery officer of the army or army group charged with PVO matters. In some cases where this was not done in the army or army-group rear areas, it turned out that PVO Voisk and PVO Strany posts were set up at the same locations. This reduced the effectiveness of coverage, and it interfered with the work of both VNOS systems by putting them in competition for the use of the same signal facilities.

Experience has shown that PVO Strany VNOS posts can work effectively with PVO Voisk VNOS posts when a PVO Voisk liaison officer is regularly stationed at the principal VNOS posts of PVO Strany in the front areas, and when there is firm line communication between the two systems.

VNOS is valuable not only as a system for air warning but also as a means of ground reconnaissance concerning the enemy. Thus, during the defense of Moscow, the army-group command and the Supreme Command both received frequent and useful reports concerning the enemy ground troops from VNOS elements in the Tula, Kashin, Klin, and other areas. This was equally true of VNOS of PVO Voisk and PVO Strany.

The summarized experience and conclusions set forth above concerning the air defense of a large place or city should be digested not only by PVO Strany Commanders but also by artillery commanders of PVO Voisk, by commanders of fighter aviation units, by the staffs of combined-arms formations, and by the staffs of the armed services.

This quick review of the air defense of a large place or city, in which all the resources and general procedures of contemporary air defense are mentioned, could be followed by a more thorough study, in which these matters could be probed right to the core, so that the results might be translated into firm overall recommendations and could be studied by all the antiaircraft personnel of our armed forces.

The Red Army made extensive use of camouflage during the Great Patriotic War. Particularly successful was its use of camouflage in sniping action as attested by the number of snipers who were awarded the title of Hero of the Soviet Union. Less is known about the Red Army's use of chemical agents such as smokescreens in both offensive and defensive operations. This chapter is perhaps the most detailed Soviet coverage of this topic under wartime conditions. Discussed in detail are tactics, the weapons used, as well as specific case studies—Ed.

12

Combat Employment by Ground Troops of Smoke for Cover and Camouflage

INERT smoke markedly diminishes the effectiveness of enemy fire and makes it much easier for our infantry and tanks to pass through the zone of enemy artillery and infantry weapons fire with minimum losses. Smoke not only reduces our losses, but it also enables us in the attack to conceal from the enemy the direction of the main effort, to disorient the enemy, and to prevent him from concentrating his firepower at the points where it would be most effective.

The combat employment of smoke by the field forces of the Red Army in most cases has created favorable conditions for the actions of our units and has facilitated their success with minimum losses.

Tactical-Technical Characteristics of Smoke and Basic Principles Governing Its Employment

Experience in the combat employment of smoke shows that the most efficient and easy method of generating smoke is the DM-11 neutral smoke generating block. This smoke generator is extremely elementary, and there are no particular difficulties in its combat use by troops not specially trained in smoke techniques.

Smoke blocks, because of their simple construction and uncomplicated characteristics, are readily used by combat troops of the various arms, and they have been used effectively by them in various combat situations.

The tactical-technical characteristics of the smoke block DM-11 are weight: 2.2 kilograms; time needed to ignite the block: 30 to 60 seconds; duration of smoke-generating time: 5 to 7 minutes; length of effective smoke screen generated by one block under normal weather conditions: 150 to 200 meters.

Smoke hand grenades are used mainly by small infantry groups and by individual tanks to conceal their activities from the enemy and interfere with aimed enemy fire.

Smoke hand grenades are issued to individual infantrymen and to tank commanders and commanders of armored cars. They are used by them at their direction as the situation warrants.

The tactical-technical characteristics of the RDG-1 smoke grenade are: overall weight: 510 to 520 grams; weight of the smoke-generating element: 450 grams; time before which smoke is generated most intensively: 10 to 50 seconds; time during which smoke is generated: 1.2 to 1.5 minutes. If weather conditions are favorable, the grenade will generate a smoke screen through which one cannot see some 15 to 20 meters in length.

The laying of smoke screens by shells and other special devices will be discussed below, when the tactical-technical considerations involved in such procedures are set forth.

Smoke screens at the front (as against those laid in the rear to conceal an air target, etc.) are classified by their appearance into frontal, flanking, and diagonal. They are classified according to their purpose as blinding, screening, and camouflage. Most smoke screens are generated with equipment fixed in place.

Smoke is used by decision of the combined-arms commander if it is used on any scale of importance. Infantry unit commanders are responsible for arranging for and seeing to the generation of smoke at the desired place.

Chemical service personnel are responsible for the technical direction necessary in the generation of a smoke screen. This includes:
- Issuing warning orders for smoke generation;
- Identifying for the troops the line at which the smoke screen will be generated, choosing the unloading point for smoke-generating apparatus and supervising the distribution of the apparatus along the line at which the smoke screen will be generated;
- Determining how much equipment will be needed to achieve the desired effect;
- Coordinating the organization of the smoke screen with tank, artillery, and infantry commanders; and

Smoke for Cover and Camouflage 157

* Supervising the actual generation of the smoke screen.

Coordination with armor, artillery, aviation, and with neighboring units in the laying of a smoke screen is accomplished in the following manner: A detailed plan is prepared, indicating precisely when the artillery preparation for the attack is to begin and end, when the tanks and infantry move out, when the smoke begins to be generated, and when smoke generation stops. As a rule, smoke generation begins directly after the end of the artillery preparation.

Generally, smoke generation (in the case of a sizable smoke screen) is accomplished by the chemical defense units of regiments and divisions. In some cases, flame-thrower teams were used, and in others, special mixed smoke-generating teams were formed and placed under command of the regimental or divisional chemical officer.

Smoke generation is directed and controlled from the command posts of the regimental, battalion, or company commander, who uses prearranged signals with the personnel actually operating the smoke-generating equipment. It has been found unnecessary to organize special headquarters for the chief chemical officer or for the officer directing the smoke-generating.

The line along which smoke-generating apparatus is placed depends on the terrain. Several lines are often used. The intervals between them depend on the mission to be accomplished, the weather, and the terrain. The amount of smoke-generating apparatus to be used also depends on the concrete situation and is determined mainly by the density and dimensions of the smoke screen desired.

The tactical employment of smoke grenades for the most part is a matter of screening combat actions, or some phase of the combat actions of small infantry groups or even individual soldiers. Here again the particular situation determines how many smoke grenades will be needed.

The employment of smoke at the front depends on the terrain, the weather, and the mission.

The direction and intensity of the wind, ascending air currents, and precipitation all have a decided influence on the use of smoke. The intensely hot layer of lower atmosphere in summer days facilitates the rapid dissemination of smoke upward and laterally. Light rain or snow have little effect on a smoke screen, whereas strong rain or snow quickly dissipate it. Fog tends to make a smoke screen even denser.

The best wind speed for making a smoke screen is 2 to 4 meters per second. If the wind is blowing faster than 7 meters per second, it will be difficult to generate a solid smoke screen without gaps and ragged spots. Morning appears generally to be the best time of day for laying a smoke screen.

There have been occasions when a well-prepared smoke screen failed to materialize on account of bad weather conditions, as in the case of the 342d Rifle Division of the Sixty-first Army.

Smoke-generating apparatus is brought up from army dumps to division and regiment by trucks. From regiment to platoon unloading points, transportation is generally by pack or cart unless trucks are available.

The smoke blocks or smoke pots are brought up to the smoke-generating line in bags by men moving on foot. One bearer can carry eight or ten smoke pots at a time. If the unloading point is, on the average, 2 kilometers from the line, one must figure 1 to $1\frac{1}{2}$ hours. If a man is to carry 40 smoke pots, it will take him, on the average, six or seven hours.

To be sure that the smoke screen will accomplish its mission, generally a reserve of smoke pots is provided for. This reserve is brought up to the line either at night or under cover of the smoke screen itself when it begins.

Usually there is one unloading point for each regiment or battalion in the line. On the average, on a division front on which smoke is to be generated, there will be three or four platoon unloading points, each with 20 or 25 men.

In the early days of the war, smoke was used very little and in a haphazard manner. Smoke was mainly used then to cover the withdrawal of small units from platoon to battalion size.

Since then, the scale and means of employment of smoke have become decidedly larger and more varied. Recently smoke has been most used on the western and Kalinin fronts. On the fronts in the south, smoke is still used relatively little.

Employment of Smoke in Offensive Operation

The widest use of smoke has been in offensive actions of the Red Army. Several useful and typical examples of such employment are set forth below.

On one occasion, the forward elements of the 104th Rifle Division during an offensive came into a mine field. They had to halt and were taken under heavy automatic weapons fire from the entrenched enemy. The units extricated themselves from this unfavorable situation under cover of a smoke screen, thanks to which their losses were very light.

During the period 12 through 29 September 1941 in the Murmansk direction, smoke screens were used to cover the offensive of our forces against an enemy fortified area. The enemy was unable to see our troops or to get an idea of how our offensive was developing because he was blinded by the smoke, so he was obliged to withdraw to his next defense line.

On 6 October 1941, the 466th Rifle Regiment went over to the attack at 0430. The attack was screened by smoke along a 500-meter sector. Some 500 smoke pots, echeloned in depth, were used to generate this smoke screen. The wind was blowing at 3 to 4 meters a second. For the first 30 minutes of the smoke screen, the Germans did not fire at all from their small arms and machine guns. The attacking units moved slowly forward behind the smoke screen and sustained no losses. Thirty minutes after the beginning of the smoke screen, the Germans opened strong artillery mortar fire and small arms automatic fire against the line from which the smoke was generated. Later that same day, on the same sector, another smoke screen was generated to cover the attack of one of our battalions. Some 125 smoke pots were used on a 300-meter front. As in the earlier instance, the Germans appeared confused; they stopped firing and did not resume for 20 minutes, by which time our infantry had crossed the danger zone without losses.

Since they had not had enough experience in the use of smoke, our infantry in this case did not take full advantage of the cover given them; they advanced extremely slowly and carefully.

On the Kalinin front on 10 October 1942 near Rzhev on the sector of the 243d Rifle Division, a smoke screen was generated with smoke pots for the purpose of concealing from the enemy the combat deployment of the division's right flank, so that he could not register his artillery on it or keep it under observation. The smoke screen was generated from 55-degree smoke pots laid out along two lines on a front of 400 meters. The smoke screen lasted over five hours (not all the smoke posts were used initially, so that the screen really was generated in two waves). The wind was blowing at 1 to 3 meters a second. Thirty-five chemical personnel did the whole job.

The mission of blinding the enemy and concealing from him the combat deployment of our units was successfully accomplished. As a result of the screen that hid their activities, our troops suffered no losses.

On 5 July 1942, on the sector of the Sixty-first Army, the enemy opened heavy artillery and mortar fire against the combat formations of our attacking troops. Our troops were pinned down. In the attack sector of the 122d Rifle Division, a smoke screen was laid down on a front of 2 kilometers with a 2 to 3 kilometer per second wind from the northwest. As soon as the smoke screen was laid down, the enemy ceased his fire; our troops resumed the attack, cut through the enemy wire, came upon the enemy fieldworks, and forced the enemy to abandon them.

At the moment when our chemical troops were beginning to ignite the smoke pots, the enemy's combat security outposts elements attacked our chemical troops to prevent them from laying the smoke screen. But our chemical troops repulsed the enemy with grenades and automatic weapons fire; the smoke screen was not interfered with, and our smoke men lost only four casualties.

Toward the end of August 1942 during the offensive battles on the Bryansk Front, a smoke screen was laid simultaneously on two nearby sectors. At the beginning of the smoke screen, the direction of the wind changed sharply, to our disadvantage. Then the wind changed again, this time blowing steadily from the northeast. Now the wind was again favorable for us.

Within a minute after the beginning of the smoke screen, the enemy opened a strong automatic small arms fire against the lines from which the smoke was being generated. The smoke men at the moment were moving back to the second line of smoke pots and were preparing to light them for the second smoke wave. Both lines had been prepared beforehand to provide cover for the chemical smoke men while they were lighting the smoke pots, and the smoke pots had been set down ahead of time, too. The actual work of lighting the smoke pots was masked on both lines by hand smoke grenades. In all, some 300 smoke pots were used in this instance.

On 5 October 1941, the chemical defense company of the 108th Rifle Division laid a smoke screen with smoke pots to cover the move of KV heavy tanks. The road had been well registered by German artillery in the vicinity of the town of Pushkin, so that the artillery could deliver accurate flanking fire to it. Twenty chemical soldiers, using 400 smoke pots, carried out the mission. The wind was blowing diagonally in relation to the road, and at a rate of 3 or 4 meters per second. The smoke screen took ten minutes to generate. The smoke pots themselves were set up in a series of lines, with each line having five smoke pots. The smoke from these lines overlapped as the wind blew it diagonally and made a solid screen, behind which the tanks moved along the road without losses. The enemy opened fire on the area where the smoke was generated after 20 minutes. The smoke men, meanwhile, covering themselves by smoke from grenades, withdrew after completing their mission without losses.

On 22 August 1942, substantial forces of infantry of the 7th Guard Rifle Corps were able to advance in quite dense formation of their assault line across open terrain under cover of smoke with no losses. The troops as they reached the assault line safely, broke into cheers of "Hurrah for the chemical troops!"

Wide use was made of smoke to mask the actions of small units and detachments.

On the Western Front, infantry of the 115th Rifle Brigade made a smoke screen with DM-11 smoke pots so that a small group of men of one of the rifle companies could advance safely to the enemy wire and cut lanes through it. As a result, the company was able to advance rapidly through the wire without losses.

On the Karelian Front, the use of smoke to cover the actions of reconnaissance groups was especially successful. Near the town of Povenents on 20 August 1942, a smoke screen was laid down on the southeast edge of the town in order to attract the attention and the fire of the Finns away from the edge of the town where a group of our reconnaissance men was in action. The smoke screen covered a front of 600 meters, and lasted for one hour and twenty minutes. One-hundred-and-fifty smoke pots were used.

The ruse worked; the Finns, expecting an attack or a parachute drop, concentrated two companies along the edge of town and fired over three-hundred artillery rounds and two-hundred mortar rounds at the line of the smoke screen. Meanwhile, the reconnaissance group seized two blocks in the edge of the town, took a number of prisoners and, having accomplished their mission, withdrew without losses.

In another area on 1 August 1942, two smoke screens were laid down that covered the actions of a reconnaissance group and enabled it to carry out its mission with insignificant losses.

On 26 August 1942 near Somovo (Bryansk Front), a smoke screen was laid down that enabled a reconnaissance patrol to withdraw with virtually no losses after it had accomplished its mission. Only one chemical soldier was wounded.

In the actions of small units and detachments, there are numerous such instances of the use of smoke for cover. Most of them turned out successfully, and the expenditure of smoke-generating equipment was very small. The smoke screens were easy to lay and required few personnel.

The use of smoke for this purpose must be popularized among the troops, and smoke must be used whenever it is advantageous.

Smoke was also used to blind enemy strong points. Thus, on the sector of the 155th Rifle Division on 6 August 1942 for the purpose of covering the actions of our assault groups that were attacking enemy earth-and-timber strong points near Toropino, a smoke screen was laid down along a 200-meter front. Ten groups of smoke pots were laid out, with 20-meter intervals between them. Smoke was generated for fifteen minutes. Two-hundred ND smoke pots were used in two waves.

One chemical platoon was used to make the smoke screen; it suffered no losses while doing its work. The results of the smoke screen were good: The enemy firing points were totally blinded, and our troops attacked with confidence and took the two strong points.

The use of smoke screens in connection with the attack of strong points and centers of resistance is of the greatest importance. It weakens the enemy to a marked degree as far as the effectiveness of his fire is concerned, and it makes it possible for our units to get close in to the enemy firing positions without serious losses. This latter factor is especially important for the morale of the assault troops.

Smoke was often useful for protecting damaged tanks on the battlefield and for covering the maintenance men who towed them off the field. Smoke can also be used to simulate fires in our tanks during the enemy artillery preparation and during enemy air attacks. Thus, for example, on 14 August 1942 while the enemy was attacking a height in the Sixty-first Army's sector, the tank crew of the political commissar's tank of the 94th Tank Battalion threw two smoke grenades out of the tank. This gave the enemy the impression that he had hit the tank, and he ceased firing on it.

Tanks crews of the 51st Tank Brigade threw smoke pots out of several tanks, creating a smoke screen under cover of which they were able to remove three damaged machines from the field and out of the area of enemy fire.

In the 50th and 192d Tank Brigades, several damaged tanks were successfully towed out of range of enemy fire behind the cover of smoke screens.

On 1 September 1941 near Murmansk, 12 tanks were evacuated under cover of smoke without losses.

This sort of employment of smoke should be brought to the attention of all of our tankers, for it is a useful device for protecting tank crews while they are repairing their tanks or for covering recovery vehicles that are towing damaged tanks out of range of enemy aimed fire. The use of individual DM-11 smoke pots to simulate a burning tank very often deceives the enemy and causes him to cease fire against the tank.

Laying False Smoke Screens

Of the overall number of smoke screens laid down along the front, a considerable number were false ones, for experience has proved that false smoke screens can be extremely effective.

Thus, for example, in August 1941, units including a detachment of naval infantry had twice attacked a hill near the southern rapids of the Litsa River. The hill commanded a ford across the river. Both attacks failed. The third time, the attack was organized with the use of smoke pots. To deceive the enemy fire, a false smoke screen was laid with 52 smoke pots in 30 minutes. The smoke men kept in touch with the infantry by means of prearranged signals. The commander of the smoke detachment stayed at the command post of the infantry commander.

As soon as the smoke started to be generated, the enemy opened strong fire toward the smoke screen line. Then a rifle platoon attacked in a different direction, took the enemy by surprise, and seized the hill. The enemy abandoned two radios, a machine gun, various small arms, and several dead.

On 12 July 1942, units of the Thirty-third Army (Western Front) attacked near Masolovka with the help of a false smoke screen that was highly effective. The infantry assembled near Masolovka in heavy underbrush that afforded good cover. But the enemy discovered our assembly area and took it under heavy artillery and mortar fire from several battalions. Our infantry was pinned down. The divisional commander decided to use a smoke screen, preparations for which had been made earlier. This false smoke screen was laid along a 1-kilometer front; the wind from the south was moving at 2 to 3 meters a second. The smoke screen was laid in 15 to 20 minutes, 200 smoke pots being used.

The enemy, evidently believing that the smoke screen was laid in order to cover fresh Soviet forces about to be committed, shifted all his fire to the area of the smoke screen. This enabled our units that had been pinned down to start advancing; they did so and, without difficulty, seized Masolovka.

On 25 August 1942 a smoke screen was laid with the object of covering the crossing of the 1172d Rifle Regiment over the Volga near Nozhkino (Kalinin Front). All the preparatory measures for laying the smoke screen had been taken in good time. But in view of the fact that the enemy had now concentrated strong automatic small-arms fire in the crossing area, it was decided to have the regiment cross the river at Paikovo. Thus it was no longer necessary to have a smoke screen at Nozhkino.

On August 26 a new action was ordered: to use the same smoke-generated equipment and smoke troops to attract the enemy's attention away from the intended crossing area. A false smoke screen was to be laid near Solomino. In view of the weather conditions, it was decided to lay a fixed smoke screen from the right bank of the Volga and a moving screen on floating rafts.

The smoke apparatus was made ready. The enemy concentrated strong fire in the smoke screen area, while the 1172d Regiment crossed the river at Paikovo further to the north, and by 1920 hours had completed its crossing and was consolidating in the northern part of Finger Wood. Its actions were not interfered with by the enemy. The smoke screen was laid in two lines, and smoke was generated for 15 minutes. The rafts, which were constructed by the engineers, were launched at five-minute intervals. There were four of them, each with eight smoke pots. In all, 100 smoke pots were used. The smoke men did their job without casualties.

In carrying out a surprise action, the 10th Guard Rifle Regiment (Bryansk Front) used two smoke screens: one a false one and the other a screening one. The screening smoke was generated from the west slope of Height 230.8 with the object of preventing the enemy at Nizhny Turovets from delivering flanking fire against the troops who were to take Height 241.9. The false smoke screen was laid from the southwest slope of Height 242.8 with the object of deceiving the enemy as to our real intentions and to draw his fire from the troops who were to assault Height 241.9.

The front of the screening smoke was 375 meters (with 300 smoke pots) while the front of the false smoke screen was 400 meters, also with 300 smoke pots.

As soon as the false smoke screen was laid, the enemy began to open fire in its direction with infantry automatic weapons. An enemy reconnaissance plane appeared shortly, and evidently radioed to its ground troops that they were firing at a false smoke screen. The enemy then opened fire toward the screening smoke coming from Height 230.8, but he still failed to concentrate his principal fire against the troops attacking Height 241.9. Thus the smokes served a useful purpose in this case.

On 6 August 1942 near Ostrov (Volkhov Front) a reconnaissance raid was organized by a group of submachine gunners of the 378th Rifle Division. In order to deceive the enemy, a false smoke screen was laid along a 1,500-meter front with 320 DM-11 smoke pots. The enemy immediately opened strong fire against the front from which the smoke was coming and wasted nearly 2,000 rounds there. Meanwhile, the submachine gunners, taking advantage of the enemy's preoccupation, suddenly attacked enemy earth-and-timber works at Ostrov with grenades and incendiary bottles. They set fire to three strong points and seized Ostrov with almost no losses.

Conclusions

False smoke screens disorient the enemy and make it extremely difficult for him to discern our true intentions. As a rule, the enemy opens extremely heavy fire with all weapons at his disposal against the line from which smoke screens are launched; this fire is usually unaimed and wasteful. The enemy tends to pay little attention to other sectors in such cases, as a result of which the main attack can be carried out with very light losses.

It is essential in combat practice for our troops to make more use of this type of smoke screen, and in planning offensive actions, they must consider the use of false smoke screens quite as much as real ones.

Examples of Unsatisfactory Use of Smoke

At the same time that there were many examples of advantageous use of smoke, there were also cases in which smoke was poorly used. Thus, for example, on 12 October 1941 at 1250 hours on the sector of the 68th Rifle Division (Leningrad Front), a 1,000-meter smoke screen was generated in ten minutes with ND smoke pots in a light wind. Units of the division advanced behind the smoke screen and often in the smoke. They suffered no losses. But when the smoke pots were burned out, the wind carried the smoke screen off in short time, and the infantry was then in plain view of the enemy who obliged it to withdraw under heavy fire.

At the same time, on a neighboring sector, a 1,500-meter smoke screen was laid down in ten minutes from 772 smoke pots. The enemy directed very heavy fire in the direction of the smoke screen. The smoke itself moved so rapidly under a strong wind that the advancing infantry had the advantage of its cover only for a short distance, after which it was pinned down by enemy fire.

Near Rzhev on 8 August 1942 in the attack of the 906th Rifle Regiment of the 243d Rifle Division on Kopytykh, a smoke screen was made in ten minutes with DM-11 pots. The infantry advanced slowly, and was still 300 meters from the enemy front line when the smoke cleared. Strong enemy artillery, mortar, and small arms fire pinned the infantry to the ground. Our aviation laid an additional smoke screen in an effort to provide cover for our infantry, but this screen was made at an altitude of 150 to 200 meters, and because of an updraft, the smoke did not settle to the ground.

On 1 August 1942, to cover the attack of the 324th and 215th Regiments together with tanks against Pushkari and Zankove (Kalinin front), a smoke screen was laid from two directions, in all covering a front of some 700 meters. The weather was favorable; 184 smoke pots were used, and the smoke was generated in 15 minutes.

After the artillery preparation, the smoke was generated. It covered both villages, and the enemy was blinded. All available enemy fire was shifted to the direction of the smoke screens. But for some unknown reason, the tanks failed to take part in the attack, and the infantry began its attack only after eight to ten minutes of the smoke screen had been wasted. The enemy fire became more intense, and our infantry, after a slow advance, was forced to halt some

50 to 80 meters short of Pushkari. Thus, our infantry in this case failed to make full use of the smoke. The attack continued thereafter without further use of smoke.

These examples are typical in showing that brief smoke screens on broad fronts designed to cover the attacks of large units are usually ineffectual. In addition, they betray ignorance in the use of smoke, for they were undertaken without regard for the concrete tactical situation, they failed to take into account the unfavorable weather conditions, and there was insufficient coordination among the various arms.

The Use of Smoke with ARS Equipment

The use of smoke generated with ARS (Artillery Smoke Shell) on a liberal scale has taken place only on the Leningrad and Western fronts. The massive use of real and false smoke screens generated with ARS has proven of substantial value and has had a decided effect in several cases in assuming the success of operations.

Below are recounted some typical examples of the use of ARS alone and in combination with smoke pots for the covering of river forcings and the covering of bridging.

Forging of the Neva River in the Nevskaya Dubravka Area

Up to the time of the crossing operation, the situation had developed as follows.

The Germans had strongly fortified the left bank of the Neva from Shlisselburg to Poroga, with a deep defense including timber-and-earth strong points, permanent-type fortifications, and numerous systems of antitank and antipersonnel obstacles, mine fields, etc. In front of their main line of defense the Germans had a deep and fast-moving river, all of the approaches to which—as well as the river itself—they were able to take under heavy fire. The organization of their fire, in combination with the other elements of their defense, made the Germans' position exceptionally favorable. The fire from the areas of Arbuzovo and First Village, which flanked the crossing points and their approaches, was especially murderous.

The only sector of the left bank of the river that was occupied by our troops was the Moskovskaya Dubravka area. Here, nearly two regiments of the 115th Rifle Division were on the defense. Their bridgehead was under constant frontal and flanking fire. They received their rations, ammunition, and supplies by boat across the river at night, and they were taking heavy losses.

The stretch of the river between Moskovskaya Dubravka and Nevskaya Dubravka was to be the scene of further crossings that would be covered by smoke.

During 20 and 21 October 1941 near Nevskaya Dubravka, crossing equipment pontoon units and the units that were to accomplish the crossings were concentrated. A careful final reconnaissance of the crossing area was carried out.

On 22 October all preparations were completed, and that night, units of the 86th Rifle Division began the crossing. This was not unexpected by the Germans, so they at once illuminated the crossing area with rockets and opened heavy fire against the crossing area and against the approaches to it. Our troops suffered heavy losses. The pontoons and other equipment were for the most part knocked out, and the work of our pontoon units during the night was slow and not very productive. The units taking part in the fording of the river became confused; direction was hard to maintain, and the whole operation seemed likely to stall.

In view of all this, the command of the Neva Operational Group decided to try to ford the river in daytime, using smoke to cover the crossing. At about this time, the weather conditions changed and became favorable for the use of smoke.

An ARS smoke platoon with five ARS machines, each with two loads of fuel, was designated to lay the smoke screen. A team of smoke troops with ND smoke pots was detailed to help.

Their task was to generate smoke screens that would cut off Arbuzovo on the right. The smoke men were to generate smoke from two points: Peski and the school at the north edge of Nevskaya Dubravka. Smoke was to be generated for six hours. Over 20 tons of ARS smoke-generating fuel and 800 smoke pots were used to accomplish the mission.

The use of smoke was totally unexpected by the enemy. For almost 45 minutes he did not open fire, and after that he began to fire in a disorganized and aimless manner toward the crossing area, causing our troops only insignificant losses. The units of the division succeeded this time in reaching the left bank of the Neva, with far fewer losses than they had suffered during their night effort.

The use of smoke had a decisive influence on the success of this operation, and it illustrates the value of screening smokes.

On 24 October 1941 on this same sector, another smoke screen was laid down with the object of covering the crossing of the river by units of the 265th Rifle Division. Weather conditions made it possible to lay down a flanking smoke screen that would run along the river and cover the left bank. Our units crossed the river completely covered by smoke and suffered few losses. The enemy opened fire as soon as he saw the smoke being generated, but because of the density of the smoke screen, his fire could not be aimed, and it was relatively ineffectual. The smoke screen was maintained by the ARS equipment generating smoke for over ten hours, consuming 27 tons of fuel. In addition, 500 smoke pots were used.

In the area of Nevskaya Dubravka, during October and November eleven similar smoke screens were laid.

These successes in the use of smoke caused our troops to change their procedure somewhat in river crossings, and thereafter, whenever weather conditions were favorable, the basic forces and the most important engineer activity in river-forcing operations were committed during daytime, under cover of smoke.

The tactical employment of ARS equipment in these cases adds up to the following. All the smoke screens were laid from fixed points. The ARS equipment was located 20 to 500 meters from the river bank, depending on weather conditions. Reloading points for ARS equipment were located 1 or $1\frac{1}{2}$ kilometers from the smoke-generating points. Barrels of S-4 ARS fuel were made ready for reloading ahead of time. Reloading of ARS equipment was carried out by the chemical troops responsible for using the equipment for smoke-generating.

When the ARS equipment was moved up to the smoke-generating points for the first time, the move was covered by smoke from ND smoke pots. Thereafter, a relief ARS generator was covered by smoke of the machine it was to relieve, as it moved up into position.

ARS crews took cover during the smoke-generating period in slit trenches or other works 20 to 30 meters from the ARS equipment itself. They kept the ARS under constant observation and were prepared if necessary to move the ARS to a switch position while it was generating smoke.

The examples cited above (and they are worthy of careful study) are proof that with as few as two ARS machines one can lay down a sufficiently dense and large smoke screen to cover the crossing of a river, in the face of enemy opposition by forces of up to divisional size.

On 3 November 1941, north of Nevshaya Dubravka smoke screens were laid with the object of covering a night crossing of the Neva from enemy artillery and mortar fire that had been conducted with the aid of rocket illumination. Smoke was laid from two points, in order to box the crossing area in a sort of corridor. The smoke screens gave good results; there were no losses during the crossing.

Smoke was generated for over two hours, with over 5,000 kilograms of fuel being consumed. Smoke was released in short ten or 15 minute waves, with intervals of seven to ten minutes. The enemy rockets were entirely unable to illuminate through the smoke screen. The Germans did not know where the crossing was to take place, so they aimlessly shot up the river and its right bank, with no useful concentration of fire.

This episode illustrates the necessity for using smoke not only during daytime, but also at night. Therefore, we must train our units to use smoke at night and in complex situations.

The mass use of smoke on the Neva both to the north and to the south of Nevskaya Dubravka on 3 December 1941 is a good example of what smoke can accomplish in covering offensive operations.

In this case, smoke was generated for 40 minutes along an 8-kilometer front.

Smoke generation began simultaneously from eight ARS machines, so that the whole 8 kilometers of front were enveloped in a dense cloud of smoke.

As soon as the smoke appeared, the enemy opened a strong fire with artillery and mortars against the smoke-released line, but his fire was not aimed, and our forces were hardly affected by it. Our troops, operating under cover of the smoke, were able to close with the enemy without suffering losses of any consequence, and they accomplished their mission.

The smoke screen achieved a depth of up to 4 or 5 kilometers. Over 13,000 kilograms of smoke-generating fuel were used.

ARS smoke generators were also used along the lower part of the Tosna River. In accordance with the plan of offense of our forces, which involved fording the river, an ARS platoon with three machines laid a smoke screen on 11 November 1941 with the object of blinding the enemy fire system near Pokrovsokoye.

Weather conditions were extremely changeable, so that it was not possible to lay a solid and continuous smoke screen. There were two gaps in it. All told, smoke was generated for over seven hours.

Before the smoke screen began, the enemy was conducting strong fire against our departure positions. From the moment the smoke screen enveloped the enemy firing positions, the intensity of the enemy fire sharply diminished, and its effectiveness dropped even more.

At the same time, as a feint our forces made a smoke screen with smoke pots for 20 minutes (240 smoke pots were used) along a 500-meter front near Kolpinsk Kolkhoz. This smoke screen drew heavy enemy fire and succeeded in drawing the enemy's attention.

Conclusion

Experience has confirmed that smoke-generating apparatus, used in various combinations and on varying scales according to the situation, is a decisive factor in most cases in facilitating the forcing of a defended river line.

A well-organized and adequately maintained smoke screen, deliberately planned and executed under favorable weather conditions, can make it possible for troops to overcome enemy resistance and accomplish the crossing of a defended river line with relatively light losses, in daytime as well as at night.

A smoke screen is particularly valuable as cover for sapper and pontoon units that have to operate under enemy fire for long periods.

The laying of false smoke screens is an especially important measure in all types of combat, but particularly in the fording of rivers. One can go so far as to say that in many situations, the laying of a false smoke screen is an absolute necessity; and commanders must assign very high priority to this form of deception in their plans.

Use of Smoke to Cover Important Objectives in Our Own Rear

The protection of the railroad bridge over the Ugra River (Western Front) by smoke is an example of such employment of smoke.

The operational importance of this bridge was especially great, for all the supply traffic for the left flank armies of the army group passed over it. The enemy was aware of this, and beginning in February, he made daily air raids with the object of knocking out the bridge and thereby making the supply of our left flank armies of the Western Front more difficult. The enemy succeeded partially in his design: twice, in February and in early March, he was able to bomb the bridge and put it out of action. In March the antiaircraft artillery protection of the bridge was strengthened, and shortly after that, smoke screen protection for the bridge was organized. This made it impossible for the German fliers to locate the bridge accurately.

For the task, a company of ARS-6 machines were used. There were eight machines, in addition to DM-11 smoke pots. Four machines were set up on the north bank of the river, and four on the south bank, so that whichever way the wind blew it would be possible to conceal the bridge with smoke. The DM-11 smoke pots were used to conceal the ARS machines. The smoke men took shelter in slit trenches and foxholes during enemy air raids. The machines themselves were not dug in nor otherwise protected by engineer works.

The signal to begin making smoke was given three to five minutes before the actual appearance of the enemy aircraft; the signal was transmitted from an operational point located in a church, about 4 kilometers south of the bridge in the direction from which the enemy aircraft customarily approached. Beginning on April 21, the enemy sent over four or five flights of three to five Ju-88s every day in an intensified effort to knock out the bridge.

On numerous occasions false smoke screens were also laid down. Whenever there were gaps in the smoke screens, these were closed by smoke generators mounted on fishing craft on the river itself.

Thanks to the well-organized smoke cover of the bridge and also to the effective false smoke screens that deceived the enemy, not a single enemy bomb fell on the target, and the bridge remained continually in action. The smoke troops, moreover, sustained no losses.

From the very beginning of the battles around Stalingrad (August to September 1942), wide and effective use was made of smoke to protect the Volga River crossings. The details of the organization of this protective smoke operation have not yet been thoroughly examined from a tactical-technical point of view, but this valuable experience must be systematically studied and its results reported for the attention of all concerned.

Conclusions

The protection by smoke of the railroad bridge across the Ugra River was a highly successful example of the use of smoke to cover operationally and strategically important objectives in our rear from enemy air action.

General Conclusions

1. By using smoke as a means of facilitating their combat actions, our troops in most cases were able to accomplish their missions with good success and with markedly lowered personnel and materiel losses.

2. When it is used in a tactically correct manner, smoke is an excellent camouflage agent that helps the troops in the accomplishment of their mission.

3. The combat experience in the use of smoke has shown that smoke can be used in various ways and combinations of ways and on varying scales, depending on the actual situation. Smoke is especially effective in combat river crossings, in attacking enemy strong points, and in blinding enemy firing points. Large-scale smoke screens, combined with false smoke screens, have also succeeded in disorienting and confusing the enemy, by blinding his operational and command posts, creating panic among his troops, and in greatly diminishing the effectiveness of his fire. In such cases, enemy fire tended to become disorganized and without aim; it was scattered along the whole front involved and was no longer able to exercise a decisive effect on the outcome of the battle. In some cases, by the correct tactical use of smoke, it is possible to cancel the enemy superiority in firepower on a given sector by greatly reducing its effectiveness during the time of the smoke screen.

4. The duration of a smoke screen is determined by the scale and nature of the projected operation and by the amount of smoke equipment available.

5. Practice has shown that the most effective use of smoke is on large scale and for a long duration.

A fast-moving five- or ten-minute smoke screen often failed to give satisfactory results. Units were frequently unable to accomplish their mission in such a short time, so that after the smoke cleared away, the main line of defense was in unfavorable positions where they could be taken under fire from all types of enemy weapons.

However, in actions involving small groups, it is often advantageous to lay small smoke screens that do not last long.

6. False smoke screens give good results at the front. This form of smoke screen has fully proved its value and should not be neglected.

7. In order to achieve best results with smoke screens and in order also to reduce losses of men and materiel to the minimum, it is desirable to complete all preparations at night or under cover of smoke from smoke pots. When smoke is being generated, the smoke personnel should be themselves well covered either by smoke or, preferably, by taking cover in slit trenches and other engineer works.

8. Smoke hand grenades (RDG-1) proved effective in combat as a light and simple smoke-generating device.

9. Combat experience with smoke shows that the greatest effect is achieved when smoke is used in favorable weather conditions, and when the use of smoke is coordinated with the actions of the various combat arms. In cases when smoke was used without such coordination, failure was not infrequent, and at best, the smoke was less than fully effective.

10. For the use of smoke in the future, the following factors will be decisive:
- Knowledge of the tactical-technical characteristics of the various types of smoke-generating equipment and the amounts of such equipment necessary to accomplish given missions;
- Correct choice of smoke-generating equipment for the concrete task;
- A clear understanding of the combat tasks of the units that are to be given smoke cover; and
- Topographically correct choice of the smoke-release line and correct utilization of weather conditions.

This chapter is critical of topographic training in the Red Army as well as waste and lack of adequate security in handling maps. The General Staff praises the Soviet maps but criticizes the quality of paper. That German units had topographic units at lower levels is praised, and there is an implicit suggestion that this model should be followed—Ed.

13

War Experience in the Topographic Support of Combat Troops

Organization of the Military-Topographic Service of the Red Army

Up to the beginning of the Patriotic War, the Military-Topographic Service was represented in military districts and in armies by a topographic section attached to the district or army staff. In corps there was a senior topographic officer. The staffs of formations below corps had no topographic representation.

Subordinate to the military district, topographic sections were stationary and field topographic units. The field topographic units included geodetic, topographic, and motorized topographic detachments. The stationary units included cartographic, map-publishing, and geodetic elements and also map-printing shops. In addition, in the military districts and in the armies, there were district and army map depots.

The number of topographic units in a military district depended on the extent and importance of the terrain embraced within the district. Both the field and the office work of the topographic units were carried out under centralized control, in accordance with annual plans put out by the Military-

172

War Experience in the Topographic Support of Combat Troops   173

Topographic Service and approved by the chief of the general staff of the Red Army.

The basic task of the field topographic units consisted of establishing repair points and surveying the frontier areas of the USSR and preparing firing data covering fortified areas.

The stationary topographic units concentrated on the assembly of data for maps and the publishing of maps and of catalogues of geodetic repair points covering the territory of the USSR and neighboring countries.

Topographic surveys of the territory covered by interior military districts within the USSR (as against frontier Military Districts) was carried out by topographic units of the Main Administration of Geodesy and Topography under the overall direction of the Council of Peoples Commissars of the USSR.

Military-Cartographic Supply and Support before the War

Up to the outbreak of the war, maps of the following scales were available for the Red Army: 1:25,000, 1:50,000, 1:100,000, 1:200,000, 1:500,000, and 1:1,000,000. The cartographic coverage of the western USSR was as follows:

1:25,000 maps—Coverage at this scale was available only for a thin frontier strip, covering mainly fortified areas as well as a considerable part of East Prussia.

1:50,000 maps—Map coverage of the scale included an area bounded on the west by Koenigsberg-Warsaw-Ketsy-Brody and then south along the Dniester River to the Black Sea. On the east, the area extended to a line from Tikhvin through Vyazma-Bryansk-Konotop to Kherson. In the middle of this area the area bounded by Grodno-Sventsyany-Pinsk-Kovel-Brest-Byalystok was covered only by older 1:42,000 maps, since this area was still undergoing basic topographic resurvey that had begun in 1941.

1:100,000 maps—This scale coverage was available for Finland, the Baltic republics, Germany up a line from Koelberg to Vienna, Czechoslovakia, Rumania, and the USSR western frontier area as far east as the Leningrad-Kiev-Odessa line.

1:200,000 maps—This coverage embraced the area bounded on the north by Tammerfors and Petrozavodsk, on the west by Danzig, Kalish, and Budapest, and on the east by Volkhov, Smolensk, Poltava, and Melitopol. It extended south to the Black Sea. However, this map series was not entirely up to date at the outbreak of the war, for after it had been published, new and better surveys were made on some of the area covered, and there were discrepancies between these larger-scale series and the maps of the 1:200,000 series.

1:500,000 maps—This series covered the area from Berlin meridian east to the Moscow meridian.

1:1,000,000 maps—This series covered all of Europe, including European USSR.

Thus it can be seen that in peacetime the territory of the USSR was not sufficiently covered by large-scale maps. Even the basic tactical 1:100,000 maps went no farther east than Leningrad–Kiev–Odessa. Therefore, when the Red Army began to withdraw eastward from our border, the topographical service was faced with the imperative task of supplying as quickly as possible maps of the territory to the east of the Leningrad–Kiev–Odessa line, with the highest priority to maps of the 1:100,000 scale. Not only were the field and stationary agencies of the Military-Topographical Service put on this task, but the widest use was made of civil agencies, mainly of the Main Administration of Geodesy and Cartography.

The measures that were taken made it possible to supply the withdrawing field forces of the Red Army with 1:100,000 maps. In this connection, in view of the extremely short time available, some of the sheets had to be printed in temporary black-and-white editions, which of course presented inconveniences in the use of such maps. The printing difficulties were further complicated by the fact that a part of the map reserves that had been printed in peacetime were lost in the first month when some map depots in the west were overrun. Thus, it was necessary to republish some sheets at the same time that new ones were being published.

The map-printing difficulties were overcome by setting up two military map-printing works in a very short time. By October 1941 both were already in production, and they took the place of the map-printing works of the Main Administration of Geodesy and Cartography, which had been evacuated from Moscow.

The scope of the map-publishing job (covering the western parts of the USSR) can be seen from the following figures: During the first year of the war, 4,085 new sheets of various scales were published, including assembly of data, drafting, etc. The overall number of maps printed amounted to nearly three hundred million sheets.

As a result of the high-pressure work of all the units of the Military-Cartographic Service and the wide-scale use of civilian resources, the additional areas of the USSR covered up to the present by 1:50,000 and 1:100,000 maps include those shown on sketches 23 and 24 (amounting generally to nearly a doubling of the total area covered). [Sketches not included—Ed.]

The experience of the Great Patriotic War as far as the supplying of maps to the field forces of the Red Army and the use of maps are concerned provides the basis for the following conclusions:

1. The various map series of the scales listed above together provide the troops with every type of map they need in wartime. There is no need to change the content of any of the regularly issued map series that existed before the war.

2. In comparison with the maps with which the German army is supplied, ours are more detailed and more accurate. However, ours are printed on poor

paper, and the ink is bad. These factors merit censure; they greatly shorten the useful life of a map and should be corrected.

3. Together with 1:100,000 and 1:500,000 maps for army groups and army staffs and for the air force and the tank forces and the rear services troops, there must be a good 1:200,000 map. The problem of producing such a series was solved for the whole theater by the middle of 1942, and by now, such maps have been furnished to the whole theater of operations, with the exceptions of the Karelian Front. According to reports received from the staffs that are using the 1:200,000 maps, this series is entirely satisfactory for the ground troops, and in addition, it is being widely used by the air force for bombing missions that are carried out in support of ground actions.

4. The 1:1,000,000 and 1:2,500,000 maps that the Military-Topographic Service have issued are absolutely essential for politico-economic orientation and for operational and strategic purposes. There is a great demand for these maps from the various Peoples Commissariats, from the headquarters of the Peoples Commissariat of Defense, the Air Force, and various staffs of high-level field headquarters.

Organization of Work and Technical Equipment

The organizational structure of the Military-Topographical Service has undergone no change during the course of the war with the exception of the streamlining of the technical department of its units. The experience of the first months of the war drew attention to the necessity of reorganizing the control structure and organizing the work of the units of the Topographical Service.

It was recognized that centralized planning of the work of topographical units was desirable only in the case of units that were supporting rear-area military commands. The work of topographical units attached to army groups must be planned by the army-group staff and must correspond to the immediate needs of the army group to which the topographical unit is attached.

In peacetime, topographical units had to work very little in actual cooperation with combat units. But in wartime, they must be closely and firmly in contact with the field forces, and they must carry out topographical-geodetic work not only on previously prepared lines, but also in areas right up to and including the front line itself.

Most of the stationary cartographic, geodetic, and map-printing units were removed from army-group control and put under centralized control. Such units were replaced in the army groups by mobile cartographic detachments, capable of making maps ready for printing and then actually printing them. It was vital and absolutely essential to have mobile topographic units including mobile map-printing sections within them.

War experience has shown that in the army there should be very simple map-printing equipment: a single lithographic press mounted on a 1½-ton truck suffices at army level.

In the beginning of the war, some of the topographic sections in armies were reorganized into topographic subsections subordinate to the operations sections of the army staffs. This proved unwise. Experience showed that it was preferable to retain the topographic sections of armies as separate elements of the staff, directly subordinate to the chief of staff of the army.

It proved necessary to have topographic elements not only in army and corps but also in division. The directive of the General Staff that divisional topographers be established has proven of great use. Though officer shortages have made it possible to have in division only one topographer rather than a section, even this has been of decided value, and such a position should be formally provided for.

Topographic work under wartime conditions has shown how our equipment is operating and makes it possible now to form a sound judgment as to what equipment is needed under what conditions.

Geodetic Instruments

The basic instrument is the 30-inch theodolite. Its accuracy and simplicity make it ideal for all types of geodetic work in combat situations. More accurate geodetic instruments are needed only for longer-term survey work in the rear areas.

From the experience in the use of the 30-inch theodolite, it can be said that this instrument, which is accurate enough for topographic work, is also quite satisfactory for artillery survey, since artillery survey is not as precise as most topographic survey. Therefore, the 20-inch theodolite developed for use by artillery survey units should be withdrawn, for it costs several times as much as the 30-inch model.

Experience has shown that the 30-inch theodolite should be equipped with some form of illumination for night work and that a periscope must be developed that can be attached to it for observation from cover. Both of these requirements have been taken up by the development people, and experimental models have been produced that are now being tried out in some units before they are finally adopted and produced in quantity as standard items.

Topographic Instruments

These include basically the plane table and the plane table alidade, which are used for survey work and instrumental terrain reconnaissance. War experience has shown that these instruments function perfectly satisfactorily for this kind of work, and no changes appear necessary.

Cartographic Equipment

The mobile cartographic team, which is part of the mobile topographic section, is equipped with a copying camera, a printing machine, and other items that are mounted on four trucks. This arrangement has proven fully satisfactory. Experience has shown that such a team is capable of producing all the cartographic material in printed form that an army group will need.

Before the war, no provision had been made for the allotment to army of map-printing resources, since it was anticipated that all army requirements for maps prepared in the theater would be taken care of by the army group. However, the experience of the first months of the war showed that it was essential for an army staff to have its own map-producing resources. Therefore, early in the war a provisional cartographic outfit for army was worked out, consisting of a small lithographic press mounted on a $1\frac{1}{2}$-ton truck. Some armies have been furnished these, but they are not yet standard items, and no provision has yet been made on the staff of army headquarters for such an outfit.

Neither had any provision been made for reproduction equipment at divisional level, though experience has shown that there must be an extremely simple reproduction machine (mimeograph allotted to divisional staff for the quick reproduction of combat charts, maps, etc.).

A simple machine, similar to a hectograph, has been developed that will reproduce up to 20 or 25 copies of charts, maps, or other combat documents. These have been distributed to the topographic sections of army groups for further distribution down through division, but not enough have yet been produced to make full distribution to all divisions in the field possible.

Combat Experience of Military-Topographical Units

The work of the units of the Topographic Service was relatively little known among the officers of the Red Army as a whole in peacetime. And conversely, the Topographic Service personnel had no experience in meeting the immediate requirements of combat units. This lack of experience extended even to the topographic people having never taken part in peacetime maneuvers in the field. Therefore, at the beginning of the war, there was some difficulty in getting commanders to assign appropriate missions, or any mission at all, to their topographic sections, and for the most part the topographic sections were little more than map-issuing agencies.

But this situation lasted only a very short time. As soon as the Red Army had halted the enemy's advance and had taken up defensive positions along prepared lines, the necessity arose at once for survey work in connection with the preparation of artillery data, and various other requirements for immediate topographic support of the combat troops.

The work of the agencies of the Topographic Service under combat conditions included the following tasks:

- Establishment of firm topographic-geodetic data for the territory in which the topographic unit is operating;
- Supplying the troops with topographical maps;

- Establishment of firm repair points for the artillery and in areas where there are prepared defenses;
- Interpretation and annotation of air photos as the basis for reconnaissance charts and overlays;
- Printing of maps, overlays, and other graphic combat documents; and
- Topographic training of the troops.

Topographic-Geodetic Study

A topographic-geodetic study of the area in which the army group is operating is one of the basic tasks of the topographic section of an army-group staff. The topographic section must know what maps are available covering its area, how good they are, what catalogues of geodetic points can be obtained, and it must provide supplementary data where necessary.

The topographic section of an army-group staff organizes the supply of maps through its own map depot and through those of subordinate topographic agencies. It distributes maps in accordance with the quantities prescribed for distribution to various units at various levels in the Ministry of Defense Directive No.085 of 1941.

A regular system for the distribution of maps has been worked out on the basis of experience in the field.

The topographic section of the army-group staff receives maps from the central depots of the Main Topographic Administration. It stores the maps in an army-group map depot, which includes a forward echelon or forward depot. This latter includes a mobile subsection. In addition, a certain supply of maps is maintained directly at the army-group staff and its rear elements. The mobile subsection delivers maps to the army map depots, and from there, they are delivered to the divisions. The divisional topographic officer, in turn, forwards maps to the units organic to and attached to the division.

The size of the task of furnishing maps to the field forces can be seen from the following table, showing the number of sheets issued by the central map depots of the Topographic Administration.

Thus the active field forces of the Red Army, excluding units in reserve in the military districts, received some 162 million sheets of maps of various scales. This amounts to about 200 railroad freight-car loads. It is evident of course that not all of these sheets have been expended. Some remain in army-group and army map depots. Still these figures give an indication of the very great expenditure of maps, as a result both of actual need and of wasteful handling.

The careless handling of maps on the part of Soviet army officers has been useful to the Germans. In the beginning of the war, the Germans did not have good map coverage of the territory of the USSR. During the course of the war, through captured maps, they have been able to a large extent to overcome this deficiency. At the beginning of the war, the best large-scale coverage the

Scale	2nd Half 1941	1st Half 1942	Total for 1 year
	Deliveries in Thousands of Sheets		
1:25,000	8,796	1,871	10,667
1:50,000	38,478	22,083	60,561
1:100,000	52,270	28,235	80,505
1:200,000 and smaller scale	7,663	2,966	10,629
Total	107,207	55,155	162,362

Germans had of the western USSR was at the 1:100,000 scale, and many of the sheets of this series were simply blowups of the 1:200,000 series. The Germans for some areas had to use the old Tsarist three-verst maps, and even the ten-verst maps. In describing their difficulties with map coverage of our country, the Germans in their manual wrote as follows: "large-scale and medium-scale [Soviet] maps were always classified secret. This classification was strictly adhered to, so that it has not been possible to assemble up-to-date data on which to base a good 1:100,000 map coverage. On Russian terrain, the enemy has the advantage of much better maps than we.... The serious lack of original maps makes it essential that any captured sheets be at once forwarded to the Army headquarters."

The Germans were no better off when it came to catalogues of geodetic bench marks on our territory. In the same manual, we find: "Together with the fact that we have thoroughly inadequate map coverage, we are not able to compile catalogues of bench mark coordinates. Thus our units are at a disadvantage in not having any firm data on which to base artillery survey and firing data."

From these passages it is clear that the Germans in peacetime had not collected cartographic material of worthwhile quality on the USSR. However, within a few months after the beginning of the war we began to capture German maps that were adapted and republished from our large-scale maps. The Germans had taken advantage of the negligence of some of our officers and units to acquire the basis for good map coverage of our country. Finally a special directive had to be issued by the chief of the General Staff prescribing procedures for the maintenance of security and economy in the use and handling of maps.

Geodetic Support for the Artillery

Geodetic support for the artillery has been provided right from the beginning of the war by topographic field units. In the defense, these units compile basic reference data in close cooperation with artillery topographic and survey units. Both organizational and functional problem of coordination in this matter have now been worked out satisfactorily on the basis of the war experience that were collected and published under the title, "Procedure for the Work of Military-Topographic Units of the Red Army Support of Artillery under Combat Conditions."

In accordance with this tentative regulation, the following tasks are the responsibility of the military-topographic units:

- Providing the artillery topographic service and long-range artillery units with a firm net of survey data; providing basic geodetic data to divisional artillery through supplementary survey and thereby increasing the density of the basic survey nets of the existing published maps in combat areas;
- Developing and increasing the density of firm geodetic data in fortified areas and in the deep rear;
- Providing catalogues or lists of the coordinates of geodetic bench marks;
- Providing artillery units with reference material concerning maps and catalogues of bench marks covering enemy-held areas;
- Training the personnel of artillery topographic units; and
- Organizing magnetometric work in the areas where heavy artillery and long-range artillery are in action.

The artillery topographic service is increasing the scope of its work, including the development of solid artillery reference data nets in artillery deployment and firing areas; establishment of coordinates of artillery firing positions, reference points, repair points, and targets; and the calculation of basic data for the conduct and direction of fire.

In spite of the fact that the tentative regulation referred to above clearly delineates the line of responsibility between military-topographical units and artillery topographical elements, in actual fact, the former continues in many cases to do work that should be done by the latter.

The field geodetic work done by the Red Army is on a massive scale. Thus, for example, the topographic units of the western front alone in one year surveyed and established some 10,200 additional repair points in connection with the job of making the geodetic net more dense, and in addition, they carried out nearly 1,000 artillery survey missions.

According to reports of artillery chiefs at army-group, army, and divisional levels, the work of the military topographic units in support of the artillery has greatly increased the accuracy of our artillery fire and has brought about a substantial saving in the expenditure of artillery ammunition. The work of these units and the results of this work in the increased effectiveness of our artillery make it clear that the topographers must be considered as valuable combat auxiliaries of the artillery. There are numerous instances when artillery fire conducted on the basis of customary registration failed to give worthwhile results, whereas the same artillery unit, firing later on the basis of geodetic data, was able to knock out its target with only a few rounds.

War experience in the support of artillery indicated that the military topographer must not only be able to handle triangulation well, but must also have mastered the theodolite; he must be able to do a geodetic survey as well as tie in base points on a map survey.

War Experience in the Topographic Support of Combat Troops

Interpretation of Air Photos

Aerial photography interpretation is done by the topographic section of army-group headquarters and is directed mainly at preparing reconnaissance maps or overlays. Air photo interpretation and photogrammetric work are done either by one of the teams of the army-group topographic section or, if the scale and object of the work justify it, by a specially formed team including air force photo interpreters and artillery topographic personnel as well as military topographic experts.

Topographic personnel have had extensive experience in air photo interpretation, and by now each army-group staff has experienced and competent experts in this work. Experience has shown that if the air photos are of good quality, up to 70 percent of the enemy phenomena on them can be correctly identified.

To check on the results of air photo interpretation, the Leningrad front took an air mosaic of a section of the terrain occupied by our troops and had it studied and interpreted by the topographical section. The results of the photo interpretation were then checked directly on the ground. The check showed that all battery positions, trenches, communications trenches, open firing positions, etc., were fully and accurately identified. Shelters, machine gun positions, permanent firing positions, earth-and-timber works, etc., were identified in 60 to 70 percent of the cases. In all, the defensive system was correctly identified in 70 to 75 percent of its elements, and this was with not very satisfactory air photos.

The check also showed that the camouflage of the elements of our defensive system was not adequate, so that the enemy would be able, just as we had, to identify the system quite satisfactorily from his point of view.

The check thus was valuable to the interpreters as a confirmation of their work and an indication of where they could improve it, while it was of equal value to our camouflage personnel in pointing out their errors and shortcomings. Their work was materially improved as a result of what they learned through the check. It is intended to carry out similar checks on other fronts.

It must also be pointed out that despite the clear value of air photos in obtaining data concerning the enemy dispositions etc., air photo reconnaissance has up to now not been used as much as it should. The photo interpreters, as a fact, are often idle for lack of photos to work on. Carrying out area air photography with a view to providing material for photogrammetric work to discover the enemy defense system and to correct our existing maps is not done nearly enough and constitutes a weakness at present in our air reconnaissance.

Combat Graphic Documents

Such documents are prepared and reproduced by army-group topographic sections. The basic documents so prepared include:

- Reconaissance charts, based on reconnaissance data received from all sources and usually overprinted on large-scale maps;
- Base maps (blank maps) with geodetic base points either tied in as a geodetic overlay or listed with their coordinates;
- Photos with photo interpretation annotations or overprints;
- City plans, printed to large scale and based on existing maps with corrections from air photos;
- Individual air photos with overprinted coordinate net;
- Annotated air photos or maps prepared from air photos of enemy air bases; and
- Orientation maps, showing all or some of the following: artillery and machine gun fields of fire, orientation points, etc.

Topographic Training of Troops

Combat experience has shown that the level of topographic training of Red Army commanders is generally low. Many commanders cannot show correctly on a map the dispositions of their troops. There have been cases of the main line of defense being shown incorrectly on maps. Routes of march have been incorrectly shown, and some officers are not able to move by azimuth.

Topographic units in the field have been able to help officers in their study of topography. They have given detailed courses for junior lieutenants. They have helped in the field by verifying and correcting where necessary data placed on maps by commanders, such as precise location of the main line of defense, etc. They have helped in training artillery survey personnel. And in reserve units, they give lessons as part of the overall officer training program.

However, as an overall proposition, the topographic training given to the officer corps by topographic units in the field is inadequate, mainly because it is on an improvised basis. Topographic training is weakest in the infantry. It is absolutely essential to have an experienced man to head up the topographic work of each division. Divisional topographic officers can (and are) markedly increasing the level of topographic training of our officers through giving courses, through practical exercises, and through helping other training officers in the division train their men in topography.

Two handbooks have been issued to help the officer in his study of topography: *Topographic Maps and Their Use* and *Units of Air Photos.*

In addition, a number of wall charts on military topography have been issued. Bubnov's textbook, *Military Topography*, is being reprinted, and a shorter handbook is being published. Shebalin's text on the subject has also been republished.

Organization of the Military-Topographic Service of the German Army

The following chart shows the agencies of the German Military-Topographical Service.

Topgraphic Section of the General Staff of the Army	Army Cartographic Point	Corps Cartographic Point	Divisional CartoGraphic Point

Thus the German army's Topographic Service extends down through division. The number of military topographic agencies in the German army and their technical equipment have not been determined. But there is evidence to suggest that even the divisional cartographic point is provided with reproduction equipment. Thus, the *Berliner Boersenzeitung* for 25 August 1941 in an article entitled "Army Cartographic Section" says, "Given the great areas and long distances that the army must deal with in its struggle with the Soviet armies, the cartographic sections play a particularly important role. They are attached to the field forces right down through divisional level. They carry with them not only regularly issued maps, but also all the equipment needed to make maps under field conditions. The cartographic sections have their own motor columns. There are trucks to carry stores of maps, paper, ink; and of particular importance are the laboratories mounted on trucks that are equipped to do cartographic work to develop and reproduce photos, to prepare and make blueprints, to do printing, etc. The topographic section has its own truck-mounted power station."

Some captured maps have carried the imprint of divisional motorized cartographic detachments, indicating that these detachments have the equipment to print maps.

General Conclusions

As a result of the high-pressure work of all elements of the Military-Topographical Service working under the centralized direction of the Military-Topographical Administration of the General Staff, all army groups have been supplied with topographic maps.

The territory of the western part of the USSR, much of which before the war was either not covered or only partially covered by large-scale maps, has now been fully (or nearly fully) covered by such maps.

Military topographic units have been widely used for the direct topographical support of the field forces; in this work they have received valuable experience, and they have become an inseparable element of the active field forces.

As a result of the work of topographic units in support of artillery, the prevailing views in the army concerning topographic preparation of artillery fire have changed markedly. On the basis of much checking of topographic basic data by actual registration, artillerymen have come to appreciate the value of such topographic data, and the demand for this type of topographic and geodetic assistance has grown. The conduct of artillery fire on the basis of topographic data has been highly successful and has done much to overcome the notion formerly prevalent among some artillerymen and some topographers that topographic data were not necessary for the artillery because "artillery uses direct fire" or because the data the artillery can get from topographic preparation can equally be obtained by expending a few extra rounds in registration.

The experience of the war shows that it is essential to have topographical elements not only on army-group and army staffs but also on corps and divisional staffs.

Combat experience provides the basis for the estimate that there should be one topographic detachment for every three armies for special topographic work that may be required by the army group.

Each army group must have a motorized topographic detachment with a cartographic subsection and printing equipment consisting of a lithographic press. There must also be a photo laboratory and various other equipment fixed-mounted in four or five trucks.

To meet the requirements of an army staff, the army topographical staff element should have a small lithographic press mounted on a $1\frac{1}{2}$-ton truck.

Each divisional topographic officer must have a hectograph or a similar machine for reproducing essential combat graphic documents.

War experience has shown that there must be standardization in the topographic-geodetic instruments used in the field. The present system by which the various arms develop their own models is a waste of money and effort.

Combat experience has shown that the artillery topographic service has proven unequal to the tasks it faces. Therefore, particular attention must be paid to the training of personnel of this service.

It is essential to point out that the inadequate topographical training of Red Army officers as a whole has led to serious trouble and embarrassment. It is a matter of urgent priority to improve as soon as possible the level of topographic training of the officers of all arms. Military topography must take its rightful place as one of the basic subjects in officer training programs.

This chapter is more of a description than a critique of the rear services, which performed well under the leadership of the tough A.V. Khrulev. The report is also interesting in the General Staff's description of rear duties that fall exclusively under the NKVD. Further reading about rear services during this period should include the memoirs of Colonel General N.A. Antipenko (Na Glavnom Napravlenii [*1967*]), *who commanded the rear area service of the western front—Ed.*

14

Regulation Concerning the Organization and Work of the Army Rear

I. General Propositions

1. The tasks of the army rear are:

a. Timely and uninterrupted supply of the troops of the army with all the items needed by them to fight and to subsist;

b. Timely accumulation in the army rear area of stocks of materiel and stores needed by the troops for their current requirements and over and above these requirements to create mobile reserves of materiel and supplies;

c. Organization of rail, road, and water transportation for supply and evacuation movements from the army regulating station up to the boundary at which troops unit supply transportation takes over;

d. Organization of the preparation and employment of local production resources, shops, rations, and other resources, locally available and that can be used in the army rear area for the support of the army;

e. Preparation and maintenance of main and secondary roads in the army rear area;

f. Organization of the repair and maintenance of materiel and equipment in local civilian establishments and in army workshops;

g. Organization of the movement of replacement units toward the front and servicing of such units as they pass through the army rear;

h. The evacuation of sick and wounded personnel and horses and the furnishing of medical treatment;

i. Receipt from combat units enemy prisoners of war and moving them to the rear;

j. Organization of the collection, reissue, and evacuation of enemy and Soviet equipment;

k. The security and defense of the principal rear installations and the maintenance of order in the army rear area; and

l. Political support of the work of the rear.

2. The army rear area is bounded on its forward edge by the rear boundary of the front line, on its flanks by the rear areas of neighboring armies, and on its rear by the forward edge of area under control of the army group.

3. The depth of the army rear area depends on the nature of the operation, the enemy's actions, the makeup of the army, the layout and nature of the communications system, the availability of local resources for storage of supplies and for repair of equipment. On the average, it runs between 75 and 150 kilometers.

II. Army Rear Units and Installations

4. In the rear area of the army, the following rear units and installations are deployed, with the task of supporting and servicing the combat elements of the army:

a. The *army base*, consisting of the headquarters of the army base and of the following army field depots: artillery, tank, supply, military-technical, medical, and veterinary.

In addition, along the evacuation route of the army there is deployed an army depot for the receipt and further evacuation of captured and damaged materiel and salvaged metal.

b. *Road exploitation and transport units*:
- Road-exploitation battalions (one or two);
- Road-construction battalions (two or three);
- Bridge-building battalion;
- Service company;
- Motor transport battalions (one or two);
- Animal-drawn transport companies (three or five);
- Fuel transport company;
- Evacuation company; and
- Company for the collection and dispatch to the rear of captured and Soviet materiel, salvage, and scrap metal.

Regulation Concerning the Organization and Work of the Army Rear

c. *Repair units and shops*:
   - Motor repair battalion (for trucks and other vehicles);
   - Army artillery workshop;
   - Mobile footgear repair vehicle;
   - Mobile workshop for repairing wagons and carts;
   - Mobile workshop for repairing leather and saddle equipment; and
   - Workshop for the repair of canvas and individual equipment.
d. [No data—Ed.]
e. *Medical installations and units*:
   - Army medical headquarters;
   - Field clearing stations (two or three, depending on the situation);
   - Mobile field hospitals (number depends on the number of wounded);
   - Hospitals for lightly wounded (normally three);
   - Infectious disease hospitals (two);
   - Pathology-analytical laboratory;
   - Medical-epidemiological company;
   - Independent medical reserve company (for reinforcement at point of main effort);
   - Disinfection company; and
   - Laundry detachments.
f. *Veterinary installations and units*:
   - Veterinary field hospitals (one or two);
   - Veterinary evacuation hospitals (one or two);
   - Mobile veterinary laboratory.
g. *Army reserve rear units and installations*:
   - Army field artillery depot;
   - Field supply depot;
   - Field fuel depot;
   - Labor company; and
   - Guard company.

5. The army reserve units and installations when present are used for the following:
   - The organization of new army bases whenever the army moves its bases; and
   - Supplementing regular real elements in cases or rapid advance in the offensive.

6. For the collection and evacuation of prisoners of war, POW collection points are set up in the army rear along rail lines but not near other supply stations or unloading points. The chief of such POW collection points is subordinated to the appropriate NKVD element. The chief of the army rear determines when and where the collection point will be set up.

7. Fixed installations, such as warehouses, workshops, factories, etc., located in the area of the army rear may be used by the army for its purposes only with the permission of the army-group chief of the rear.

8. In order to ensure uninterrupted supply of the combat troops, there are set up in the army field depots stocks of *mobile* reserves and of *maneuver* reserves.

These special reserves include all the basic categories of supplies. The quantities maintained depend on the nature of the projected operation, the distance from the army-group bases and depots, the density and efficiency of the rail and road network within both army and army-group rear areas, and the possibility of interruption in the flow of supplies forward to the army bases.

9. On the average, the following mobile reserves are maintained in the army field depots:

a. Ammunition—up to one unit of fire;
b. Rations and fodder—up to three or four days' supply;
c. Fuel—up to two refills.

The quantities of other categories of supplies will depend on the specific situation and on the nature of the projected operation.

In addition, the army commander may set up maneuver reserves on the following order of magnitude:

a. Ammunition—up to $\frac{1}{4}$ unit of fire;
b. Rations and fodder—up to two days' supply;
c. Fuel—up to one refill.

10. In setting up reserves of supplies in army field bases, the following are used:

a. Cargoes consigned by army-group or by General Headquarters and, in the case of rations and fodder, whatever local resources are available;

b. Captured items, including weapons and equipment that are suitable for use by our troops.

11. The issue to the troops of blocks of supplies from army field depots, or the routing directly to troops of consignments as they arrive from army group, is accomplished on the basis of orders issued by the army chief of the rear to the appropriate depot commanders or to the commandant of the army distribution station.

12. In army-scale operations, it is particularly important that the task of collecting, evacuating, and reissuing captured equipment and abandoned friendly equipment is organized on a clear-cut and efficient basis. Such utilizable items include weapons, equipment, trucks, and even combat vehicles.

The chiefs of the various arms and services should have their own plans already worked out for the collection, repair, evacuation, and reissue of such equipment; and these plans should be worked out on a basis of a realistic appraisal of the projected operation.

III. Organization of the Bringing up of Supplies and of Evacuation

13. The bringing up of supplies and evacuation are accomplished at army level by means of rail, motor, and water transportation and, in exceptional cases, by air transport as well.

14. In order to ensure an uninterrupted supply of the troops, the following installations are set up:
a. The army railway sector;
b. The army distributing point;
c. Supply stations, loading, and unloading stations;
d. Army military truck roads;
e. Army routes for bringing up of supplies and for evacuation.

15. The basic army lines of communication is the army railway sector. If the rail system is inadequate, then the basic line may consist of a truck road sector or even a water transportation route sector. The rail sector of the army extends from the regulating station (distributing point) to the supply stations or unloading points located closest to the troops.

16. The army regulating station is usually located at a major existing rail station near the rear boundary of the army rear area. If there is no such station, then the regulating station is set up in and around two or three secondary rail stations adjacent to each other. All supplies addressed to the army must clear through the regulating station.

17. The chief of the army base commands the army regulating station and all installations in its vicinity. He is the commander of the garrison of the regulating station; he is responsible for the overall order, defense, and security of the installation, and he must take measures as quickly as possible to restore any damage caused by enemy air raids.

18. The following tasks are accomplished at the army regulating station:
a. The reception, checking, reorganization where necessary, and dispatch of all supply and medical trains sent by higher headquarters to the army;
b. The unloading, or provision for unloading, of all trains bearing freight addressed to the army base.

19. The army base is located near the regulating station; the various army depots that make up the army base are set up near stations adjacent to the regulating station.

These army field depots are dispersed; those containing inflammable supplies (ammunition and fuel) are located $1\frac{1}{2}$ or 2 kilometers from other depots and from rail stations. Generally small spur lines are laid from the main railway line leading to these installations. The chiefs of the various army depots are subordinated to the chief of the army base, though for technical matters, their subordination is to their own respective chiefs of arms and services.

20. The chief of the army base is subordinated to the army rear services chief.

21. Within the headquarters of the chief of the army base, there are positions for representatives of the following supply elements: artillery, supplies, and fuel. These representatives are deputies to the chief of the army base. The regulating station commandant, as the commander of its garrison, is responsible for security and defense, and is a deputy to the chief of the army base.

22. For the purpose of operating the army base (loading and unloading

work, road service including traffic control and security), the army base chief has a service company at his disposal.

23. Supply station is the term used to describe a rail station and the area around it (to a radius of 3 to 5 kilometers) in which the individual army depots are dispersed, including those that contain mobile reserves, and the medical and veterinary installations as well.

The supply station is the transfer point between rail and truck transportation. One supply station is set up, on the average, for every two or three rifle divisions.

Mechanized and cavalry formations as a rule are based on supply stations that serve rifle units, but sometimes separate supply stations may be set up specially to serve mobile formations or groups.

24. At each supply station normally there are set up an artillery depot, supply depot, fuel depot, main field evacuation point (medical headquarters, clearing station, mobile hospital), and a veterinary field hospital.

The commandant of the railway station at the supply station is responsible for loading and unloading of supplies and materiel, etc. He carries out these tasks at the order of the chief of the supply station. The army chief of the rear details guard and labor units to see to the defense of the area and the work that must be done in connection with loading and unloading.

25. In a situation where rapid movement is taking place, usually an unloading station is set up, rather than a supply station. An unloading station in effect is a railway station where trains or special motor columns unload goods destined for formations and separate units that are temporarily based on that station. At the unloading station there may be some or all of the customary army depots (as found at a supply station) with their complement of mobile reserves of supplies.

The army rear services chief assigns the necessary labor troops and security forces to the unloading station, and if needed the formations and units served by the unloading station may themselves have to contribute personnel also for these purposes.

26. The various army field depots are subordinated to the chief of the unloading station (or supply station) in matters having to do with labor tasks, security, location of the depots within the station area, etc.

27. Water route sectors, if they exist within the area of the army rear, may be the basic lines of communication of the army, especially if no railway stations or facilities are available. The chief of the water route sector is subordinated to the chief of military communications.

28. Military motor roads in the army rear area are organized and put into working order by the rear services chief.

29. Army routes for bringing up of supplies and for evacuation are laid out from the supply stations (or unloading stations) up to the rear boundary of the troop rear.

30. Army supply and evacuation routes are set up at the initiative of the army rear services chief, who uses army resources for the purpose.

31. Supplies are moved forward from supply stations or unloading stations to the troops by transport vehicles belonging to the troops in cases where the supply or unloading stations are less than 45 kilometers behind the line of the troop rear. In case of necessity, army transportation may be used to supplement transportation belonging to troop formations and units.

Supplies that are moved over army motor roads travel in army transport vehicles. Supplies moved over army supply routes are carried either in divisional or in army vehicles, depending on the circumstances.

32. If the troops units are over 150 kilometers from the supply station or unloading station, the army rear services chief sets up intermediate forward army bases, containing the various essential types of army field depots. Supplies are moved up to the forward army base by army transport.

33. All available metaled and suitable dirt roads are used in the system of military motor roads and army supply routes.

34. Motor transport assigned for movement of supplies and for evacuation along military motor roads becomes subordinated operationally to the chief of the military motor road along which it is moving.

35. Army military motor roads and army supply routes are handled by traffic control elements and road service troops, and telegraph or telephone systems are set up along such roads whenever possible.

36. The following elements carry out the work of maintaining order and movement along military motor roads and army routes of supply:

 a. Road maintenance battalions;

 b. Transportation units (truck, tractor drawn, animal drawn, pack);

 c. Special units (road construction, chemical decontamination, signal, labor, etc.);

 d. Security and defense units.

37. The chiefs of the military motor roads within the army area are subordinated to the chief of motor transportation and road services of the army.

38. Air supply (either by dropping cargoes or by having the aircraft land and discharge their cargoes) is resorted to in cases when land transport is not practicable or is insufficient to ensure timely arrival of needed supplies to the troops.

Most frequently air supply is used in cases when troops are encircled or are fighting in the enemy's rear. Therefore, this form of supply must be carefully prearranged: the landing or drop area must be thoroughly reconnoitered, the dispositions of our troops must be accurately determined, and signals must be firmly understood both by air and ground elements.

IV. Medical Service of the Army

39. The following elements take part in the medical service of an army:

 a. Mobile field hospitals, which are set up along the evacuation routes within the troops' rear, some 15 to 30 kilometers behind the front line (first-echelon or first-line hospitals), and also in the army rear mainly near railway stations (second-echelon or second-line hospitals);

b. Clearing stations, which are located as a rule at railway loading stations. They are equipped to handle lightly wounded personnel and are equipped to care for and load up wounded personnel onto evacuation medical railway trains;

c. Hospitals for lightly wounded, which are located in the army rear and take care of cases who, it appears, will be able to return to their units within a short period, say, ten to fifteen days;

d. Independent medical reinforcement companies, used to reinforce the work in army medical installations and to increase their clearing capacity. In essence, medical reserve forces, available where the traffic is heaviest;

e. Separate ambulance company, which evacuates wounded from the clearing stations of units and formations;

f. Medical-epidemiological detachment, which carries out preventive work designed to forestall epidemics, etc.;

g. Infectious-diseases hospital;

h. Disinfection and delousing company;

i. Laundry detachments, which launder the clothing of military personnel;

j. Pathological-analytical laboratory;

k. Field medical depot, which furnishes troops and medical units with the supplies they require.

In addition, depending on the circumstances, the army medical chief may have at his disposal animal-drawn sleds and medical air evacuation detachments, evacuation hospitals, etc.

40. The army-group medical chief sets up within the army areas various elements that assist in the treatment and timely evacuation of sick and wounded. These include field evacuation points and forward field evacuation points. The former consists of a headquarters, field and evacuation hospitals, laundry and disinfection detachment, a military-medical commission, and ambulance detachments. A forward field evacuation point includes a headquarters, a 500-bed clearing hospital, and two or three mobile field hospitals.

Both may either remain under the control of the army-group medical chief or be attached to the army medical chief, at the discretion of the army-group medical chief.

41. The field evacuation point as a rule is set up in the vicinity of the army regulating station, while the forward evacuation point is generally set up near a railway loading point or supply station. The army-group medical chief, at his discretion, sends special medical evacuation railway trains to the army to pick up wounded.

42. In organizing the medical service of the army, the army medical chief draws up a "medical treatment, and plan" in accordance with instructions received from his own army commander and from the army-group medical chief.

43. The medical service at army level depends most heavily on the mobile field hospitals; these are designed to afford competent and timely medical aids and, if possible, to retain and bring back to health cases where the prognosis is for early recovery. Only cases that give promise of recovery within ten to fifteen days (according to the instructions of the army-group medical chief) and retained within army medical installations for treatment and eventual discharge back to their troop units.

V. Administration of the Army Rear

44. The army commander carries full responsibility for the overall direction of the work of the army rear and the timely and adequate provision of supplies to the troops.

Having taken his operational decision, the army commander must also make his decision as to the role and task of his rear, assigning its mission in the context of his overall responsibilities. During the course of an operation, the army commander, who is in touch with the general situation and capabilities of his rear services, assigns changed or additional missions to his rear services in accordance with changes in the situation or changes in the capabilities of the rear services.

To ensure direct and continuous control and direction of the rear—and in the interests of ensuring continuous supply for the troops—one of the members of the military council of the army is assigned to supervise the rear.

45. In his decision concerning the rear, the army commander indicates:

a. Where the formations of the army will be based;
   (1) Railway sectors;
   (2) Supply stations and unloading stations;

b. Rate of issue and norms of consumption of supplies for the various formations of the army;

c. Priorities among formations in the army for receipt of supplies;

d. The extent that local resources will be used;

e. Special measures for the defense and security of the rear areas and assigning of forces to accomplish these measures.

46. The army chief of staff must be always up-to-date as to the situation of the army rear; he must know thoroughly the supply situation, and he must keep a close control over the work of the rear. When necessary, he must report to the army commander concerning the situation of the rear together with his ideas as to how it should be organized for operation.

47. The army chief of staff must also communicate in good time to the army chief of the rear all changes in the operational situation and all changes of plan, so that the latter can take measures accordingly.

48. The army chief of the rear is also a deputy commander of the army: he himself organizes the army rear and plans and executes the movement of supplies and evacuation in accordance with the operational situation.

49. The chiefs of the arms and services carry out their responsibilities in respect to the supply and servicing of the troops, each according to his particular speciality, for which he is fully responsible.

The chiefs of the arms and services operate under the following directives:
* The army commander's order for the rear;
* Orders and special instructions concerning rear services work issued by the chief of the rear;
* Orders concerning appropriate special and technical matters issued by the next highest echelon of their respective arms and services.

50. The army chief of the rear has a headquarters consisting of a staff and the following sections: military communications; motor and road services; supplies, rations, and fodder supply; fuel supply; medical, veterinary services; and salvage sections, including those that deal with captured materiel.

51. The staff of the headquarters of the chief of the rear is his working apparatus. It:

a. Collects and prepares data concerning the situation of the rear and the supply situation;

b. Organizes reconnaissance of the army rear area;

c. Works out the details flowing from the army commander's order for the rear and prepares the necessary detailed orders and instructions;

d. Determines the army's needs, in terms of rear service units and installations;

e. Draws up overall plans for the evacuation of materiel and supplies, in cases where the army is withdrawing to new defensive lines;

f. Works out, in connection with the operational section of the army staff, a plan for the operational security of the rear;

g. Keeps a record of captured materiel and organizes the collection and evacuation of such materiel;

h. Keeps a running record of losses in materiel and weapons;

i. Checks the rear plans of the formations within the army, and checks to see that these plans are being carried out;

j. Draws up periodic reports concerning the rear situation in the army and submits these to the headquarters of the army-group rear;

k. Keeps the chiefs of the arms and services and the staffs of subordinate units within the army informed of the rear situation.

52. The staff of the rear services headquarters works in close coordination with the section for the setting up of the operational rear of the army staff.

53. The chief of military communications of the army, who is both a chief and a staff officer, is subordinated to the chief of the rear of the army. The chief of military communications of the army is also subordinated, for technical matters, to his own next highest echelon at army-group headquarters. The field units dealing with military communications in the army are subordinated to the army chief of military communications.

54. The military communications section of the army:

Regulation Concerning the Organization and Work of the Army Rear

a. Plans the movement of all types of cargo to the supply station and to the unloading points and supervises the movement of these cargoes;

b. Draws up plans for the improving and strengthening of the rail and water route sectors' carrying capacity. These plans are made to cover each day and each phase of an operation;

c. Organizes the work of setting up and developing the rail aspects involved in laying out the army distributing point and the supply station;

d. Checks on the accomplishment of defense and security tasks carried out by combat troops in the rear and by NKVD elements; such tasks include the security of rail lines, bridges, water routes, etc.

55. The motor transportation and road section of the army:

a. Collects and organizes data concerning the layout and capacity of the net of roads in the area in which the army is operating;

b. Organizes the movement of supplies along roads within the army rear and in some cases within the troop rear as well;

c. Facilitates the movement along motor roads and along army supply routes of march columns of personnel and horse replacements, seeing to their rationing, quartering, etc.;

d. Provides transportation for the evacuation along motor roads and army routes of wounded and sick men and animals and also for the evacuation of damaged materiel and weapons that must be repaired in army or army-group workshops. Also facilitates the evacuation of captured materiel;

e. Organizes the correct deployment and utilization of road-exploitation units, transport units, and other rear service elements that contribute to the effective utilization of road communications in the rear area.

All motor transportation and road units within the army are subordinated to the army chief of the motor transportation and road section, who is a member of the rear services staff.

56. The chiefs of the arms and services inform the chief of the rear arm, through his staff, concerning the following:

a. The needs of the formations within the army for their respective special types of supplies, expressing quantity where possible in terms of conventional loads, days of supply, etc.

b. Their proposals for the organization of the rear as it affects their particular specialties;

c. Data concerning their specialties that are to be included in the order for the rear;

d. In the case of chiefs of services who are totally subordinate to the army chief of the rear—i.e., chief of motor transportation, but not the chief of artillery—expenditure and wastage of materiel and equipment and evacuation needs and repair requirements resulting from such wastage or damage;

e. Data concerning the extent to which the capacity of medical and veterinary installations and evacuation facilities are being utilized;

f. Requests for transportation space for movement and evacuation by motor and rail transport; road time and space requirements for such movements.

57. The basic documents involved in the organization and administration of the army rear are the army order for the rear and separate orders and instructions concerning the rear.

Secondary documents include:
- Periodic reports concerning the rear situation;
- Plans governing traffic over rail, motor roads, army supply routes, for movement of supplies and for evacuation;
- Requisitions, special reports, and memoranda;
- The master working map for the rear, logs, and tables and charts showing consumption norms.

58. The order for the rear, as the basic document for the organization of the rear and the conduct of its work in supplying the army, usually contains the following elements:

a. Boundaries of the army rear area;

b. Army communications, including rail or water-route sector, and the army distributing point;

c. The basing of the formations (divisions) of the army, showing the supply station or unloading stations, with indication of which formations will be supplied by which stations and when these stations will go into action;

d. Military motor roads of the army and army routes of supply and evacuation;

e. The amounts of supplies—ammunition, fuel, rations—figured for every formation within the army, that will be issued, figured either for the entire operation or for one or more phases of it;

f. Basic instructions concerning medical and veterinary service and evacuation;

g. Arrangements for repair and evacuation of arms and equipment, indicating army collection points for damaged equipment, mobile army repair shops, order and routes of evacuation, and army-group resources that will be available;

h. Location of the second echelon of the army headquarters.

i. Time and frequency for rear service reports.

Instructions concerning the security and defense of the rear area and the organization of signal communications in the rear are issued in separate orders.

The order for the rear is signed by the army commander, a member of the military council of the army, and the chief of rear services. The order for the rear is distributed immediately after the operational order has been distributed.

59. Signal communications in the rear area are organized by the army chief of signal troops, in accordance with the requirements as determined by the army chief of rear services.

In order to conduct and control the work of the rear, the army chief of the

rear sets up the signal facilities:
- With the chief of the army base;
- With the chiefs of the military motor roads within the army rear area;
- With the headquarters of the formations (divisions) of the army; and
- With the military commandant of the army regulating station.

60. Telephone, telegraph, and radio are the signal communications means used for sending of messages in the rear area. Along military motor roads and army routes of supply and evacuation, the road repair equipment and trucks are used. Units and formations assigned to tasks in the army rear establish signal communications with the appropriate rear services agency, using their own signal resources.

V1. Defense and Security of the Army Rear

61. The basic means used by the enemy to attack our rear and to disrupt its work is aviation. The enemy uses air attacks against the army rear in order to strike at distributing points, field dumps, stationary bases, rail lines, bridges, tunnels, viaducts, etc. Therefore, it is particularly important that there should be an efficient and well-organized antiaircraft defense of the basic air targets within the army rear area.

In all cases of enemy air attack against our rear, the army chief of the rear must take all possible measures to ensure the uninterrupted flow of supplies to the troops; he must maneuver his reserves of supplies to overcome interruptions caused by air attack, and for this purpose, he must on occasion concentrate his reserves of transport facilities at the emergency points.

62. The following elements are employed in the defense and security of the army rear:

   a. Combat units of the various arms, assigned to the defense of the rear and used as mobile reserves;

   b. Combat units assigned as garrisons for the defense of particularly important rear service installations;

   c. All rear service units and installations, which must take measures to ensure their own security. Included also are NKVD units, units of the Peoples Commissarist of Communication, and other personnel and units of civil commissariats in the army rear area;

   d. Combat units that happen to be in the army rear.

63. The army chief of the rear is responsible for organizing the security and defense of the army rear area. Defense of the army rear is broken down into two zones: the first is the defensive zone of the troop rear, and the second is the defensive zone of the army rear. In the first zone, defensive arrangements are the responsibility (on the orders of the army chief of the rear) of the units and formations occupying this zone; in the second zone, the defensive tasks are carried out by NKVD units and by combat units deployed in the army rear area.

64. The defense and security of the army regulating station, the army base, supply station, unloading points, military motor roads, and other rear installations must be organized by the chiefs of these installations, in accordance with orders from the army chief of the rear.

These various chiefs are responsible for the following:

a. To set up air warning services;

b. To conduct combat reconnaissance in their areas;

c. To assign to their subordinate elements specific security and defense tasks;

d. To assign specific tasks to all antiaircraft and antitank elements within their areas;

e. To assign concrete tasks to any combat troops that may be attached to them for security or defense missions;

f. To draw up specific plans for the defense of their areas and installations.

65. In the plan for the defense of an area or installation, there should be the following elements:

a. Location of antiaircraft and antitank warning posts;

b. Specific deployment of the defensive forces available;

c. Specific warning and signal communications within the installations or area;

d. Setting up of special teams, including antiaircraft, antitank, and firefighting.

Appendix 1

Order of Battle of Soviet Forces during the Battles of Moscow

Unit	Commander	Political Commissar	Chief of Staff
West Front 10-1-1941 to the end	Col. Gen. I.S. Konev. 10—10-1941 Army Gen. G.K. Zhukov	N.A. Bulganin, I.S. Khokhlov D.A. Lestev (until 11-1941)	Lt. Gen. V. D. Sokolovskii. 1-25-1942 Maj. Gen. V.S. Golushkevich
Reserve Front 1-10-1941 to 10-12-1941	Marshal of the Soviet Union S.M. Budennyi	Commissar State Security (NKVD) 3d rank S.N. Kruglov,[1] G.M. Popov	Maj. Gen. A.F. Anisov
Bryansk Front (first formation) 10-1-1941 to 11-10-1941	Lt. Gen. E.I. Ermenko 10-14-1941 Maj. Gen. C.F. Zakharov	Division Commissar P.I. Mazepov, Division Commissar V.E. Makarov	Maj. Gen. G.F. Zakharov, 10-14-1941 Col. L.M. Sandalov
Bryansk Front (second formation)	Col. Gen. Ia.T. Cherevichenko	Corps Commissar A.F. Kolobiakov, Brigade Commissar S.I. Shabalin	Maj. Gen. V.Ia. Kolpakchi, 1-17-1942 Maj. Gen. M.I. Kazakov
Kalinin Front 10-19-1941 to the end	Col. Gen. I.S. Konev	Corps Commissar D.S. Leonov, Division Commissar	Maj. Gen. I.I. Ivanov, 11-11-1941 Maj. Gen. E. P. Zhuravlev. 11-26-1941 Col. A.A. Katsnelson. 1-1-1942 Maj. Gen. M.V. Zakharov
Southwestern Front 11-11-1941 to 12-24-1941	Marshal of the Soviet Union S.K. Timoshenko. 12-18-1941 Lt. Gen. F.Ia. Kostenko	N.S. Krushchev. 1-12-1942 Division Commissar K.A. Gurov	Lt. Gen. P.I. Bodin
1st Sapper Army	Maj. Gen. of Engineers M.P. Vorob'ev	Brigade Commissar P.M. Lakhtarin	Military Engineer First Rank P.I. Gorbunov

200   Battle for Moscow

Unit	Commander	Political Commissar	Chief of Staff
1st Guard Cavalry Corps (formerly 2d Cavalry)	Maj. Gen. from 1-2-1942, Lt. Gen. P.A. Belov	Brigade Commissar A.V. Shchelakovskii	Col. M.D. Gretsov, 1-9-1942, Col. M.M. Zaikin
2d Guard Cavalry Corps (formerly 3d Cavalry Corps)	Maj. Gen. L.M. Dovator 12-19-1941 Maj. Gen. I.A. Pliev	Brigade Commissar F.F. Tulikov	Lt. Col. A.I. Radzievskii
3d Guard Cavalry Corps (formerly 5th Cavalry Corps)	Maj. Gen. V.D. Kriuchenkin	Regimental Commissar F.P. Luchko	Lt. Col. I.I. Shchimov-Izmov
5th Airborne Corps	Lt. Col. I.S. Bezuglyi 12-6-1941 Col. S.S. Gur'ev	Regiment Commissar from 2-12-1942 Brigade Commissar N.N. Korolev	Lt. Col. A.A. Nestesov
1st Antiaircraft	Maj. Gen. from 10-28-1941 Lt. Gen. of Artillery D.A. Zhuravlev		
20th Army (first half of October 1941)	Lt. Gen. F.A. Ershakov (taken prisoner)	Corps Commissar F.A. Semenovskii, Brigade Commissar V.Ia. Vlasov	Maj. Gen. N.V. Korneev
20th Army (from 11-30-1941)	Lt. Gen. A.A. Vlasov	Division Commissar P.N. Kulinkov	Colonel from 12-17-1941 Maj. Gen. L.M. Sandalov
22nd Army	Maj. Gen. (NKYD) V.A. Iushkevich. 10-19-1941 Maj. Gen. V.I. Vostrukhov	Corps Commissar D.S. Lenov. 10-20-1941 Division Commissar Katkov	Colonel from 1-17-1942 Gen. M.A. Shalinin
24th Army 10-1-1941 to 10-20-1941	Maj. Gen. (NKVD) K.I. Rakutin	Division Commissar N.I. Ivanov	Maj. Gen. A.K. Kondrat'ev
29th Army	Lt. Gen. (NKVD) I.I. Maslennikov. 12-11-1941 Maj. Gen. V.I. Shvetsov	Brigade Commissar K.A. Gurov. 1-13-1942 Brigade Commissar N.N. Savkov	Maj. Gen. V.M. Sharapov
30th Army	Maj. Gen. (NKVD) V.A. Khomenko. 11-18-1941 Maj. Gen. D.D. Leliushenko	Brigade Commissar N.V. Abramov Division Commissar A.M. Krivulin (from 12-18-1941)	Col. A.I. Vinogradov 11-25-1941, Maj. General of Artillery G.I. Khetagurov
31st Army	Maj. Gen. (NKVD) V.N. Dolmatov 10-19-1941, Maj. Gen. (NKVD) V.A. Iushkevich	Brigade Commissar A.G. Russkikh	Col. Z.I. Khominskii 10-6-1941, Col. N.P. Anisitov. 10-26-1941, Col. V.A. Gluzdovskii
32d Army 10-1-1941 to 10-12-1941	Maj. Gen. S.V. Vishnevskii (taken prisoner)	Brigade Commissar M.I. Zhilenkov[3]	Col. N.S. Bushmanov

Appendix 1

Unit	Commander	Political Commissar	Chief of Staff
33d Army	Kombrig (NKYD) D.P. Onuprienko 10-25-1941 Lt. Gen. M.G. Efremov	Brigade Commissar M.D. Shliakhtin	Col. I.K. Prostov 10-20-1941 Maj. Gen. A.K. Konkrat'e
39th Army (from 12-22-1941)	Lt. Gen. (NKVD) I.I. Maslennikov	Corps Commissar A.Ia. Fominykh[4] Regiment Commissar G.T. Klishin	Col. P.P. Morushnichnko
43d Army	Maj. Gen. P.P. Sobennikov. 10-10-1941 Lt. Gen. S.D. Akimov. 10-29-1941 Maj. Gen. K.D. Golubev	Brigade Commissar S.I. Iakovleev. 10-25-1941 Division Commissar S.I. Shabalov Brigade Commissar A.D. Seriukov	Col. F.A. Zuev. 1-17-1942 Maj. Gen. A.N. Bogoliubov
49th Army	Lt. Gen. Zakharkin	Brigade Commissar A.I. Litvinov	Col. P.M. Verkholovich
50th Army	Maj. Gen. I.E. Petrov. 10-13-1941, Maj. Gen. A.N. Ermakov. 11-22-1941 Lt. Gen. I.V. Boldin	Brigade Commissar N.A. Shliapin, 11-12-1941. Brigade Commissar K.L. Sorokin. 11-30-1941 Brigade Commissar V.G. Zhavoronkov	Col. from 10-8-1941 Maj. Gen. L.A. Pern. 10-26-1941, Col. from 1-2-1942 Maj. Gen. N.E. Argunov. 3-10-1942 Maj. Gen. I.T. Grishin.
61st Army (from 12-9-1941)	Col. Gen. F.I. Kuznetsov. 12-18-1941 Lt. Gen. M.M. Popov	Corps Commissar A.F. Kolobianov. 12-28-1942 Division Commissar D.G. Dubrovskii, Regiment Commissar N.T. Zhelobanov	Maj. Gen. M.I. Glukhov 12-16-1941 Col. D.I. Samarskii
1st Assault Army (29-11-41 to 1-21-1942)	Lt. Gen. V.I. Kusnetsov	Brigade Commissar D.I. Kolesnikov Division Commissar Ia.S. Kolesov	Maj. Gen. N.D. Zakhvataev 12-16-1941
3d Army	Maj. Gen. Ia.G. Kreizer. 12-13-1941 Lt. Gen. P.S. Pshennikov. (KIA) 12-28-1941, Lt. Gen. P.I. Batov. 2-11-1942 Maj. Gen. F.F. Zhmachenko	Division Commissar F.I. Shlykov	Maj. Gen. A.S. Zhadov
5th Army (from 10-11-1941)	Maj. Gen. D.D. Leliushenko. 10-10-1941 Maj. Gen. from 11-9-1941 Lt. Gen. of Artillery L.A. Govorov.	Brigade Commissar P.P. Ivanov	Col. Z.I. Khominskii. 10-24-1941 Maj. Gen. A.A. Filatov. 1-12-1942, Maj. Gen. B.A. Pigarevich
10th Army (from 12-1-1941)	Lt. Gen. F.I. Golikov. 2-2-1942,		

Unit	Commander	Political Commissar	Chief of Staff
	Maj. Gen. V.S. Popov	Corps Commissar T.L. Nikolaev, Corps Commissar S.K. Kozhevnikov	Maj. Gen. N.S. Dronov. 12-13-1941, Maj. Gen. S.I. Liubarskii.
13th Army	Maj. Gen. A.M. Gorodnianskii. 1-25-1942 Maj. Gen. N.P. Pukhov	Brigade Commissar M.A. Kozlov	Kombrig from 12-27-1941 Maj. Gen. A.V. Petrushevskii
16th Army	Lt. Gen. K.K. Rokossovskii	Division Commissar A.A. Lobachev	Col. from 10-7-1941 Maj. Gen. M.S. Malinin
19th Army (first part of October)	Lt. Gen. M.F. Lukin	Division Commissar I.P. Sheklanov	Maj. Gen. V.F. Malyshkin[5]
6th Interceptor Corps	Maj. Gen. of Aviation I.D. Klimov. 11-19-1941 Col. A.I. Mitenkov	Brigade Commissar I.A. Orlov. 12-1-1941 Brigade Commissar I.T. Chernyshev	Col. I.I. Komarov

Editor's Notes

1. Kruglov was the Minister of Internal Affairs under Stalin and Nikita Khrushchev.
2. For obvious reasons, the Soviet sources list this army under its deputy commander, Major A. I. Liziukov, killed in action in 1942 and branded a traitor by Stalin but rehabilitated during the deStalinization period.
3. Future Vlasovite.
4. Former commissar of the Belorussian Military District at the start of the war who survived the holocaust of the Western Front and the execution of its command staff.
5. Future Vlasovite. Soviet sources incorrectly list the chief of staff as Colonel A. G. Mazlov (deputy chief of staff) but strangely enough correctly list the commissar of the 32nd Army M. N. Zhilenkov, another Vlasovite.

Appendix 2

Soviet Forces in the Battle of Moscow (*Voenno istoricheskii zhurnal*, 3–1967)

Units	1 October 1941			
	Western Front	Reserve Front	Bryansk Front	Total
General Armies	6	6	3	15
Airborne Corps	–	–	–	–
Rifle Divisions	30	28	25	83
Motorized Divisions	2	–	–	3
Tank Divisions	–	–	1	1
Cavalry Divisions	3	2	4	9
Tank and Motorized Brigades	5	5	4	14

Units	15 November 1941			
	Kalinin Front	Western Front	Southwestern Front	Total
General Armies	3	7	2	12
Airborne Corps	–	1	–	1
Rifle Divisions	14	35	12	61
Motorized Divisions	–	3	–	3
Tank Divisions	–	3	–	3
Cavalry Divisions	1	12	4	17
Tank and Motorized Brigades	2	16	2	20

Soviet Manpower and Armament in the Battle of Moscow

Manpower and Armament	1 October 1941			
	Western Front	Reserve Front	Bryansk Front	Total
Troops	540,375	471,912	240,304	1,252,591
Rifles	339,862	322,581	169,156	831,599
Machine Guns	2,678	3,490	2,826	8,994
Artillery (field)	7,585	9,313	3,767	20,665
Artillery (antiaircraft)	350	285	104	739
Tanks	464	301	84	849

Battle for Moscow

Soviet Units in the Battle of Moscow

1 October 1941

Front and Armies	Rifle Divisons	Rifle Brigades	Front and Armies	Rifle Divisions	Rifle Brigades
Western Front			*Bryansk Front*		
22d Army	6	–	50th Army	8	–
29th Army	4	1	3d Army	6	–
30th Army	4	–	13th Army	8	–
19th Army	5	–	Group Ermakov	5	2
16th Army	4	1	From Reserve Front	3	1
20th Army	4	–			
From Reserve Front	8	3			
Total	35	5	Total	30	3
Reserve Front					
24th Army	6	2			
43d Army	1	2			
31st Army	4	–			
	11	4			

Soviet Units in the Battle of Moscow

15 November 1941

Front and Armies	Rifle Divisons	Rifle Brigades	Front and Armies	Rifle Divisions	Rifle Brigades
Kalinin Front			*Western Front*		
22d Army	6	1	30th Army	7	2
29th Army	5	–	16th Army	8	3
31st Army	4	–	5th Army	5	5
			33d Army	5	1
			43d Army	4	6
			49th Army	6	–
			50th Army	10	2
			From Reserve Front	6	–
Total	15	1	Total	51	19

Place and Name Index

Akhtyrka 93
Aleksandrovka 84
Alekseyevka 84, 86, 87
Alekseyevka-Sivash 88
Andreapol 11, 28, 34
Andreyevka 81
Antipenko 185
Anton-Antonov-Ovseenko iii
Arbuzovo 165, 166
Artemovka 94
Arzhukhova 60
Arzhukhova-Vyazovka 60

Balaklaya 2, 81, 88
Balta 80, 92
Balta-Yelenovka-Eftodiya 92
Baranov, General 91
Bargartion v
Barsukovo 97
Barvenkovo 77, 80
Belov, General 82, 91
Beltsy 91
Bereka 87, 88
Bialystok iii
Boldin, General 82, 91
Bolshaya Vishera 16
Borisenki 143
Brezhnev iv
Brody 173
Bryansk iv, 84, 173
Bryansk Front 46, 48, 56, 70, 159, 161
Budnitsa 96
Bychkovsky, General 86, 91, 94
Bykovo 81

Chepchugovo 97
Chernovo 97
Chervony Shakhter 20, 39
Chukhalovo 81
Chulaev 116

Crimean Front 46, 48

Demidovo 40
Demidovo-Dukhovshchina 96
Denisikha 89
Dnieper River 93, 141, 142
Dniester 92, 173
Dovator, General 89, 196

Efremovka 87, 88

Feodosia 61
Fess 115-117
Fomino 96

Galvshkin 93
Gareev 1
Glazunovka 81, 86, 87
Glukhoye 40, 73
Gnilovskaya 13
Gorbachev iv
Gorbovo 89
Gorodishche 97
Grechko, General 77
Gridino 97
Grigorenko, P. G. iii
Gruzino 16
Guderian, General 82, 83, 94, 95

Istra 10

Kalinin iv, 2, 10, 28, 58
Kalinin Front 43, 60, 62, 64, 67, 158, 159, 164, 175
Kaluga 10, 28, 33, 34
Kamkov, General 76

Kandalaksha 100, 105
Karelian Front 99, 101, 109, 143, 160, 162
Kashin 154
Kashira 82
Kashira-Stalinogorsk 83
Kastornoye 84
Kestenga 100, 105, 106
Ketsy 173
Kharkov 45
Kherso 173
Khmelevaya 84
Khodunovo 39
Kholm 39
Khomyakova Khrushchevka 83
Khorol-Beyevo 93
Khrulev 185
Khrushchev iv
Khukhlova 84
Kiev iv, 131, 140, 174
Kiseli 87
Kishinev 90, 91
Kishinev-Orgeyev 91
Kleist, General 80
Klin 10, 154
Knesh River 84
Koenigsberg 173
Kolpinsk-Kolkhoz 168
Konotop 173
Kopytykh 164
Korotkov 113
Kostenko, General 84
Kozminka 84
Krasnograd 81, 86, 87
Krasny Lug 84
Kravtsovka 86
Krememchug 93
Krichev-Chavsi 94
Krioleni-Dubossary 91, 92
Kryuchenkin, General 76, 84
Kryukovka 83
Kubinka 88
Kuibyshev iv
Kukuruzeni 91
Kukuruzeni-Serateni 91

Lake Ilmen 39
Lake Ladoga 39
Leningrad 131, 134, 142, 146, 174
Leningrad Front 37, 38, 43, 48, 50, 53, 164, 165, 181
Likhachevo 86, 87
Likhachevo Station 86
Liman 81
Litsa River 162
Lokotnya 89
Losovaya 77, 80
Lukashevka 91

Lukhi-Kestenga 105, 106
Lutsinovka-Markovka 93
Lysovo 98

Maidenov 115, 116
Maksimovka 86
Malaya Vishera 9, 13
Malinovo 85
Malinovskii 74
Maloyaroslavets 10
Marchenko 115
Masolovka 162
Medvezhegorsk 103, 107, 143
Medyn 10
Merefa 87
Mezha River 96
Mikhailov 83
Mikhailovka 86
Mikheyev 1
Minsk iii, 76, 118
Mironovka 86, 87
Mius River 46, 51
Model, Walter iv
Mordves 83
Morkaya Sura River 20
Moscow iii-vi, 2, 16, 24, 28, 76, 82, 88, 131, 137, 142
Moscow-Minsk Highway 97
Motus 116
Mozhaysk iv
Murmansk 100, 102, 103, 105, 106, 158, 161

Neckrich, A. M. iii
Nelidovo 33, 34
Neva River 141, 165, 167
Nevskaya Dubravka 165-167
Nikitino-Nikolskoye 85
Nizhnorel 86, 88
Nizhny 163
North Donets River 81
Northern Donets River 20
Northwestern Front 24, 29, 34, 39, 58, 60, 69
Novaya Russa 40

Odessa 141, 174
Okhrincha 91
Olym River 84
Orel-Mtsensk iv
Orgeyev 91
Ostashkova 97
Ostrov 163

Paikovo 162, 163, 166
Pavlenkovo 93

Index

Pervomaisk 92
Ploskoye 84
Podoprigory 93
Pokrovskoye 89, 168
Porogo 165
Povenents 160
Prilepy 84
Pryakhivio 83
Pushkari 164, 165
Pushkin 160

Ramushevo 39
Reitlinger, Gerald iii
Rogachev 142
Roslavl 94
Rossosh 77, 85
Rostov 10, 13
Rozhano 96
Ryazan 82
Rzhev v, 2, 3, 159, 164

Safonikha 89
Sebezh 41
Selizharovsk 34
Semenovka 87
Semlevo 97
Sergievo 83
Serpukhov 82
Severny Donets River 86
Sharov 113
Shatilovo 85
Shcbelinka 81, 87
Shlisseburg 165
Shtepovka 93, 94
Shtepovka-Vasilievka 94
Shtepovski 93
Shtern 131
Shturmoviks 115
Shumovka 94
Sivash 86
Slavyansk 2, 48
Smolenk 98
Solomino 163
Solyony Hill 63
Somovo 161
Sorge, Richard iv
Southern Front 43, 45, 48, 51, 54, 63, 92
Southwestern Front 2, 48, 52, 54, 70, 93
Spalshchino 89
Stalin iii, iv, v, vi, 131
Staraya Russia 39
Starshavka 94
Strasheni 91
Sumy 93

Taganrog 45, 63

Telegino 84
Telegino-Ploskoye 85
Temernik 13
Terekhovo 89
Tikhvin 10, 173
Toropets 10, 23, 28-35
Toropino 161
Tosna River 168
Tula iv, 10, 28, 82, 142, 154
Tula-Oryol 83
Tyunezh 83

Ugra River 169
Ustye-Podvyazie 96
Uzlovaya 83

Vasilievka 93
Vechnyi vi
Velichkov 34
Velizh 23
Velizha 9
Venev 82, 83
Verkh-Bishkin 87, 88
Verkhovya 85
Vershina-Vosochek 41
Vitebsk 23
Volga 162, 163, 169
Volkhov Front 10, 53, 69, 70, 163
Vokhovski 46
Volokolamsk 10
Volovenkovo 86
Volovo 84
Voronezh 142
Voronov 131
Voznesensk 80
Vyazma iv, v, 2, 97, 98, 173
Vyazovaya-Pokrovskoye 84
Vyazovka 83
Vykova 83

Warsaw 173
Western Front 2, 43, 45, 46, 48, 50, 53, 58, 70, 82, 88, 94, 96, 160, 162, 165, 169

Yamnovo 97
Yarsolavl iv
Yeletakoye 76
Yelets 84, 85
Yelets Group 76
Yukhnov 10

Zagorye 89
Zagorye-Safonikha 89

Zakharovka 84
Zanikove 164
Zaovrazhye 89
Zelenkov-Kozelyonnoye 93

Zhelyukhovo 97
Zhitomir 141
Zhukov iv, v
Zmiyev 86, 87

Unit Index

1st Guards Cavalry Corps 82, 83
1st Guards Cavalry Division 82
1st Guards Rifle Division 77, 84
1st Rumanian Infantry Division 80
1st Tank Brigade 93, 94
2nd Cavalry Corps 80, 91-94, 97, 98
2nd Guards Cavalry Corps 78, 81, 88, 89
2nd Guards Motorized Rifle Division 76, 97
2nd Guards Cavalry Division 82, 83
2nd Guards Artillery Regiment 49
2nd Guards Rifle Division 46
2nd Panzer Army 94
3rd Motorized Rifle Brigade of the Romanian
   Army 3rd Army 8, 23, 27
3rd Alpine Division, 39
3rd Cavalry Division 76, 80, 84, 85, 88
3rd Guards Cavalry Division 81, 88, 89
3rd Tank Brigade 76
4th Guards Cavalry Division 81, 88, 89
4th Guards Mortar (Rocket Launcher)
   Group 76
4th Army 8, 10, 23, 27, 28, 30, 31, 32, 34
5th Army 44, 45, 48, 89
5th Cavalry Division 80, 91-93
5th Guards Tank Brigade 80, 86, 87
5th Cavalry Corps 76, 77, 80, 81, 83-87, 99
6th Army 76-78, 80, 81, 86, 88, 97
6th Rifle Division 57
6th Cavalry Corps 76, 78, 80, 81, 86
7th Guard Rifle Corps 160
7th Independent Army 39
9th Division 93
9th Panzer Division 93, 94
9th Army 91, 92
9th Cavalry Division 80, 91, 93, 94
9th Tank Brigade 82
10th Army 82
10th Guard Rifle Regiment 163
11th Cavalry Corps 76
11th Cavalry Regiment 93
11th Guard Rifle Corps 63
12th Tank Brigade 77
13th Independent AA Battalion 143
14th Cavalry Division 76, 80, 84, 85
15th Guards Rifle Division 54

15th Motorized Rifle Division 91
16th Army 97
16th Motorized Division 93
17th Panzer Division 83
17th Army 77
18th Army 80
18th Cavalry Division 97
18th Panzer Division 83
19th Motorized Divison 92
20th Motorized Division 83
20th Army 78, 81
20th Cavalry Division 88, 89
20th Tank Brigade 51
21st Army 93, 94
21st Cavalry Division 94
22nd Panzer Division 48
22nd Tank Brigade 81, 89
24th Cavalry Division 97
25th Motorized Division 93, 94
26th Army 95
26th Cavalry Division 80, 86, 87
26th Rifle Brigade 69
28th Army 94, 95
28th Cavalry Division 80, 86, 87
29th Army 20
29th Cavalry Division 86
32nd Cavalry Division 76, 84, 85
33rd Army v, 162
34th Army Corps 77, 85
34th Cavalry Division 77, 80
34th Independent AA Battalion 143
34th Motorized Rifle Brigade 76, 77, 84
35th Rifle Corps 91
38th Army 81
39th Army 97
40th Army 93, 94
41st Independent Armored AA Train 142
43rd Infantry Division 94
44th Army Corps 84
45th Infantry Division 85
47th Rifle Corps 91, 92
48th Army 56
49th Cavalry Division 80, 86, 87
50th Cavalry Division 96
50th Motorized Division 91

Index

50th Army 82, 93
50th Tank Brigade 161
51st Army 61
51st Tank Brigade 161
52nd Cavalry Division 77, 84, 94
53rd Cavalry Division 96
55th Cavalry Division 77, 84
56th Army 63
57th Army 77
57th Rifle Brigade 69
60th Cavalry Division 77
61st Army 157, 159, 161
61st Ski Brigade 39
63rd Motorized Rifle Division 61
64th Independent AA Battalion 142
68th Rifle Division 164
70th Motorized Division 83
72nd Cavalry Regiment 91, 92
78th Infantry Division 89
79th Cavalry Division 77
81st Rifle Division 76
82nd Cavalry Division 97
82nd Motorized Rifle Division 58
86th Rifle Division 166
94th Tank Battalion 161
95th Infantry Division 77, 84, 85
96th Cavalry Regiment 93
104th Rifle Division 158
108th Rifle Division 160
111th Ski Brigade 39
113th Infantry Division 80
113th Rifle Brigade 160
114th Rifle Division 39
121st Rifle Division 84
122nd Rifle Division 48, 84, 159
123rd Cavalry Regiment 86
125th Cavalry Regiment 87
126th Cavalry Regiment 86
129th Tank Brigade 76, 84, 85
130th Cavalry Regiment 87
131st Cavalry Regiment 93
132nd Cavalry Regiment 86
134th Infantry Division 77, 85
137th Cavalry Regiment 86
140th Regiment 58
141st Independent AA Battalion 143
141st Tank Battalion 12
142nd Tank Brigade 76
143rd Division 57
155th Rifle Division 161
155th Ski Battalion 31, 40
160th Cavalry Regiment 92, 93
167th Infantry Division 83
171st Tank Battalion 29
173rd Rifle Division 75, 82
178th Artillery Division 52
179th Infantry Regiment 87
183rd AA Regiment 141

191st Ski Battalion 39
192nd Ski Battalion 39
192nd Tank Brigade 161
205th Ski Battalion 39
208th Infantry Division 97
210th Motorized Rifle Regiment 58
212th Rifle Division 76
212th Ski Battalion 39
213th Ski Battalion 39
215th Regiment 164
243rd Rifle Division 159, 164
249th Division 9, 23
249th Rifle Division 20, 21, 63
254th Ski Battalion 40
255th Ski Battalion 11
256th Antiaircraft Battalion 141
256th Ski Battalion 41
257th Rifle Division 9, 20
270th Artillery Regiment 33
270th Rifle Division 20, 21
272nd Rifle Division 39
273rd Rifle Division 82
275th Rifle Division 20
288th Rifle Division 69
293rd Infantry Division 92
297th Infantry Division 92
297th Rifle Division 76
298th Independent AA Battalion 143
310th Rifle Division 69, 70
320th Red Banner Artillery Regiment 49
322nd Rifle Division 75, 83
324th Regiment 164
327th Rifle Division 69
331st Rifle Division 45
334th Rifle Division 32, 33, 62
342nd Rifle Division 157
351st AA Regiment 139–141
358th Rifle Division 11, 29, 30
360th Division 8, 9, 23, 29
368th Rifle Division 39
371st Rifle Division 62
379th Rifle Division 70
390th Rifle Division 60
393rd Division 70, 86
411th Division 70, 80, 87, 88
411th Rifle Division 76, 81, 86
430th Infantry Regiment 97
450th Infantry Regiment 96
466th Rifle Regiment 158
478th Infantry Regiment 98
531st Road Construction Battalion 87
638th AA Regiment 141
745th AA Regiment 142
906th Rifle Regiment 164
1014th Rifle Regiment 69
1172nd Rifle Regiment 162, 163
1191st Rifle Regiment 33

About the Editor

MICHAEL PARRISH, the foremost student of Soviet military historiography in the West, is the author of over 50 publications including the encyclopedic *USSR in World War II* (1982), an annotated bibliographic survey of books published in the USSR about the Great Patriotic War. He holds degrees from Berea College in Kentucky, and Indiana University, where he has been a member of the faculty since 1974.